CONCEPTS IN STRATEGIC MANAGEMENT

CONCEPTS OF STRATEGIC MANAGEMENT

FORMULATION AND IMPLEMENTATION

THIRD EDITION

Lloyd L. Byars

Clark Atlanta University

HarperCollinsPublishers

Sponsoring Editor: Debra Riegert
Project Editor: Susan Goldfarb
Design Supervisor: Lucy Krikorian
Text and Cover Design: Edward Smith Design
Production Administrator: Paula Keller
Compositor: ComCom Division of Haddon Craftsmen, Inc.
Printer and Binder: R. R. Donnelley & Sons Company
Cover Printer: The Lehigh Press

Concepts of Strategic Management: Formulation and Implementation,
Third Edition

Library of Congress Cataloging-in-Publication Data

Byars, Lloyd L.
    Concepts of strategic management : formulation and implementation
/ Lloyd L. Byars. — 3rd ed.
      p. cm.
    Includes bibliographical references and index.
    ISBN 0-06-500673-9
    1. Strategic planning. 2. Strategic planning—Case studies.
I. Title.
  HD30.28.B897 1992
  658.4'012—dc20

91-18128
CIP

92 93 94 9 8 7 6 5 4 3 2

To my wife, Linda

A good wife is her husband's pride and joy.

Proverbs 12:3

CONTENTS

Preface xv
About the Author xxi

PART ONE INTRODUCTION TO THE STRATEGIC MANAGEMENT
PROCESS 1

CHAPTER 1 STRATEGIC MANAGEMENT: AN OVERVIEW 3
THE STRATEGIC MANAGEMENT PROCESS 5
Defining the Organization's Philosophy (or Creed) 5
Developing an Organizational Culture 8
Origin of Organizational Cultures 9
Identifying Organizational Cultures 10
Changing Organizational Cultures 10
Defining the Organization's Mission or Purpose 11
Establishing Long- and Short-Range Objectives 12
Selecting a Strategy 13
Hierarchy of Strategies 13

INTEGRATING PHILOSOPHY, MISSION, OBJECTIVES, AND STRATEGY 14
STRATEGIC MANAGEMENT AND ORGANIZATIONAL SUCCESS 14
STRATEGIC BUSINESS UNITS (SBUs) 16
MAKING STRATEGIC DECISIONS 16
ETHICS AND STRATEGIC MANAGEMENT 19
SUMMARY OF LEARNING OBJECTIVES 20
REVIEW QUESTIONS 21
DISCUSSION QUESTIONS 22
REFERENCES AND ADDITIONAL READING 22
Strategy in Action Case Study: FORD MOTOR COMPANY 23

PART TWO STRATEGY FORMULATION 33

CHAPTER 2 ANALYZING THE EXTERNAL ENVIRONMENT 35
COMPETITIVE ANALYSIS 36
Industry Structure Analysis 37
Individual Competitor Analysis 37
Sources of Competitive Information 41

ENVIRONMENTAL SCANNING 41
Economic Forces 42
Technological Forces 43
Political and Regulatory Forces 43
Social Forces 44
ESTABLISHING AN ENVIRONMENTAL SCANNING PROGRAM 45
ENVIRONMENTAL FORECASTING METHODS 46
Qualitative Forecasting Techniques 47
    Jury of Executive Opinion 47
    Sales Force Composite 47
    Customer Evaluation 47
    Delphi Technique 47
    Anticipatory Surveys 48
Quantitative Forecasting Techniques 48
    Time-Series Analysis 48
    Regression Modeling 48
    Econometric Modeling 48
**FRAMEWORK FOR INTEGRATING COMPETITIVE ANALYSIS AND
    ENVIRONMENTAL SCANNING AND FORECASTING 49**
SUMMARY OF LEARNING OBJECTIVES 50
REVIEW QUESTIONS 50
DISCUSSION QUESTIONS 51
REFERENCES AND ADDITIONAL READING 51
Strategy in Action Case Study: FORD MOTOR COMPANY 52

CHAPTER 3   ANALYZING THE INTERNAL ENVIRONMENT AND ESTABLISHING
    ORGANIZATIONAL OBJECTIVES 63
INTERNAL ORGANIZATIONAL ANALYSIS 64
Financial Position 64
Product Position 65
Marketing Capability 65
Research and Development Capability 66
Organizational Structure 66
Human Resources 66
Condition of Facilities and Equipment 67
Past Objectives and Strategies 67
Responsibility for Performing an Internal Organizational Analysis 69
ESTABLISHING ORGANIZATIONAL OBJECTIVES 69
Mix of Organizational Objectives 70
Procedure for Establishing Objectives 71
Setting Objectives in Strategic Business Units and Functional Areas 74
SUMMARY OF LEARNING OBJECTIVES 75
REVIEW QUESTIONS 78
DISCUSSION QUESTIONS 78
REFERENCES AND ADDITIONAL READING 78
Strategy in Action Case Study: FORD MOTOR COMPANY 79

PART THREE THE STRATEGY SELECTION PROCESS 89

CHAPTER 4   IDENTIFYING STRATEGIC ALTERNATIVES 91
             STRATEGIC ALTERNATIVES 92
             Stable Growth Strategy 92
             Growth Strategies 94
                 Concentration on a Single Product or Service 95
                 Concentric Diversification 97
                 Vertical Integration 98
                 Horizontal Diversification 99
                 Conglomerate Diversification 100
             Endgame Strategies 101
             Retrenchment Strategies 102
                 Turnaround Strategy 103
                 Divestment Strategy 104
                 Liquidation Strategy 105
             Combination Strategies 105
             GENERIC COMPETITIVE (OR BUSINESS UNIT) STRATEGIES 105
             Overall Cost Leadership Strategy 106
             Differentiation Strategy 106
             Focus Strategy 107
             **IMPLEMENTING STRATEGIES THROUGH MERGERS AND
                 ACQUISITIONS 108**
             Reasons for Mergers and Acquisitions 108
             Carrying Out Mergers and Acquisitions 109
             Guidelines for Successfully Implementing Mergers and Acquisitions 110
             IMPLEMENTING STRATEGIES THROUGH JOINT VENTURES 112
             Reasons for Entering Joint Ventures 113
             Strategies Used in Joint Ventures 113
             Considerations in Forming a Joint Venture 114
             SUMMARY OF LEARNING OBJECTIVES 114
             REVIEW QUESTIONS 116
             DISCUSSION QUESTIONS 116
             REFERENCES AND ADDITIONAL READING 116
             Strategy in Action Case Study: FORD MOTOR COMPANY 117

CHAPTER 5   STRATEGY EVALUATION AND SELECTION 123
             BUSINESS PORTFOLIO ANALYSIS 124
             Growth-Share Matrix 124
                 Strategy Selection 126
                 Criticisms of the Growth-Share Matrix 127
             Industry Attractiveness–Business Strength Matrix 128
                 Defining and Assessing Critical External Factors 129
                 Defining and Assessing Critical Success Factors 129
                 Forecasting Critical External Factors 129
                 Specifying the Desired Position on Critical Success Factors 129

Corporate-Level Strategies 129
Business Unit Strategies 130
Functional-Area Strategies 130
Criticisms of Industry Attractiveness–Business Strength Matrix 130
Life-Cycle Approach 131
Strategy Selection 132
Product-Market Evolution Matrix 133
COMPETITIVE STRATEGY ANALYSIS 135
PIMS ANALYSIS 135
VALUE-BASED PLANNING 137
**QUALITATIVE FACTORS IN THE STRATEGY EVALUATION AND SELECTION
PROCESS 139**
Managerial Attitudes Toward Risk 139
Environment of the Organization 141
Organizational Culture and Power Relationships 141
Competitive Actions and Reactions 141
Influence of Previous Organizational Strategies 142
Timing Considerations 142
SUMMARY OF LEARNING OBJECTIVES 142
REVIEW QUESTIONS 143
DISCUSSION QUESTIONS 144
REFERENCES AND ADDITIONAL READING 144
Strategy in Action Case Study: FORD MOTOR COMPANY 145

PART FOUR STRATEGY IMPLEMENTATION 151

CHAPTER 6 STRATEGY, STRUCTURE, AND ORGANIZATIONAL LEADERSHIP 153
STRATEGY AND STRUCTURE 154
DEPARTMENTATION 155
Functional 155
Product or Service 156
Geographic 156
Customer 157
Other Types 157
CONTINGENCY APPROACH TO ORGANIZING 157
Organizational Size and Growth Stage 158
Organizational Environment 159
Technology and Structure 159
ASSESSING AN ORGANIZATION'S STRUCTURE 160
**GUIDELINES IN DESIGNING EFFECTIVE ORGANIZATIONAL
STRUCTURES 161**
Simple Structures 161
Simple Form, Lean Staff 162
REASONS FOR RESTRUCTURING AN ORGANIZATION 162
**MANAGEMENT ACTIONS REQUIRED IN RESTRUCTURING AN
ORGANIZATION 163**

ORGANIZATIONAL LEADERSHIP   164
BOARDS OF DIRECTORS   167
Composition of the Board   168
Structure of the Board   169
    Executive Committee   169
    Audit Committee   169
    Compensation Committee   169
    Nominating Committee   169
    Finance Committee   169
    Social Responsibility Committee   170
    Planning Committee   170

Legal Responsibilities of the Board   170
SUMMARY OF LEARNING OBJECTIVES   171
REVIEW QUESTIONS   172
DISCUSSION QUESTIONS   173
REFERENCES AND ADDITIONAL READING   173
Strategy in Action Case Study: FORD MOTOR COMPANY   175

APPENDIX TO CHAPTER 6:   Strengths and Weaknesses of Organizational Structure Types   181

CHAPTER 7   DEVELOPING BUDGETS, FUNCTIONAL STRATEGIES, AND MOTIVATIONAL SYSTEMS   187
DEPLOYMENT OF RESOURCES THROUGH BUDGETING   188
Flexible Budgets   189
Zero-based Budgeting   189
Participative and Nonparticipative Budgets   189
Dangers in the Budgeting Process   189
Strategy and the Budgeting Process   190
DEVELOPING FUNCTIONAL STRATEGIES   190
Marketing Strategies   191
Financial Strategies   195
    Capital Budgeting   195
    Cash Flow Analysis   196

Production/Operations Strategies   197
Human Resource/Personnel Strategies   197
Research and Development Strategies   199
STRATEGY AND MOTIVATIONAL SYSTEMS   202
SUMMARY OF LEARNING OBJECTIVES   204
REVIEW QUESTIONS   205
DISCUSSION QUESTIONS   206
REFERENCES AND ADDITIONAL READING   206
Strategy in Action Case Study: FORD MOTOR COMPNANY   207

CHAPTER 8   THE STRATEGIC CONTROL PROCESS   213
STRATEGY FORMULATION AND THE STRATEGIC CONTROL PROCESS   214
THREE ELEMENTS OF THE STRATEGIC CONTROL PROCESS   214

Objectives of the Business 214
Evaluating Organizational Performance 217
Feedback or Corrective Action 218
METHODS USED IN STRATEGIC CONTROL SYSTEMS 220
Budgets 220
Audits 220
   Independent Auditors 221
   Government Auditors 221
   Internal Auditors 221
   Management Audits 221

DESIGNING EFFECTIVE STRATEGIC CONTROL SYSTEMS 222
ROLE OF MANAGEMENT INFORMATION SYSTEMS IN THE STRATEGIC
   CONTROL PROCESS 223
CONDUCTING A STRATEGY REVIEW 224
SUMMARY OF LEARNING OBJECTIVES 224
REVIEW QUESTIONS 227
DISCUSSION QUESTIONS 228
REFERENCES AND ADDITIONAL READING 228
Strategy in Action Case Study: FORD MOTOR COMPANY 228

PART FIVE   APPLICATION OF STRATEGIC MANAGEMENT 233

CHAPTER 9   GLOBAL STRATEGY: FORMULATION AND IMPLEMENTATION 235
REASONS FOR INTERNATIONAL BUSINESS INVOLVEMENT 236
DEFINING GLOBAL INDUSTRY, GLOBAL STRATEGIES, AND
   MULTINATIONAL CORPORATIONS 236
UNIQUE ENVIRONMENTAL FORCES IN GLOBAL STRATEGY
   FORMULATION 240
Cultural Differences 240
Payment for International Transactions 240
Tariffs 241
Quotas 241
Government Control over Profits 241
Taxation 242
Coalitions of Cooperating Countries 242
Human Rights 242
Terrorism 243
GENERIC GLOBAL STRATEGY OPTIONS 243
Product Standardization 243
Broad-Line Global Strategy 243
Global-Focus Strategy 243
National-Focus Strategy 244
Protected-Niche Strategy 244
SELECTING A GLOBAL STRATEGY 244
ORGANIZING INTERNATIONAL BUSINESS ACTIVITIES 244

**GUIDELINES FOR SUCCESSFULLY FORMULATING AND IMPLEMENTING
    GLOBAL STRATEGY 248**
SUMMARY OF LEARNING OBJECTIVES 248
REVIEW QUESTIONS 249
DISCUSSION QUESTIONS 250
REFERENCES AND ADDITIONAL READING 250
Strategy in Action Case Study: FORD MOTOR COMPANY 250

PART SIX   **USEFUL INFORMATION FOR ANALYZING STRATEGIC
MANAGEMENT CASES 255**

APPENDIX A: Preparing a Case Analysis 257
APPENDIX B: How to Conduct Financial Analysis for Business Policy
Casework 261

Index 289

PREFACE

The publication of the first edition of *Concepts of Strategic Management* had gratifying results. Hundreds of colleges and universities adopted the book and thousands of students have learned about the strategic management process from it. As a result of its success, I was tempted to do a minor revision and continue on with a proven product.

However, much has happened in the world since the publication of the first edition. The savings and loan debacle will cost taxpayers billions of dollars. The investigation of the disaster pinpointed widespread abuse and mismanagement. Drexel Burnham Lambert, the firm that led the mergers and acquisitions mania of the 1980s, went bankrupt, and yet had paid millions of dollars to its management team just months before the bankruptcy.

In the global arena, the Iron Curtain across Eastern Europe has disappeared. As a result, a unified Germany is expected to have even more significance in the European and world economy. Deteriorating conditions in the planned economies of the Communist world signal the likelihood of even more changes in the political and economic structures of those countries. Japan continues to increase its business presence throughout the world. As a result of these and other changes, firms must continue to adapt to new and changing global conditions and competition.

In a similar fashion, textbooks must adapt to new and changing conditions. As a result, HarperCollins and I decided to make major revisions in this edition. Relying on the suggestions of instructors who have used the book, reviewers who provided valuable insights, and my own study, I have retained the strongest parts of previous editions and have strengthened the weaker parts. The text has been reorganized: some material has been eliminated, other material has been revised and updated, and new material has been added.

Topical Coverage of the Book

Concepts of Strategic Management: Formulation and Implementation is organized around a model that graphically depicts the steps involved in the strategic management process. This model has been used in previous editions and has been very positively received by students and professors. I believe the model is helpful because it gives in one diagram a picture of the complex process of strategy formulation and implementation. The model is used to open each part and chapter of the text. Part One of the text introduces the student to the strategic management process. Part Two describes the strategy formulation process, and Part Three discusses the strategy selection process. Part Four describes strategy implementation. Global strategy formulation and implementation are covered in Part Five, and Part Six explains how to prepare a case analysis and how to conduct financial analysis for casework.

Changes in the Third Edition

This third edition is a major revision of the earlier edition. In Part One, Chapter 1, I now cover organizational culture, an integral part of the strategic management process. Ethics, a subject that was not stressed in the second edition, is now specifically addressed to reflect its increasing significance in today's business world.

In Part Two, Chapter 2, which analyzes the external environment, has been completely revised. Competitive analysis has been strengthened by the addition of significant new material on industry structure analysis and individual competitor analysis. New material on environmental forecasting methods has been added. Chapter 3—"Analyzing the Internal Environment and Establishing Organizational Objectives"—is also a complete revision. A new series of checklist questions for performing an analysis of each of the functional areas of a business has been added. A new section on setting objectives in strategic business units and functional areas has also been added.

Both chapters comprising Part Three had been identified by reviewers as being very strong in earlier editions. As a result, this part of the book has received the least revision. Strategic alternatives, generic competitive strategies, mergers, acquisitions, and joint ventures are described in detail in Chapter 4. Strategy evaluation techniques and qualitative factors in strategy selection are discussed in Chapter 5. One significant addition to this latter chapter is a discussion of value-based planning.

Part Four, on strategy implementation, has been completely revised. Chapter 6—"Strategy, Structure, and Organizational Leadership"—contains new material on restructuring a business and on organizational leadership. A unique feature of this chapter is the discussion of the structure and responsibilities of a firm's board of directors. An appendix of the end of Chapter 6 describes the strengths and weaknesses of organizational structure types. Chapter 7—"Developing Budgets, Functional Strategies, and Motivational Systems"—has new material on functional strategies and on the budgeting process. Functional strategies are analyzed in depth, and new material on strategy implementation and motivational systems has been added. Chapter 8—"The Strategic Control Process"—contains new material on the elements of strategic control and on the role of management information systems in strategic control. New material on conducting a strategy review has also been added.

Part Five—"Application of Strategic Management"—is totally new and describes global strategy formulation and implementation. The addition of this chapter recognizes the increasing globalization of business activity. Global industries, global strategies, and multinational corporations are all examined, and unique environmental forces in global strategy formulation are presented. Generic global strategy options and methods of global strategy selection are also discussed.

Part Six provides useful information for strategic management casework. Appendix A describes how to prepare a case analysis. It offers typical questions that an instructor might pose during classroom discussion of a case and gives helpful suggestions on how to analyze and write up cases. Appendix B, which is totally new, describes how to conduct financial analysis for business policy casework. Prepared by Professors Manab Thakur and Amir Jassim of California State University, Fresno, this appendix describes in detail ratio analysis, working capital analysis, capital budgeting, business acquisitions analysis, and pro forma financial statement analysis.

❑ *Pedagogy*

Several features of this book are designed to facilitate the learning process. Each chapter opens with the *model of the strategic management process.* The particular component of the process that is being analyzed in the chapter is highlighted to shows its relationship to the other components in the process. Immediately following the model are statements of *learning objectives* for the chapter. *Key terms and definitions* are highlighted throughout each chapter. Within each chapter, several examples are given of actual companies applying concepts from the chapter. Entitled *"Strategy in Action,"* these examples describe both large and small businesses.

At the end of each chapter, the learning objectives are repeated, followed by a brief recapitulation of the corresponding concepts from the chapter. *Review questions* that require the student to provide specific responses are also included. Following the review questions are three to four *discussion questions* that require analysis and amplification based on material from the chapter.

A major feature new to this edition is an *integrative case.* This feature is designed to illustrate the strategic management process in more detail by following an actual case study of the Ford Motor Company. Ford Motor Company was chosen because it is one of the oldest and best-known American organizations, it is one of the leading American companies in the international business arena, and it has faced strong competition from foreign manufacturers. This integrative case, parts of which appear at the end of each chapter in sections entitled "Strategy in Action Case Study: Ford Motor Company," describe how Ford has used concepts and methods discussed in each chapter in following the strategic management process. This continuing case study should enable the student to understand how an actual company would apply concepts from the text.

❑ *Supplemental Material*

In addition to the materials in the book, several ancillary items are provided to promote the learning environment.

Instructor's Manual Written by James Spee of the California State University, Fullerton, the Instructor's Manual contains unique features such as an overview of the case method and instructions on the use of task groups, computerized materials, videos, simulations, and group projects in the teaching of strategic management. It also includes summaries, objectives, an outline, key terms, and answers to review and discussion questions for each chapter, along with a detailed analysis of each case. The Instructor's Manual is also available on disk for the IBM PC and compatibles.

Test Bank   Written by Donald McCarty of the University of Pittsburgh, this extensive test bank contains nearly 1500 multiple-choice, true/false, fill-in, and essay questions. A unique feature is the inclusion of multiple-choice questions about each of the cases in the text.

Harper Test   The test bank on this highly acclaimed computerized test-generation system with full word-processing capabilities is available. Harper Test produces customized tests and allows instructors to scramble questions and/or add new ones. Available for the IBM and some compatibles.

Transparency Acetates   Seventy-five acetates of key figures are available free to adopters.

HarperCollins Business Video Library   Adopters may choose from a variety of original and archival business videos related to the text.

Grades   HarperCollins offers to adopters this grade-keeping and class management package for the IBM-PC that maintains data for up to 200 students.

Acknowledgments

As in previous editions, I am indebted to many colleagues and students for the assistance and support I have received. Special thanks are due to the following reviewers of this edition:

Sheila Adams, University of North Carolina at Wilmington
Helen Deresky, State University of New York at Plattsburgh
Massoud Farahbakhsh, Salem State College
Theodore Herbert, Rollins College
Ed Lyell, Metropolitan State College
Donald R. McCarty, University of Pittsburgh Johnstown
Joseph G. P. Paolillo, University of Mississippi
Daniel James Rowley, University of Northern Colorado
Joseph A. Schenk, University of Dayton
Brad Shrader, Iowa State University of Science and Technology
Daniel L. White, Drexel University

. . . and to the reviewers of previous editions:

Pierre A. David, Baldwin-Wallace College
Eliezer Geisler, Northeastern Illinois University
Peter M. Ginter, University of Alabama at Birmingham
Kenneth W. Olm, University of Texas at Austin

Joseph A. Schenk, University of Dayton
Scott A. Snell, Michigan State University
Wilma D. Strickland, Northern Illinois University
Rajaram Veliyath, Virginia Polytechnic Institute and State University

I would also like to thank a special group of students who assisted greatly with the analysis of the Ford Motor Company. They are Karla Bailey, Ansumana Bangura, Michelle Bonner, Marvin Davis, M. A. Ekon, Biram Fall, Pamela Foster, Daniel Grissom, Annjennette Hall, Traci Jackson, Andrea Lucas, Dawn Moore, Javier Ramos, and Angelo Veney.

I am excited about this new edition and hope it meets your needs. I am interested in any feedback you may be inclined to send.

LLOYD L. BYARS

ABOUT THE AUTHOR

Lloyd L. Byars is professor and chairman of the Department of Management at Clark Atlanta University and has recently served as a visiting professor at the Georgia Institute of Technology. He received his bachelor's degree in electrical engineering and his master's degree in industrial management from the Georgia Institute of Technology; he was awarded his Ph.D. degree in management from Georgia State University. Dr. Byars currently teaches courses in business policy and strategic management, human resource management, and organizational behavior.

Prior to joining Clark Atlanta University, Dr. Byars was on the faculty of the College of Business Administration of Georgia State University. Early in his career he worked as a marketing representative in the data processing division of the IBM Corporation. Dr. Byars has given lectures in management development programs for many organizations, including the U.S. Department of Defense, the U.S. Social Security Administration, the University of Florida—Medical School, Duke Power Company, and South Carolina Electric and Gas Company. Dr. Byars also serves as a labor arbitrator, certified by both the Federal Mediation and Conciliation Service and the American Arbitration Association. He has arbitrated cases in the United States, Europe, Central America, and the Caribbean.

Dr. Byars has published numerous articles in leading professional journals. In addition, he has coauthored three other textbooks in the field of management.

CONCEPTS OF STRATEGIC MANAGEMENT

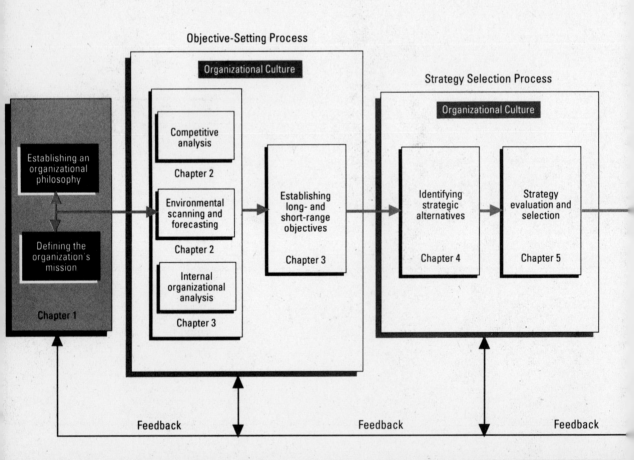

STRATEGIC MANAGEMENT PROCESS

Strategy Formulation

Objective-Setting Process

Organizational Culture

Strategy Selection Process

Organizational Culture

Establishing an
organizational
philosophy

Defining the
organization's
mission

Chapter 1

Competitive
analysis

Chapter 2

Environmental
scanning and
forecasting

Chapter 2

Internal
organizational
analysis

Chapter 3

Establishing
long- and
short-range
objectives

Chapter 3

Identifying
strategic
alternatives

Chapter 4

Strategy
evaluation and
selection

Chapter 5

Feedback   Feedback   Feedback

PART ONE
INTRODUCTION TO THE STRATEGIC MANAGEMENT PROCESS

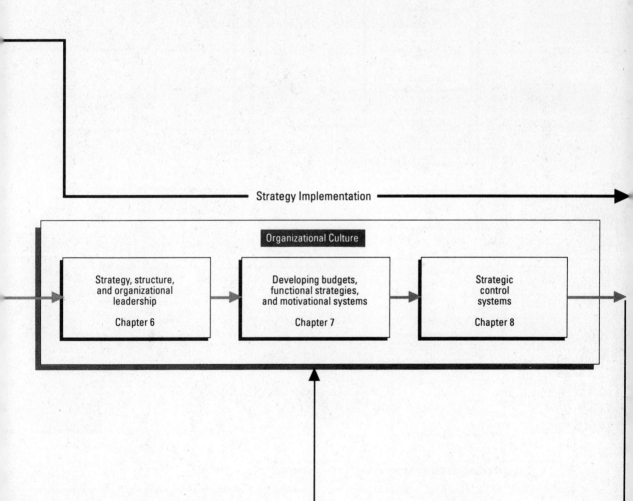

Strategy Implementation

Organizational Culture

Strategy, structure, and organizational leadership	Developing budgets, functional strategies, and motivational systems	Strategic control systems
Chapter 6	Chapter 7	Chapter 8

Feedback   Feedback

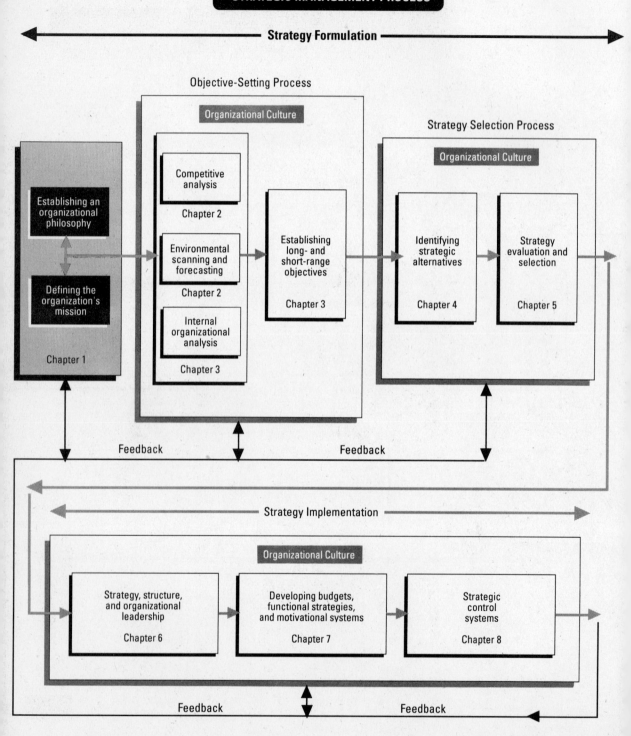

STRATEGIC MANAGEMENT PROCESS

Strategy Formulation

Objective-Setting Process

Organizational Culture

Competitive analysis

Chapter 2

Environmental scanning and forecasting

Chapter 2

Internal organizational analysis

Chapter 3

Establishing long- and short-range objectives

Chapter 3

Strategy Selection Process

Organizational Culture

Identifying strategic alternatives

Chapter 4

Strategy evaluation and selection

Chapter 5

Establishing an organizational philosophy

Defining the organization's mission

Chapter 1

Feedback   Feedback

Strategy Implementation

Organizational Culture

Strategy, structure, and organizational leadership

Chapter 6

Developing budgets, functional strategies, and motivational systems

Chapter 7

Strategic control systems

Chapter 8

Feedback   Feedback

CHAPTER 1
Strategic Management:
An Overview

LEARNING OBJECTIVES

After studying this chapter, you should be able to

1. Define strategic management.
2. Explain the steps involved in strategy formulation.
3. Identify the steps involved in strategy implementation.
4. Define organizational philosophy.
5. Describe organizational culture.
6. Define organizational mission.
7. Differentiate between long- and short-range objectives.
8. Define strategy.
9. Explain strategic business units.
10. Describe ethics in business.

Some organizations grow to be extremely large and profitable, while others go bankrupt. Some organizations diversify into many new business activities, while others do not. Each year *Fortune* magazine lists America's largest companies by sales volume. As can be seen from Example 1.1, some companies, such as IBM, were not on the list in 1955. Others, such as International Harvester, were on the list in 1955 but not in 1989.

In the decades to come, the increased rate of environmental, social, and technological change, the increased internationalization of business organizations, and the increased scarcity and cost of natural resources will make the environment of organizations even more complex. How do organizations make decisions about their future in this complex and changing environment? The process used is called strategic management. *Strategic management* involves

---

STRATEGY IN ACTION Example 1.1

The Top 25 Companies As Ranked by Sales Volume

Rank	1955	1970	1989
1	General Motors	General Motors	General Motors
2	Standard Oil of N.J. (Exxon)	Standard Oil of N.J. (Exxon)	Ford Motor
3	U.S. Steel	Ford Motor	Exxon
4	General Electric	General Electric	IBM
5	Swift	IBM	General Electric
6	Chrysler	Mobil Oil	Mobil
7	Armour	Chrysler	Philip Morris
8	Gulf Oil	ITT	Chrysler
9	Socony-Vacuum Oil (Mobil)	Texaco	du Pont
10	du Pont	Western Electric	Texaco
11	Bethlehem Steel	Gulf Oil	Chevron
12	Standard Oil (Ind.)	U.S. Steel	Amoco
13	Westinghouse Electric	Westinghouse Electric	Shell Oil
14	Texas Co. (Texaco)	Standard Oil (Calif.)	Procter & Gamble
15	Western Electric	LTV	Boeing
16	Shell Oil	Standard Oil (Ind.)	Occidental Petroleum
17	National Dairy Products	Boeing	United Technologies
18	Standard Oil (Calif.)	du Pont	Eastman Kodak
19	Goodyear Tire & Rubber	Shell Oil	USX
20	Boeing Airplane	GTE	Dow Chemical
21	Sinclair Oil	RCA	Xerox
22	International Harvester	Goodyear Tire & Rubber	Atlantic Richfield
23	RCA	Swift	PepsiCo
24	Union Carbide	Union Carbide	RJR Nabisco
25	Firestone Tire & Rubber	Procter & Gamble	McDonnell Douglas

Source: Fortune, July 1955; May 1971; and April 23, 1990.

making those decisions that define the organization's mission and objectives, determine the organization's most effective utilization of its resources, and seek to assure the effectiveness of the organization within its environment.

Strategic management is equally applicable to public, private, not-for-profit, and religious organizations. Strategic management concepts are as useful to a local restaurant, a small office supplies firm, or a college football team as to giant corporations such as Coca-Cola, IBM, or General Motors. Strategic management also applies to Georgia Tech, the Mayo Clinic, the Baptist church, Kiwanis International, the U.S. Department of Defense, the Ford Foundation, Sigma Mu Fraternity, and the NAACP. An attempt is made in this book to show the applicability of strategic management to all types of organizations, but the emphasis is on private-enterprise organizations.

THE STRATEGIC MANAGEMENT PROCESS

A description of the strategic management process involves the use of terms and expressions that have a variety of meanings and interpretations depending on the author and source. For example, some of the phrases used interchangeably with strategic management are *strategy and policy formulation, long-range planning,* and *business policy.* The purpose of this section is to define the terminology used in this book and to present a framework for analysis of the strategic management process.

Basically, strategic management can be broken down into two phases: strategy formulation and strategy implementation. *Strategy formulation* is concerned with making decisions with regard to

1. Defining the organization's philosophy and mission
2. Establishing long- and short-range objectives to achieve the organization's mission
3. Selecting the strategy to be used in achieving the organization's objectives

Strategy implementation is concerned with aligning the organizational structure, systems, and processes with the chosen strategy. It involves making decisions with regard to

1. Matching strategy and organizational structure and providing organizational leadership pertinent to the strategy
2. Developing budgets, functional strategies, and motivational systems for the successful achievement of organizational objectives
3. Monitoring the effectiveness of the strategy in achieving the organization's objectives

Defining the Organization's Philosophy (or Creed)

Organizational philosophy (or creed) establishes the values, beliefs, and guidelines for the manner in which the organization is going to conduct its business. It establishes the relationship between the organization and its *stakeholders:* employees, customers, shareholders, suppliers, government, and the public at large. The importance of having an organizational philosophy was stated by Thomas J. Watson, Jr., former chairman of the board of IBM, as follows:

> This, then, is my thesis: I firmly believe that any organization, in order to survive and achieve success, must have a sound set of beliefs on which it premises all its policies and actions.
>
> Next, I believe that the most important single factor in corporate success is faithful adherence to these beliefs.
>
> And finally, I believe that if an organization is to meet the challenges of a changing world, it must be prepared to change everything about itself except those beliefs as it moves through corporate life.[1]

Watson went on to describe IBM's philosophy:

1. Respect for the individual. This is a simple concept, but at IBM it occupies a major portion of management time. We devote more effort to it than anything else.
2. We want to give the best customer service of any company in the world.
3. We believe that an organization should pursue all tasks with the idea that they can be accomplished in a superior fashion.[2]

Over 25 years after Watson stated these three basic beliefs, IBM Board Chairman Frank Cary stated: "We've changed our technology, changed our organization, changed our marketing and manufacturing techniques many times, and we expect to go on changing. But through all this change, those three basic beliefs remain. We steer our course by those stars."[3]

The philosophy of an organization is normally a rather permanent statement that is usually articulated by the chief executive officer. For small businesses, the owner establishes the philosophy either in writing or through his or her personal behavior. In many larger organizations, the founder of the business established the corporate philosophy and it is maintained throughout the life of the organization. For example, J. C. Penney and Thomas Watson, Sr., established philosophies for their organizations that are still in existence.

The content and specific wording of organizational statements of philosophy vary from organization to organization. However, Thomas Peters and Robert Waterman found that the philosophies of excellent companies included the following basic beliefs:

1. Belief in being the best.
2. Belief in the importance of the details of execution, the nuts and bolts of doing the job well.
3. Belief in the importance of people as individuals.
4. Belief in superior quality and service.
5. Belief that most members of the organization should be innovators, and its corollary, the willingness to support failure.
6. Belief in the importance of informality to enhance communication.
7. Belief in a recognition of the importance of economic growth and profits.[4]

Example 1.2 presents the organizational philosophy of Johnson & Johnson, one of the world's most respected drug companies. In this statement, Johnson & Johnson clearly spells out its responsibilities toward its customers, its employees, the communities it serves, and its stockholders.

STRATEGY IN ACTION *Example 1.2*

Credo of Johnson & Johnson

Johnson & Johnson (J&J) makes and sells a wide variety of products in the health care and related industries, including such well-known products as baby shampoo, Tylenol, and Band-Aid adhesive bandages. Over the last ten years its earnings growth has averaged 13 percent annually. In 1988, it had over $9 billion in sales and $1.8 billion in profits. All of this was accomplished by selling basically consumable or disposable health-care-related products. Johnson & Johnson operates under the following corporate philosophy:

We believe our first responsibility is to the doctors, nurses, and patients, to mothers and all others who use our products and services. In meeting their needs everything we do must be of high quality. We must constantly strive to reduce our costs in order to maintain reasonable prices. Customers' orders must be serviced promptly and accurately. Our suppliers and distributors must have an opportunity to make a fair profit.

We are responsible to our employees, the men and women who work with us throughout the world. Everyone must be considered as an individual. We must respect their dignity and recognize their merit. They must have a sense of security in their jobs. Compensation must be fair and adequate and working conditions clean, orderly, and safe. Employees must feel free to make suggestions and complaints. There must be equal opportunity for employment, development, and advancement for those qualified. We must provide competent management, and their actions must be just and ethical.

We are responsible to the communities in which we live and work and to the world community as well. We must be good citizens—support good works and charities and bear our fair share of taxes. We must encourage civic improvements and better health and education. We must maintain in good order the property we are privileged to use, protecting the environment and natural resources.

Our final responsibility is to our stockholders. Business must make a sound profit. We must experiment with new ideas. Research must be carried on, innovative programs developed and mistakes paid for. New equipment must be purchased, new facilities provided, and new products launched. Reserves must be created to provide for adverse times. When we operate according to these principles, the stockholders should realize a fair return.

Source: Patrick E. Murphy, "Creating Ethical Corporate Structures," *Sloan Management Review,* Winter 1989, p. 83.

If an organization's philosophy is to have meaning, it must be adhered to in all situations. Ignoring the organizational philosophy in crisis situations is a major mistake for management. It is through the day-to-day decisions and actions of management that philosophies are confirmed and strengthened or become meaningless words on a piece of paper.

Finally, an organization's philosophy provides the general framework for the establishment of organizational policies. *Organizational policies provide guides to action for employees of the organization.* For example, after describing IBM's corporate philosophy, Thomas Watson, Jr., outlined one policy as follows:

> Open-door policy—Every employee has the right to talk to whomever they wish including any member of top management concerning problems, or concerns they have about management actions or decisions.[5]

Policies help to ensure that all units of an organization operate within the corporate philosophy. They also facilitate coordination and communication between various organizational units.

Several other factors influence the formulation of policies. One important factor has been federal, state, and local government. Government regulates organizations in areas such as competition (antitrust and monopoly), product standards (safety and quality), pricing (utilities), hiring practices (civil rights), working conditions (Occupational Safety and Health Administration, or OSHA, regulations), wages (minimum wages), accounting practices (income tax regulation), and issuance of stock (Securities and Exchange Commission, or SEC regulations). Policies need to be developed to guide employees in following these regulations. For example, as a result of government regulation, many organizations have developed a policy statement that declares the organization's unqualified opposition to all forms of discrimination.

Policies of competitors also influence an organization's policies. This is especially true with personnel policies such as wages, benefits, and working conditions.

An extremely important consideration in policy formulation is that policies should facilitate the successful accomplishment of organizational objectives. All too frequently policies emerge from history, tradition, and earlier events. Changing environmental conditions and changed organizational objectives should trigger an evaluation of organizational policies to ascertain if they are still appropriate or should be changed.

Developing an Organizational Culture

Culture in an organization compares to personality in a person. Humans have fairly enduring and stable traits that help them protect their attitudes and behaviors. So do organizations. In addition, certain groups of traits or personality types are known to consist of common elements. Organizations can be described in similar terms. They can be warm, aggressive, friendly, open, innovative, conservative, and so forth. An organization's culture is transmitted in many ways, including long-standing and often unwritten rules, shared standards about what is important, prejudices, standards for social etiquette and demeanor, established customs for how to relate to peers, subordinates, and superiors, and other traditions that clarify to employees what is and is not appropriate behavior. Thus, *organizational culture* refers to the collective assumptions and beliefs of an organization's employees that shape the behavior of individuals and groups in the organization. Simply stated, organizational culture means how things are done in an organization.

Origin of Organizational Cultures

There is no question that different organizations develop different cultures. What causes an organization to develop a particular type of culture? Many trace their culture to one person who provided a living example of the major values of the organization. Robert Wood Johnson of Johnson & Johnson, Harley Procter of Procter & Gamble, Walt Disney of Walt Disney Productions, and Thomas J. Watson, Sr., of IBM all left their imprints on the organizations they headed. Additional aspects of an organization's culture appear to develop in response both to the environment in which the business operates and to the needs of the employees. Four separate factors have been identified that contribute to the development of an organization's culture: its history, its environment, its staffing process, and its socialization processes.

1. *History* Employees are aware of the organization's past, and this awareness builds culture. Much of the "way things are done" is a continuation of how things have always been done. The existing values, which may have been deliberately established, are continuously and subtly reinforced by experiences. The status quo is also reinforced by the tendency of people to strongly resist changes in beliefs and values. For example, executives of Walt Disney Productions reportedly pick up litter unconsciously because of the Disney vision of an immaculate Disneyland.

2. *Environment* Because all organizations must interact with their environment, the environment plays an important role in shaping an organization's culture. Organizations that operate in a highly regulated environment, such as public utilities, develop cultures totally different from those in organizations that face fierce competition in industries with rapidly changing technology, such as the computer industry. In fact, since deregulation, many organizations in the communications, banking, and airlines industries are no longer sheltered by their regulated environment and must change their cultures. The question is whether the change can come fast enough to ensure their success and survival.

3. *Staffing Process* Organizations tend to hire, retain, and promote people who are similar to current employees in important ways. A person's ability to fit in can be an important criterion, helping to ensure that current values are accepted and that potential challenges of "how we do things" are screened out.

4. *Socialization Processes* New employees also learn the organization's culture from their orientation program and their actual work experiences. Companies such as IBM, Procter & Gamble, General Electric (GE), and McDonald's have formal orientation programs that teach the basic values of these

companies. Furthermore, compensation, performance appraisal, and promotion systems communicate and reinforce the organization's culture.

Identifying Organizational Cultures   Seven characteristics have been identified that, when taken together, define or describe an organization's culture. Each of these characteristics should be viewed as lying on a continuum that ranges from low to high. A picture of the overall organizational culture can be developed by appraising an organization on each of the following characteristics:

1. *Individual Autonomy.* Degree of responsibility, independence, and opportunities for exercising initiative that individuals in the organization have.
2. *Structure.* Number of rules and regulations and amount of direct supervision that is used to oversee and control employee behavior.
3. *Support.* Degree of assistance and warmth that managers give their subordinates.
4. *Identification.* Degree to which employees identify with the organization as a whole rather than with their particular work group or field of professional expertise.
5. *Performance-Reward.* Degree to which reward allocations in the organization (i.e., salary increases, promotions) are based on performance criteria.
6. *Conflict Tolerance.* Degree of conflict present in relationships between peers and work groups as well as a willingness to be honest and open about differences.
7. *Risk Tolerance.* Degree to which employees are encouraged to be aggressive, innovative, and risk-seeking.

In developing and reinforcing their cultures, many organizations have emphasized one or more of the seven characteristics. Delta Air Lines, for example, has stressed assistance and warmth, which has, in turn, developed a family feeling among its employees. This feeling has led to a strong sense of teamwork among employees and loyalty to the company.

Changing Organizational Cultures   Organizational objectives are sometimes not achieved and strategies are ineffective because of their incompatibility with the organization's culture. However, changing a corporate culture is a long, difficult process. How can management change an organization's culture to meet its needs? A starting point is a clear written statement of corporate philosophy that is consistently reinforced by the company policies and managerial practices. It is essential for managers to remember that culture must be practiced, not just preached.

On the other hand, many organizations that are hard pressed to change their culture seem to find it easier just to fire the senior management team and replace it with a new team. This view is based on the assumption that most organizations promote people who fit the prevailing norms of the organization so the easiest if not the only way to change the culture is to change the senior management.

Defining the Organization's Mission or Purpose

An organizational *statement of mission or purpose* outlines why the organization exists. It should define the organization's line or lines of business, identify its products and services, and specify the markets it serves at present and within a time frame of three to five years. A clear, written statement of mission provides a sense of direction and a guide to decision making for all levels of management. Without a concrete statement of mission, it is virtually impossible for an organization to develop objectives and strategies.

Peter Drucker has postulated that an organization's mission is not determined by the organization itself but rather by its customers.[6] Customer satisfaction with an organization's products and services defines its mission. Thus, defining an organization's mission starts with a clear description of its customers. Questions that need to be answered are as follows:

1. Who is the customer?
   a. Where is the customer located?
   b. How does the customer buy?
   c. How can the customer be reached?
2. What does the customer buy?
3. What does the customer consider value? (What does the customer look for when he or she buys the product?)[7]

Since a mission statement is also concerned with an organization's future business activities, its potential customers must also be described. The following questions need to be answered:

1. What are the market trends and market potential?
2. What changes in market structure might occur as a result of economic developments, changes in styles or fashions, or moves by the competition?
3. What innovations will alter the customer's buying habits?
4. What needs does the customer currently have that are not being adequately met by available products and services?[8]

One final question needs to be addressed in determining an organization's mission. Is the organization in the right business, or should it change its business?[9]

Example 1.3 gives the corporate mission statement of American Telephone and Telegraph (AT&T). This statement illustrates a clear, written statement of mission.

An organization's mission not only must be defined at its inception but also must be reexamined regularly. Several factors can signal a need for a reexamination: declining profits and market share, changes in competitive position or top-level management personnel, new technologies, decreased availability or

STRATEGY IN ACTION Example 1.3

Mission Statement of AT&T

1. To strengthen and enhance the profitability and market position of the company's core businesses. The core businesses include

   - Domestic long-distance services
   - The design, manufacture, and sale of network telecommunications equipment for operating companies
   - The design, manufacture, and sale of custom-premises telecommunications equipment, which includes stand-alone computers as well as component computers in our information systems

2. To build on AT&T's strength and reputation to bring a new generation of data-networking solutions to our customers.
3. To establish a major position in the international market for information movement and management. To accomplish this we will pursue overseas partners that are established in the information industry.

Source: Adapted from James E. Olson and Thomas A. Cooper, "CEOs on Strategy: Two Companies, Two Strategies," *Journal of Business Strategy*, Summer 1987, pp. 52–53.

increased cost of resources, and changes in market demographics, government regulations, or consumer demand. Often the need for a change in mission is sensed by top management in vague or undefined terms (i.e., things simply do not seem to be going right). Top managers' skill in recognizing the need for a change in mission and their ability to clearly delineate the new mission play a significant role in the future success of the organization.

Finally, it is important to note that organizational statements of philosophy and mission are not always separate and distinct documents. Often these statements are combined into one document, but that document still embodies the essential features of the philosophy and mission statements described in the previous paragraphs.

Establishing Long- and Short-Range Objectives

Long-range objectives specify the results desired in pursuing the organization's mission and normally extend beyond the current fiscal year. Short-range objectives are performance targets, normally of less than one year's duration, that management uses to measure progress toward the achievement of long-range objectives.

An organization's objectives depend on the particular organization and its mission. Although objectives can vary widely from organization to organization, normally they can be categorized as follows: (1) profitability; (2) service to customers, clients, or other recipients; (3) employee needs and well-being; and (4) social responsibility. The entire objective-setting process will be described in much more detail in Chapters 2 and 3.

Selecting a Strategy

The word *strategy* came from the Greek word *strategos,* which means "a general." Originally, strategy literally meant the art and science of directing military forces. Today, the term is used in business to describe the steps taken by an organization in achieving its objectives and mission. Most organizations have several options available to them. Strategy is concerned with deciding which option is to be used. *Strategy is the determination and evaluation of alternatives available to an organization in achieving its objectives and mission and the selection of the alternative to be pursued.* Strategy selection is examined in more depth in Chapters 4 and 5.

Hierarchy of Strategies Strategies exist at different levels in an organization; they are classified according to the scope of what they are intended to accomplish. Most organizations can be segmented into business units (or strategic business units as they are frequently called). Strategic business units (SBUs) are described in more detail later in this chapter.

Strategies that address what businesses a multiple-business-unit organization will be in and how resources will be allocated among those businesses are referred to as *corporate strategies.* They are established at the highest levels of management and involve a long-range time horizon. *Business strategies* focus on how to compete in a given business. Narrower in scope than a corporate strategy, business strategy generally applies to a single business unit. A third level of strategy is the functional strategy. *Functional strategies* are narrower in scope than business strategies and deal with the activities of the functional areas—production, finance, marketing, personnel, and the like. Functional strategies must support business strategies, but they are mainly concerned with "how-to" issues. Figure 1.1 illustrates the hierarchical relationships between mission, objectives, corporate strategy, business unit strategies, and functional strategies.

Figure 1.1 *Hierarchy of Strategies*

INTEGRATING PHILOSOPHY, MISSION, OBJECTIVES, AND STRATEGY

Figure 1.2 shows a framework that will be used throughout this book to analyze the strategic management process. Although the framework depicts a separate and sequential process, the entire process requires considerable feedback from the various components. In fact, the components are interdependent and inseparable. For example, a change in an organization's environment may require a change in its mission and objectives. Or a particular strategy may not have achieved the objectives of the organization, possibly because of unrealistic objectives, an inappropriate strategy, or the wrong organizational structure. Thus, as the dashed line in Figure 1.2 shows, feedback from each component in the strategic management process has the potential to influence the others.

STRATEGIC MANAGEMENT AND ORGANIZATIONAL SUCCESS

Many studies have examined a large number of organizations over different time periods, in different environments, and with different research methodologies to analyze the relationship between strategic management and organizational success.

One of the earliest and most comprehensive studies of this relationship involved companies in the drug, chemical, machinery, oil, food, and steel industries.[10] The study divided the companies into one of two groups: those with formal and those with informal strategic management systems. Companies were classified as having a formal system if they determined objectives for at least three years ahead and if they established specific action programs, projects, and procedures for achieving the objectives. Companies that did not meet these requirements were classified as having an informal strategic management system. The performance of companies in each of these categories was then analyzed in terms of sales, stock prices, earnings per share, return on equity, and return on total capital. Those organizations with formal strategic management systems significantly outperformed the others on earnings per share, return on equity, and return on total capital. Although the sales and stock price appreciation for those organizations with formal systems were also greater, the figures were strongly influenced by a single company and therefore no inferences were drawn on those two items. The study also compared the performance of the organizations with formal systems over an equal period of time before and after they initiated the system. After initiation of the formal system, the organizations surpassed their performance over prior years. A follow-up study of these same companies showed that those with formal strategic management systems continued to outperform those with informal systems and had, in fact, widened their margin.[11]

A study of 70 large commercial banks examined the financial performance (increase in net income and return on owner's equity) of those institutions with regard to whether they had a formal or informal strategic management system.[12] Again, those organizations with formal systems outperformed the other organizations.

Later studies on the relationship between the use of formal strategic management systems and organizational success have produced mixed results.[13]

Figure 1.2 The Strategic Management Process

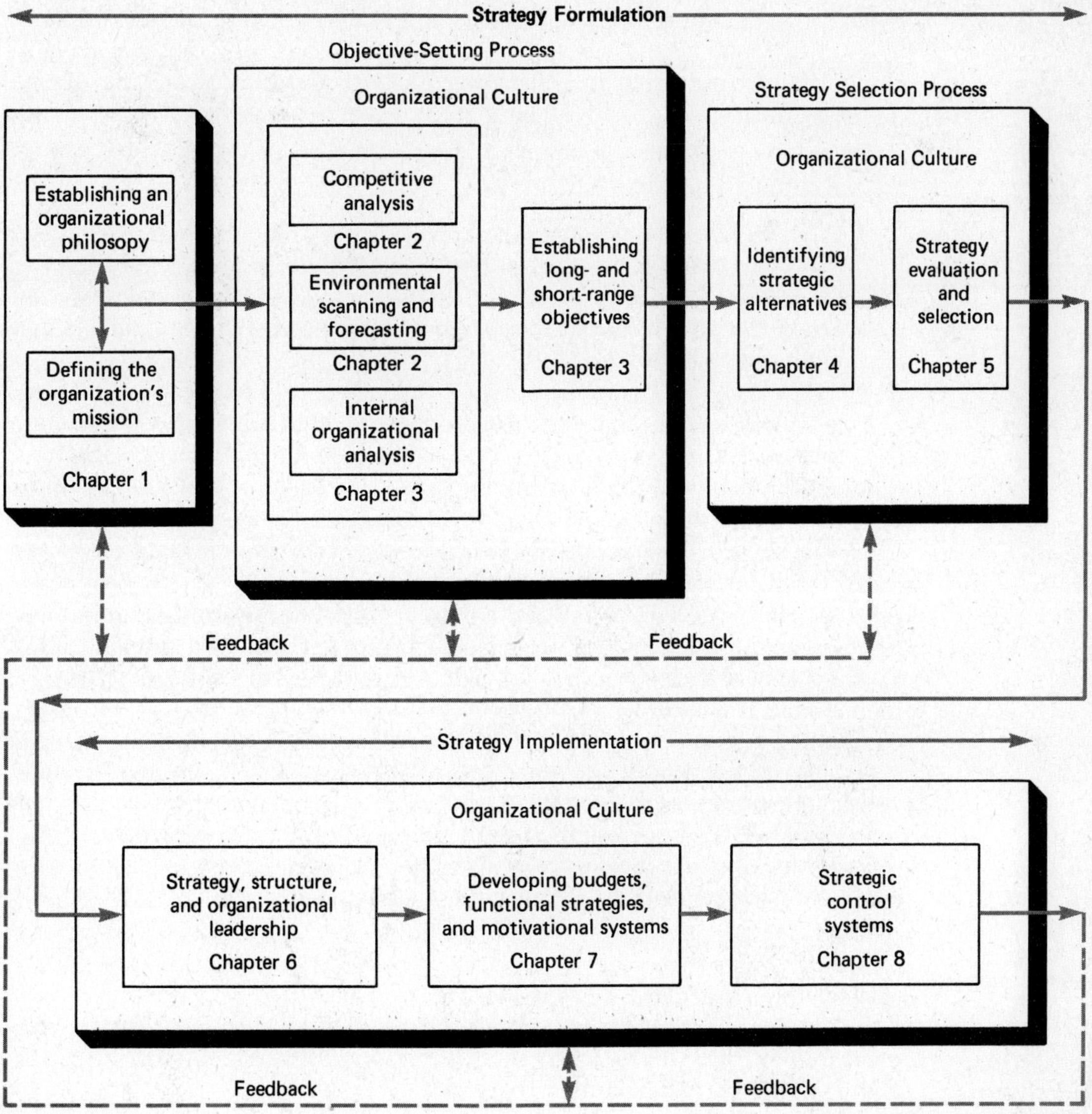

Apparently some organizations, either through luck or the intuitive genius of their leadership, have been successful without formal strategic management systems. However, most research evidence would support the conclusion that engaging in a formal strategic management process significantly enhances the likelihood of organizational success.

STRATEGIC BUSINESS UNITS (SBUs)

One additional term needs to be discussed before the strategic management process is analyzed in detail. Normally, an organization's activities can be segmented into business units. *A business unit is an operating unit in an organization that sells a distinct set of products or services to an identifiable group of customers in competition with a well-defined set of competitors.* A business unit is normally referred to as a strategic business unit, or SBU for short.

Generally, the following criteria should be considered in classifying an organizational unit as an SBU:

- First, an SBU should serve an external, rather than an internal, market; that is, it should have a set of external customers and not merely serve as an internal supplier.
- Second, it should have a clear set of external competitors, which it is trying to equal or surpass.
- Third, it should have control over its own destiny. This means that it must be able to decide for itself what products to offer, how and when to go to market, and where to obtain its supplies, components, or even products. This does not mean that it cannot use pooled resources such as a common manufacturing plant, or a combined sales force, or even corporate R&D. The key is choice. It must be able to choose and not merely be the victim of someone else's decisions. It must have options from which it may select the alternative(s) that best achieves the corporate and the business objectives.
- Fourth, its performance must be measurable in terms of profit and loss; that is, it should be a true profit center.[14]

SBUs operate within the objectives and strategy set by top management. Within that framework, each SBU performs its own strategic management process. The SBU's operations are either strengthened or weakened depending on the resources allocated to it at the corporate level. Example 1.4 shows the strategic business units in the General Electric Company.

MAKING STRATEGIC DECISIONS

The making of strategic decisions is a function and responsibility of managers at all levels, but the final responsibility rests with top management. The top

STRATEGY IN ACTION Example 1.4

Strategic Business Units of GE

Strategic Business Unit	Revenues (dollars in millions)		
	1988	*1987*	*1986*
Aerospace	$5,343	$5,262	$4,318
Aircraft engines	6,481	6,773	5,977
Broadcasting (NBC)	3,638	3,241	1,888
Industrial (lighting, transportation systems, motors, electrical distribution and control)	7,061	6,662	6,770
Major appliances	5,289	4,721	4,352
Materials (plastics and chemicals)	3,539	2,751	2,331
Power systems	4,805	4,995	5,262
Technical products and services (medical and communications systems)	4,431	3,670	3,021
Financial services (GE Capital Corporation, Employers Reinsurance Corporation, and Kidder, Peabody Group)	10,655	8,225	5,814
International operations	10,800	9,200	8,300

Source: Annual reports of GE; public documents.

managers are ultimately responsible for developing the organization's philosophy and mission statements, establishing its objectives, and selecting its strategy. The strategic management responsibilities of managers at lower levels vary depending on the nature and size of the organization and their position in the organizational hierarchy.

In fact, most large organizations have a multilevel strategic management process. Generally, the cycle of events goes as follows:

- Top management determines the corporate philosophy, mission, objectives, and strategy for the organization as a whole as well as guidelines for each of the strategic business units (SBUs).
- Each business unit or SBU then does its own strategic planning.
- If the organization has a planning department, its function is to assist the SBUs in their strategic planning or to supply information that the SBU may need.
- Top management then reviews and approves the strategic plans of each SBU.
- Each SBU then moves to develop a strategic plan for each of its functional areas (marketing, production, finance, R&D).
- After the development of strategic plans for each of the functional areas of the business or SBU unit, budgets are developed. As can be seen from

this description, virtually all levels of management become involved in the strategic management process at some point.

Because this chapter defines such a large number of terms, Figure 1.3 is presented in order to summarize them.

Figure 1.3 Definition of Terms

Business strategies focus on how to compete in a given business.

Corporate strategies address what businesses a multiple-business-unit organization will be in and how resources will be allocated among those businesses.

Functional strategies deal with the activities of the functional areas of a business—production, finance, marketing, personnel, and the like.

Long-range objectives specify the results desired in pursuing the organization's mission and normally extend beyond the current fiscal year of the organization.

Organizational culture is the collective assumptions and beliefs held by an organization's employees that shape the behavior of individuals and groups in the organization.

Organizational mission defines an organization's line or lines of business, identifies its products and services, and specifies the markets it serves at present and in a time frame of three to five years.

Organizational philosophy establishes the values, beliefs, and guidelines for the manner in which the organization is going to conduct its business.

Short-range objectives are performance targets, normally of less than one year's duration, that management uses to measure progress toward the achievement of long-range objectives.

Strategic business units are operating units in an organization each of which sells a distinct set of products or services to an identifiable group of customers in competition with a well-defined set of competitors.

Strategic management involves making those decisions that define the organization's mission and objectives, determine the most effective utilization of its resources, and seek to assure the effectiveness of the organization in its environment.

Strategy is the determination and evaluation of alternatives available to an organization for achieving its objectives and mission and the selection of the alternative to be pursued.

Strategy formulation is the making of decisions to define an organization's philosophy and mission, establish objectives, and select the strategy to be used in achieving the objectives.

Strategy implementation is the making of decisions with regard to matching strategy and organizational structure; developing budgets, functional strategies, and motivational systems; and monitoring the effectiveness of the strategy.

ETHICS AND STRATEGIC MANAGEMENT

Ethics are principles of conduct that govern the decision making and behavior of an individual or group. Since strategic management is concerned with making decisions about the future direction of an organization, the ethics of the individual or group making those decisions has significant implications for an organization's stakeholders—its employees, customers, shareholders, and suppliers—as well as the government and the public at large. In earlier times, the principle of caveat emptor—"let the buyer beware"—governed the decision making and behavior of too many organizations. Recently, scandals on Wall Street and corporate misconduct have called into question the ethics of the management of many organizations. As a result, the role of ethics in strategy decisions is now receiving increased emphasis. More and more colleges and universities are offering courses concerned with ethics in business.

The role of ethics in strategy decisions is a difficult issue, partly because it is emotionally charged and partly because of the many and varied ethical problems faced by managers. What, for example, are the ethical implications involved in the promotion and sale of cigarettes by U.S. companies in foreign countries while the U.S. government acts to diminish consumption of what is considered a dangerous product in the U.S. market? Or how about the ethical implications of forbidding purchasing agents from accepting gifts from vendors while encouraging the sales force to give gifts to prospective buyers? What about managers who are aware of unethical practices in their companies? Should they blow the whistle and risk their jobs? Should they quit and allow unethical practices to continue? Should they just ignore the practices? These are only a few of the difficult and complex ethical decisions faced by managers.

One outcome of questionable business ethics is the passage of laws to regulate organizational behavior. In fact, there are many laws directly relating to the issues of ethics in business. For example, the Federal Fair Packaging and Labeling Act of 1966 regulates labeling procedures for businesses. The Truth in Lending Act of 1967 regulates the extension of credit to individuals. The Consumer Product Safety Act of 1972 protects consumers against unreasonable risks of injury associated with consumer products. The Foreign Corrupt Practices Act of 1977 made it illegal to obtain or retain business through payments to influence foreign officials and governments improperly.

Laws, of course, do not stop all unethical behavior. One response by many organizations to the question of ethics has been to develop a code of ethics and communicate it to all employees. A *code of ethics* is a written document that outlines the principles of conduct to be used in making organizational decisions. Codes of ethics are based on one or more of the following philosophical approaches: justice, individual rights, and utilitarianism.[15] According to the *principle of justice*, ethical decisions are based on truth, a lack of bias, and consistency. Under the *principle of individual rights*, ethical decisions are based on the protection of human dignity; managers, for example, would not force employees to act in a way that is contrary to their moral beliefs. According to the *principle of utilitarianism*, ethical decisions are directed toward promoting the greatest good for the greatest number of people.

Codes of ethics should be formal, written, and communicated to all employees. Although ethics codes differ in content, one study found that those of manufacturing firms often include the following elements:

1. Conduct business in compliance with all laws.
2. Comply with all antitrust and trade regulations.
3. Provide products and services of the highest quality.
4. Perform assigned duties to the best of your ability.
5. Conserve resources and protect the environment.
6. Comply with safety, health, and security regulations.[16]

This same study found that the codes of ethics of service organizations more often include the following elements:

1. Avoid outside activities that impair duties.
2. Do not use company's property for personal benefit.
3. Illegal drugs and alcohol at work are prohibited.
4. Manage personal finances well.
5. Make decisions without regard for personal gain.
6. Dress in businesslike attire.[17]

Obviously, codes of ethics do not end unethical behavior, but they are a positive step in addressing the problem. Finally, however, it is important to note that having a written code of ethics probably does more harm than good if management does not put into practice what is written. "Actions speak louder than words" is an old statement that is especially true in matters of ethics.

SUMMARY OF LEARNING OBJECTIVES

1. Define strategic management.
   Strategic management may be defined as those decisions that define the organization's mission and objectives, determine the most effective utilization of its resources, and seek to assure the effectiveness of the organization in its environment.
2. Explain the steps involved in strategy formulation.
   The three steps involved in strategy formulation are (1) defining the organization's philosophy and mission, (2) establishing long- and short-range objectives to achieve the organization's mission, and (3) selecting the strategy to be used in achieving the organization's objectives.
3. Identify the steps involved in strategy implementation.
   The three steps involved in strategy implementation are (1) matching strategy with organizational structure and providing organizational leadership pertinent to the strategy; (2) developing budgets, functional strategies, and motivational systems for the successful achievement of organizational objectives; and (3) monitoring the effectiveness of the strategy in achieving the organization's objectives.

4. Define organizational philosophy.
   Organizational philosophy establishes the values, beliefs, and guidelines for the manner in which the organization is going to conduct its business.
5. Describe organizational culture.
   Organizational culture is the employees' collective assumptions and beliefs held by an organization's employees that shape the behavior of individuals and groups in the organization.
6. Define organizational mission.
   Organizational mission defines an organization's line or lines of business, identifies its products and services, and specifies the markets it serves at present and within a time frame of three to five years.
7. Differentiate between long- and short-range objectives.
   Long-range objectives specify the results desired in pursuing the organization's mission and normally extend beyond the current fiscal year of the organization. Short-range objectives are performance targets, normally of less than one year's duration, that management uses to measure progress toward the achievement of long-range objectives.
8. Define strategy.
   Strategy is the determination and evaluation of alternatives available to an organization for achieving its objectives and mission and the selection of the alternative to be pursued.
9. Explain strategic business units.
   Strategic business units are operating units in an organization each of which sells a distinct set of products or services to an identifiable group of customers in competition with a well-defined set of competitors.
10. Describe ethics in business.
    Ethics are principles of conduct that govern the decision making and behavior of an individual or group.

REVIEW QUESTIONS

1. What is strategic management?
2. Define the following terms:
   a. Strategy formulation
   b. Strategy implementation
   c. Organizational philosophy
   d. Organizational culture
   e. Organizational mission
   f. Long-range objectives
   g. Short-range objectives
   h. Strategy
3. Explain the four factors that contribute to an organization's culture.
4. Outline questions that must be answered in defining an organization's present and potential customers.
5. Describe the factors that signal a need for a reexamination of an organization's mission.

6. Outline four general categories of organizational objectives.
7. Define corporate strategies, business strategies, and functional strategies.
8. What is a strategic business unit (SBU)?
9. Outline the cycle of events in making strategic decisions.
10. What is a code of ethics?

DISCUSSION QUESTIONS

1. In Example 1.1, pick a company that was on the list in 1955 but not in 1989 and do library research to find out what happened to the company.
2. The final responsibility for strategic management decisions rests with top management. Since you are unlikely to enter an organization at the top management level, why is strategic management a required course at your college or university?
3. What do you think would be the major differences in strategic management decisions made by a private enterprise and a not-for-profit organization?

REFERENCES AND ADDITIONAL READING

1. Thomas J. Watson, Jr., *A Business and Its Beliefs* (New York: McGraw-Hill, 1963), p. 5.
2. Ibid., pp. 13, 29, 34.
3. Frank T. Cary, "The Remaking of American Business Leadership," *Think* 47, no. 6 (November–December 1981):24.
4. Thomas J. Peters and Robert H. Waterman, Jr., *In Search of Excellence* (New York: Harper & Row, 1982), p. 285.
5. Watson, *A Business and Its Beliefs*, pp. 19–21.
6. Peter F. Drucker, *The Practice of Management* (New York: Harper & Row, 1954), pp. 50–57.
7. Ibid., pp. 52–54.
8. Ibid., p. 56.
9. Ibid., p. 57.
10. Stanley Thune and Robert House, "Where Long Range Planning Pays Off," *Business Horizons*, August 1970, pp. 81–87.
11. David Herold, "Long Range Planning and Organizational Performance: A Cross Validation Study," *Academy of Management Review*, March 1972, pp. 91–102.
12. Robley D. Wood, Jr., and R. Lawrence La Forge, "The Impact of Comprehensive Planning on Financial Performance," *Academy of Management Journal* 22, no. 3 (1979):516–526.
13. See, for instance, C. B. Shrader, L. Taylor, and D. R. Dalton, "Strategic Planning and Organizational Performance: A Critical Appraisal," *Journal of Management*, Summer 1984, pp. 149–179; G. E. Greenley, "Does Strategic Planning Improve Company Performance?" *Long Range Planning*, April 1986, pp. 101–109; J. A. Pearce III, E. A. Freeman, and R. B. Robinson, Jr., "The Tenuous Link Between Formal Strategic Planning and Financial Performance," *Academy of Management Review*, October 1987, pp. 658–675; and L. C. Rhyne, "The Relationship of Strategic Plan-

ning to Financial Performance," *Strategic Management Journal,* September–October 1986, pp. 423–436.

14. Based on William E. Rothschild, "How to Ensure the Continued Growth of Strategic Planning," *Journal of Business Strategy,* Summer 1980, p. 14.

15. George A. Steiner and John F. Steiner, *Business, Government, and Society,* 4th ed. (New York: Random House, 1985), p. 150.

16. Fred R. David, Don Robin, and Mike Giallourakis, "The Nature of Codes of Business: A Strategic Perspective," *Journal of Business Strategies,* Spring 1989, p. 7.

17. Ibid., p. 7.

Strategy in Action Case Study: Ford Motor Company

Chapter 1: Strategic Management: An Overview

The Strategy in Action Case Study, new to this edition of the text, is designed to illustrate the strategic management process in more detail with an actual case study of the Ford Motor Company. In this chapter the case study is introduced. At the end of each subsequent chapter, specific examples of how Ford has utilized the principles discussed in that chapter in its strategic management process will be discussed.

Ford Motor Company was chosen as a subject for several reasons:

1. *It is one of the oldest and best-known American organizations.*
2. *It is one of the leading American companies in the international business arena.*
3. *It represents an industry that has faced strong competition from foreign manufacturers and has been quite successful in responding to this competition.*

At this point you are strongly encouraged to read Appendix A, "Preparing a Case Analysis," which begins on page 257 of this book. This appendix will enable you to better understand the case study method and will provide background information that will help you understand the various aspects of Ford's strategic management process.

It should also be noted that material from other sources will be brought to bear on the Ford case at the end of each chapter. This is a typical approach to case analysis. You are encouraged to research the company and use other material in analyzing the case.

Ford Motor Company joined the business world at a time when automobile companies were making fast starts—and even faster fades. In 1903 alone, more than 80 new auto companies were started. Ford survived and is closely identified with the history and development of American business throughout the twentieth century.

Ford Motor Company was founded on June 16, 1903, when the late Henry Ford and 11 of his associates filed incorporation papers at Michigan's state capitol in Lansing. The company started with just 10 employees in a small converted wagon factory on Detroit's Mack Avenue. Its assets consisted

Henry Ford, 1863–1947

mainly of some tools, blueprints, plans, patents, and $28,000 in cash scraped together by 12 investors.

Along with Henry Ford, the first stockholders were a coal dealer, the coal dealer's bookkeeper, a banker who trusted the coal dealer, two brothers who owned a machine shop that would make the engines and running gear for the new cars, a carpenter, two lawyers, a clerk, the owner of a notions store, and a man whose company made air rifles. A doctor also offered to invest, but Ford declined, fearing that 13 investors might bring bad luck.

The first Ford Motor Company car, the 1903 Model A, was advertised as "the most perfect machine on the market" and "so simple that a boy of 15 can run it." The car may have been perfect and simple, but business wasn't. In about a month, the new company had all but run through its cash. Then, on July 15, a check arrived from a Chicago dentist—the first person to buy a car from the company. The stockholders, who had seen the bank balance dwindle to $223.65, breathed a collective sigh of relief as Dr. Ernst Pfennig's check for $850 was deposited.

Between 1903 and 1908, Henry Ford and his engineers used the letters of the alphabet to name their cars. Some of the cars were experimental and never reached the public. In the first 15 months of operation, 1700 cars—Model A's—were produced in the old wagon factory. The most successful of the early production cars was the Model N, a small, light, four-cylinder machine that went on the market at $500. A $2500 six-cylinder luxury car, the Model K, sold poorly.

The Model K's failure, along with Henry Ford's insistence that the company's future lay in the production of inexpensive cars for a mass market, caused increasing friction between Henry Ford and Alexander Malcomson, a Detroit coal dealer who had been instrumental in raising the original $28,000. As a result, Malcomson left the company and Henry Ford acquired enough of his stock to increase his holdings to 58½ percent. Ford became president in 1906, replacing John S. Gray, a Detroit banker.

Squabbles among the stockholders did not threaten the company's future as seriously as did a man named George Selden. Selden had a patent on "road locomotives" powered by internal combustion engines. To protect his patent, he formed a syndicate to license selected manufacturers and collect royalties for every "horseless carriage" built or sold in America. Hardly had the doors been opened at the Mack Avenue factory when Selden's syndicate filed suit against the Ford company, which had gone into business without a Selden license. Faced with the choice of closing the doors or fighting a battery of attorneys, Henry Ford and his partners decided to fight. Eight years later, in 1911, after complicated court proceedings, Ford Motor Company won the battle that freed it and the entire auto industry from Selden's patent.

Throughout this time, Ford kept improving its cars, making its way through the alphabet until it reached the Model T in 1908. A considerable improvement over all previous models, this car was an immediate success. Model T production topped 10,000 units in its first year, an industry record at the time. But even that didn't satisfy the demand. Building each car by hand was too slow.

Henry Ford began to subdivide the work, bringing parts to employees and scheduling the parts to arrive at the right spot at the right time. In 1913, after nearly three years of development, he and his staff devised a moving assembly line system for automotive assembly. This mass production system eventually made it possible to provide all the cars the public wanted, at affordable prices.

On January 5, 1914, Henry Ford announced that he would pay his employees $5 for an eight-hour day. That was twice the existing rate for a nine-hour day, and it caused a sensation. The next morning, 10,000 job applicants lined up at the Highland Park, Michigan plant. Henry Ford theorized that he could afford to pay the higher wage because he could sell more cars if his employees earned enough to buy them. "If you cut wages," he reasoned, "you just cut the number of your customers."

By 1919, Henry Ford had bought out all outside stockholders—at a cost of over $105 million. In the 16 years after incorporation of the company, more than $30 million had been paid out in dividends, and earnings were running at the rate of $60 million a year.

During those years of expansion, Ford Motor Company

- Began producing trucks and tractors (1917)
- Bought the Lincoln Motor Company (1922)

- Built the first of 196 Ford Tri-Motor airplanes used by America's first commercial airlines (1925)

By 1927, however, time had run out on the Model T. Improved, but basically unchanged for so many years, it was losing ground to more stylish, more powerful cars being offered by Ford's competitors. On May 31, 1927, Ford plants across the country closed down for six months while the company retooled for the Model A. It was a vastly improved car in all respects. More than 4.5 million Model A's, in several body styles and a wide variety of colors, rolled onto the nation's highways between late 1927 and 1931.

The Model A, too, eventually reached the end of the line when consumers demanded even more luxury and power. Ford Motor Company's next entry, the Ford V-8 was seen by the public for the first time on April 1, 1932. Ford was the first company in history to successfully cast a V-8 engine block in one piece. Experts had told Henry Ford it couldn't be done. It was many years before Ford's competitors learned how to mass-produce a reliable V-8. In the meantime, the car and its powerful engine became a best-seller. In 1938, six years after the V-8 was introduced, production started on the Mercury, which became Ford's entry in the growing medium-priced field.

In 1942, civilian car production came to a halt as the company threw all its resources into the U.S. war effort. Initiated by Edsel Ford, Henry Ford's son and president of Ford Motor Company, this giant wartime program produced, in less than three years, 8,600 four-engined B-24 "Liberator" bombers, 57,000 aircraft engines, over 250,000 jeeps, tanks, tank destroyers, and other pieces of war machinery.

Edsel Ford died in 1943 just as his program was reaching its maximum efficiency. Henry Ford resumed the presidency until the war's end, when he resigned for the second time. His oldest grandson, Henry Ford II, became president on September 21, 1945.

In 1945, as Henry Ford II drove the industry's first postwar car off the assembly line, he was already making plans to reorganize and decentralize the company. Losing money at the rate of several million dollars a month, Ford Motor Company was in critically poor condition to resume its prewar position as a major force in the fiercely competitive auto industry.

Henry Ford II's postwar reorganization plan rapidly restored the company's health. The company that had lost $50 million in the first seven months of 1946 ended the year with a profit of $2000. Profits soared to a net of $265 million four years later through a rebuilding program that has been called the most phenomenal comeback in American industrial history.

Having relinquished his company's operation to his grandson, Henry Ford lived quietly with his wife, Clara, until he died on April 7, 1947, at age 83.

In 1948, Ford Motor Company was faced with a significant problem. It was well known in the automobile industry that lower-income car owners traded in their lower-priced cars for higher-priced cars as soon as their yearly income exceeded $5000. Ford had kept pace quite well with the other members of the

"Big Three" (General Motors, Chrysler, and Ford) in the lower-priced market. But what was perplexing to Ford was that as the lower-income Ford car owners moved up the income ladder, they traded up to medium-priced cars made by Ford's competitors, particularly General Motors.

Ford's response to this problem was the development of a new car called the Edsel. Over the next ten years Ford spent considerable time and effort developing this new, medium-priced car. Production of the car in the Edsel Division of Ford began on July 15, 1957.

While any new car has its bugs, the Edsel, having been brought to the height of public attention as a result of Ford's continuous advertising and promotion activities, was no exception—just a bigger public spectacle.

The first day's sales totaled more than 6,500 Edsels—a good showing. However, sales dropped sharply over the next few days. As this decline continued, Ford pumped more and more time, effort, and money into promoting the Edsel in order to meet the necessary 200,000 cars that was calculated as the break-even point. Sales continued to move downward until January 14, 1958, when Ford Motor Company announced that it was consolidating the Edsel Division with the Lincoln-Mercury Division to form the Mercury-Edsel-Lincoln Division under the management of the former manager of the Lincoln-Mercury Division.

All told, 110,810 Edsels were produced and 109,466 were sold. Although exact estimates cannot be found, it is generally estimated that Ford lost something like $200 million on the Edsel after it appeared on the market. In addition to the initial investment of about $250 million, a net loss of about $350 million resulted after accounting for salvageable plant and equipment. Thus, according to these rough estimates, every Edsel produced lost about $3,200, which was just about equal to the cost of an Edsel. In other words, Ford Motor Company would have saved itself money if it had decided not to produce the Edsel at all but had simply given away 110,810 specimens of its comparably priced car, the Mercury.

Another significant event in the company's history occurred in January 1956, when Ford Motor Company common stock was sold to the public for the first time. As of December 31, 1988, the company had 271,000 stockholders.

On October 1, 1979, Henry Ford II retired as chief executive officer, handing over that responsibility to Philip Caldwell. Caldwell also succeeded Ford as chairman of the board on March 13, 1980. Ford retired as an officer and employee of the company on October 1, 1982, but continued to serve on the company's board of directors and as chairman of the finance committee until his death on September 29, 1987.

When Philip Caldwell retired as chairman of the board and chief executive officer, Donald Petersen succeeded him on February 1, 1985.

During 1980, 1981, and 1982, Ford again faced a major crisis. During that time, it had operating losses totaling over $3.5 billion. Its common stock reached a low of $7.00 per share. However, as will be seen in the following sections, its turnaround has been remarkable.

INTERNATIONAL BUSINESS OPERATIONS

Paralleling Ford's domestic growth has been a foreign expansion program which got its start just one year after the company was formed. On August 17, 1904, a modest plant opened in the small town of Walkerville, Ontario, with the imposing name of Ford Motor Company of Canada, Ltd.

Today, Ford has manufacturing, assembly, or sales affiliates in 22 countries outside the United States and Canada. In addition, the company has international business relationships with auto manufacturers in 9 countries and sells through Ford dealerships in more than 180 direct-market countries.

FORD TODAY

Ford Motor Company is the world's fourth largest industrial corporation and the second largest car and truck producer. Its approximately 360,000 employees serve the automotive, agricultural, financial, and communications needs of customers worldwide. The diverse fields in which Ford operates include electronics, glass, plastics, automotive replacement parts, space technology, satellite communications, defense work, land development, equipment leasing, and car rentals. It operates through three strategic business units—the automotive group, the diversified products group, and financial services.

Automotive Group   The automotive group, which operates the company's core business, has two main components—North American Automotive Operations (NAAO) and International Automotive Operations (IAO). NAAO has more than 50 assembly and manufacturing facilities in the United States, Canada, and Mexico. IAO has operations in 22 countries, grouped into three principal regions—Europe, Latin America, and Asia-Pacific. In addition, the company has international business relationships with auto manufacturers in 9 countries. Ford vehicles are sold in more than 180 direct-market countries.

Diversified Products Operations (DPO)   Ford is more than just cars and trucks. Most Ford activities in areas other than vehicle manufacturing are grouped within Ford Diversified Products Operations (DPO). Operating in 34 countries, DPO employs more than 85,000 people in a multitude of high-technology fields. If it were a separate entity, DPO would rank among the top 30 industrial concerns in the United States. It encompasses the following separate businesses, including automotive-related and nonautomotive operations:

- *Climate Control Division* is one of the largest manufacturers of heat exchange products in the world.
- *Plastic Products Division* supplies 30 percent of Ford's plastics requirements and 50 percent of its vinyl needs.
- *Rouge Steel Company* ranks among the top ten steel makers in the United States.
- *Casting Division* is one of the world's leading producers of automotive castings and forgings.
- *Ford Glass Division*, North America's second largest glass producer, provides virtually all the glass for Ford's North American cars and trucks and

also supplies glass to other auto manufacturers. In addition, the division is a major supplier to the construction, specialty glass, and mirror industries and to the automotive aftermarket.

- *Electronics Division (ED)* is a leading innovator in automotive electronics. ED manufactures sophisticated electronic engine and vehicle controls, instrumentation and displays, driver conveniences, and an extensive line of entertainment systems.
- *Electrical and Fuel Handling Division* manufactures starters, alternators, small motors, fuel senders, and other parts for Ford vehicles. It was formed in 1988.
- *Ford New Holland, Inc.,* is one of the world's largest tractor and farm equipment manufacturers. This subsidiary was formed January 1, 1987, consolidating Ford Tractor Operations with New Holland, a farm equipment manufacturer acquired from the Sperry Corporation in 1986. Ford New Holland subsequently acquired Versatile Equipment, Ltd., North America's largest manufacturer of four-wheel-drive tractors.
- *Ford Aerospace Corporation* is a world industry leader in satellite and terrestrial communications, defense systems, and high-speed information systems. Ford Aerospace designs and produces communications satellites for a global network that provides telecommunication services to more than 165 countries, and it is a leader in tactical air defense as well as command, control, communications, and intelligence systems for the United States and its allies.
- *Ford Microelectronics, Inc.,* at Colorado Springs, was formed in 1982 to provide integrated circuit design and test services for the aerospace and automotive industries.
- *Ford Motor Land Development Corporation* is involved in the development, management, acquisition, and sale of Ford-owned land and facilities.
- *Hertz Corporation* is the world's number one daily car rental company. It was purchased in December 1987 by Park Ridge Corporation, which is owned by Ford and certain members of Hertz senior management.

Financial Services   Ford reaffirmed its commitment to the financial services business in October 1987 with the establishment of the Ford Financial Services Group. The group is responsible for overseeing operations of Ford Motor Credit Company, the financing operations in Ford's overseas automotive affiliates, First Nationwide Financial Corporation, and United States Leasing International, Inc.

- *Ford Motor Credit Company* and the overseas financing operations provide, among other services, essential financial support to dealers and retail automotive customers. Ford Credit is the second largest finance company in the world with assets of $56.3 billion at year-end 1988. In the United States, Ford Credit provided financing for 1.6 million vehicles in 1988.
- *First Nationwide Financial Corporation,* purchased by Ford in December 1985, is the second largest savings and loan organization in the United States. First Nationwide operates in 14 states, with more than 370 retail branch offices and approximately $19 billion in assets.

- *United States Leasing International, Inc.,* purchased by Ford in November 1987, more than doubled the size of its managed assets to $5 billion in 1988. The transformation was accomplished by the transfer to U.S. Leasing of management responsibility for specialized leasing and financing operations of Ford Motor Credit Company. The combined operations are involved in business and commercial equipment financing, leveraged lease financing, municipal financing, commercial fleet leasing, transportation equipment leasing, test instrument rentals, and corporate and real estate financing. Organized in 1952, U.S. Leasing was the first equipment-leasing company in the United States.

ANALYSIS OF FORD MOTOR COMPANY: AN OVERVIEW

The primary focus of Chapter 1 has been to provide a framework for studying the strategic management process and to define the key terms used in studying it. Most of the components in the strategic management process are examined in greater depth in later chapters. However, three of the key terms defined in Chapter 1 are *organizational philosophy, organizational culture,* and *organizational mission.* As you will recall, organizational philosophy establishes the values, beliefs, and guidelines for the manner in which the organization is going to conduct its business. Organizational culture refers to how things are done within an organization. Organizational mission defines why the organization exists.

Ford's Mission and Philosophy

As you have read, Ford experienced some difficult days in the early 1980s. The company learned a pivotal lesson during those bleak days: If it was to be successful it had to focus on the basics of its business and engage the full support of its employees. From this realization emerged a clear understanding of what Ford stands for and what its priorities must be. This understanding was expressed in a written statement of the company's mission, values, and guiding principles:

Mission

Ford Motor Company is a worldwide leader in automotive and automotive-related products and services as well as in newer industries such as aerospace, communications, and financial services. Our mission is to improve continually our products and services to meet our customers' needs, allowing us to prosper as a business and to provide a reasonable return for our stockholders, the owners of our business.

Values

How we accomplish our mission is as important as the mission itself. Fundamental to success for the Company are these basic values:

People—Our people are the source of our strength. They provide our corporate intelligence and determine our reputation and vitality. Involvement and teamwork are our core human values.

Products—Our products are the end result of our efforts, and they should be the best in serving customers worldwide. As our products are viewed, so are we viewed.

Profits—Profits are the ultimate measure of how efficiently we provide customers with the best products for their needs. Profits are required to survive and grow.

Guiding Principles

Quality comes first—To achieve customer satisfaction, the quality of our products and services must be our number one priority.

Customers are the focus of everything we do—Our work must be done with our customers in mind, providing better products and services than our competition.

Continuous improvement is essential to our success—We must strive for excellence in everything we do, in our products, in their safety and value—and in our services, our human relations, our competitiveness, and our profitability.

Employee involvement is our way of life—We are a team. We must treat each other with trust and respect.

Dealers and suppliers are our partners—The Company must maintain mutually beneficial relationships with dealers, suppliers, and our other business associates.

Integrity is never compromised—The conduct of our Company worldwide must be pursued in a manner that is socially responsible and commands respect for its integrity and for its positive contributions to society. Our doors are open to men and women alike without discrimination and without regard to ethnic origin or personal beliefs.

Notice that Ford's mission statement describes exactly what businesses Ford is in and why it exists. Notice also that Ford does not use the term *organizational philosophy*. It uses the terms *values* and *guiding principles*. Regardless of the terms used, however, Ford spells out the values and beliefs of the company. Ford's philosophy puts product quality at the forefront, draws employees together, encourages the contributions of all for the good of all, and fosters teamwork, mutual respect, and trust among everyone in the workplace.

Organizational Culture at Ford

From this organizational philosophy and mission a new culture has emerged at Ford. Before the 1980s, Ford had an autocratic management style with little participation by employees. Today, however, the company encourages employee involvement and practices participatory management. Ford's culture also encourages lifelong education for its employees by providing numerous educational courses on-site.

Management feels strongly that Ford's philosophy, culture, and mission have played a key role in the company's success during the 1980s. In Ford's 1988 annual report, Donald E. Petersen, chief executive officer, and Harold A. Poling, chief operating officer, state: ". . . if we concentrate on our core values, and if we keep applying ourselves diligently to the basics of running the business, we will maintain our momentum—and Ford will continue to perform strongly in the years ahead!"

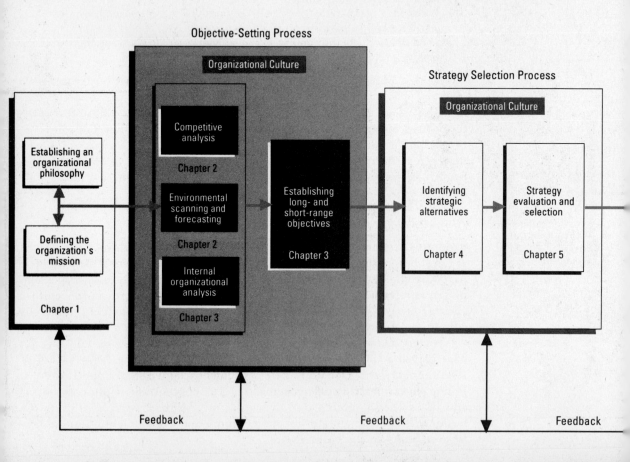

STRATEGIC MANAGEMENT PROCESS

Strategy Formulation

Objective-Setting Process

Organizational Culture

Strategy Selection Process

Organizational Culture

Establishing an organizational philosophy

Defining the organization's mission

Chapter 1

Competitive analysis

Chapter 2

Environmental scanning and forecasting

Chapter 2

Internal organizational analysis

Chapter 3

Establishing long- and short-range objectives

Chapter 3

Identifying strategic alternatives

Chapter 4

Strategy evaluation and selection

Chapter 5

Feedback

Feedback

Feedback

PART TWO
STRATEGY FORMULATION

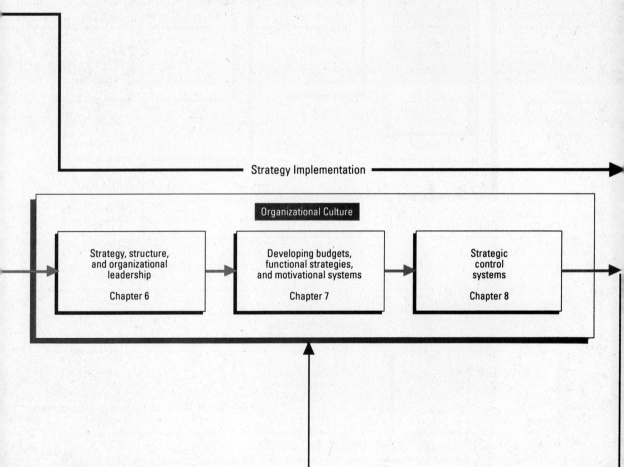

Strategy Implementation

Organizational Culture

Strategy, structure, and organizational leadership	Developing budgets, functional strategies, and motivational systems	Strategic control systems
Chapter 6	Chapter 7	Chapter 8

Feedback

Feedback

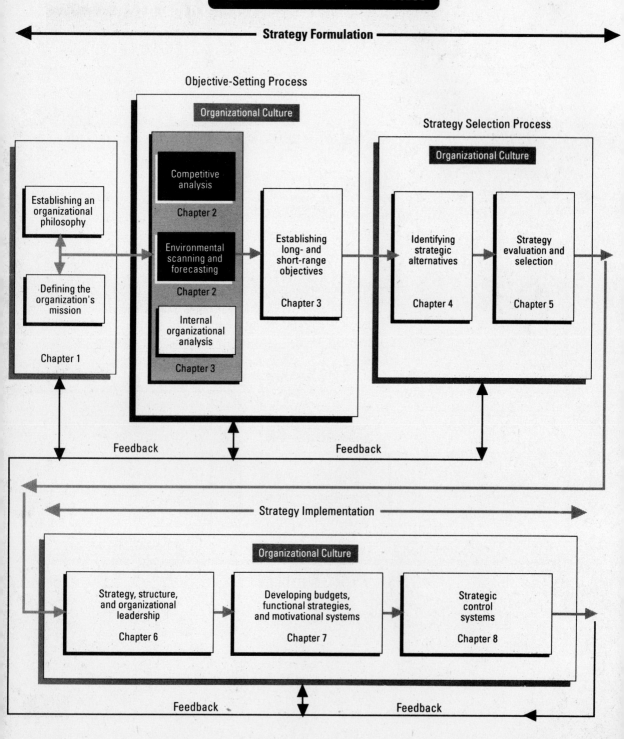

STRATEGIC MANAGEMENT PROCESS

Strategy Formulation

Objective-Setting Process

Organizational Culture

Competitive analysis

Chapter 2

Environmental scanning and forecasting

Chapter 2

Internal organizational analysis

Chapter 3

Establishing an organizational philosophy

Defining the organization's mission

Chapter 1

Establishing long- and short-range objectives

Chapter 3

Strategy Selection Process

Organizational Culture

Identifying strategic alternatives

Chapter 4

Strategy evaluation and selection

Chapter 5

Feedback   Feedback

Strategy Implementation

Organizational Culture

Strategy, structure, and organizational leadership

Chapter 6

Developing budgets, functional strategies, and motivational systems

Chapter 7

Strategic control systems

Chapter 8

Feedback   Feedback

CHAPTER 2
Analyzing the
External Environment

LEARNING OBJECTIVES

After studying this chapter, you should be able to

1. Explain the five forces that shape the intensity of competition in an industry.
2. Describe the purpose of individual competitor analysis.
3. Outline questions that must be answered in a competitor response profile.
4. Describe the two basic sources for collecting competitive data.
5. Define environmental scanning.
6. Describe the four areas in which organizations should perform environmental scanning.
7. Outline qualitative and quantitative techniques for forecasting.

In deciding on an organization's future direction, management must answer three basic questions:

1. Where is the business now?
2. Where does management want the business to be (i.e., what are its objectives)?
3. How does the business move from where it is now to where management wants it to be (i.e., what strategy is to be used)?

To answer the first question, management needs to analyze the organization's external and internal environment. The external environment is analyzed through competitive analysis and environmental scanning and forecasting, which are examined in detail in this chapter. The internal environment is analyzed through a process called internal organizational analysis, which is described in detail in Chapter 3.

Figure 2.1 illustrates the relationships between competitive analysis, environmental scanning and forecasting, and internal organizational analysis. Competitive analysis and environmental scanning and forecasting identify threats to and opportunities for the business. Competitive analysis and internal organizational analysis identify the strengths and weaknesses of the business. This kind of analysis is often referred to as strengths, weaknesses, opportunities, and threats (SWOT) analysis.

COMPETITIVE ANALYSIS

Organizations do not exist in a vacuum. They operate in a competitive industry environment. Analyzing this competitive environment not only enables an organization to identify its own strengths and weaknesses but also helps it

Figure 2.1 *Identifying Strengths, Weaknesses, Opportunities, and Threats (SWOT)*

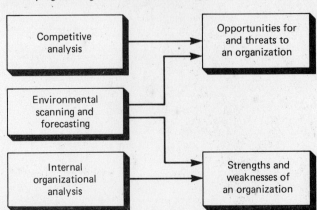

identify opportunities in and threats from its industry environment. Competitive analysis consists of two basic phases: industry structure analysis and individual competitor analysis.

Industry Structure Analysis

An *industry structure analysis* identifies the major forces affecting competition in an industry and determines the strengths and weaknesses of the business relative to the industry. Michael Porter has postulated that the intensity of competition in an industry is determined by its underlying economic structure. He further contends that the industry structure is shaped by five basic competitive forces: the threat of new entrants into the industry, the bargaining power of suppliers to the industry, the threat of substitute products or services, the bargaining power of customers, and the maneuvering for position among current competitors.[1] Figure 2.2 diagrams these competitive forces.

Figure 2.3 summarizes information about the five major forces that govern competition in an industry. This framework should be used to identify the crucial structural features in a particular industry. Knowledge of these features enables a company to identify its strengths and weaknesses.

Individual Competitor Analysis

An *individual competitor analysis* identifies what is driving the competitor and what the competitor is doing and can do. A basic framework, shown in Figure 2.4, for performing individual competitive analysis has been postulated by Michael Porter.[2]

Figure 2.2 Forces Governing Competition in an Industry

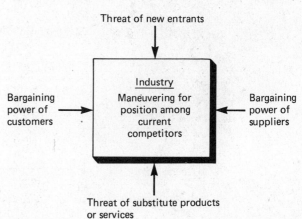

Figure 2.3 Description of Forces Governing Competition

Maneuvering for Position Among Competitors

Competition is higher when

1. Number of competitors is larger, and they are all roughly equal in size.
2. Industry growth is slow.
3. Product/service lacks differentiation or switching costs. Switching costs are fixed costs buyers face in changing suppliers.
4. Fixed costs are high or product is perishable.
5. Exit barriers are high.
6. Rivals are diverse in stategies, origins, and culture.

Threat of New Entrants

Threat of entry into an industry depends on presence of barriers to entry, which include

1. Economies of scale.
2. Product differentiation.
3. Capital requirements.
4. Switching costs.
5. Access to distribution channels.
6. Government policy.

Bargaining Power of Suppliers

Suppliers are powerful when

1. Their industry is dominated by a few companies and is more concentrated than industry it sells to.
2. Their product is unique, differentiated, or has built up switching costs.
3. They pose a credible threat of integrating forward.
4. Industry is not an important customer of the supplier group.

Bargaining Power of Customers

Customers are powerful when

1. They are concentrated and buy in large volume.
2. The products they purchase are standard or undifferentiated.
3. The products they purchase form a component of their product and represent a significant fraction of its cost.
4. They earn low profits.
5. The products are unimportant to the quality of the customer's product or service.
6. The products do not save the customer money.
7. The customers pose a threat of integrating backward to make the industry's product.

Threat of Substitute Products or Services

Substitute products that deserve the most attention from an organization are those that

1. Have trends improving their price performance trade-off with the industry's products.
2. Are produced by industries earning high profits.

Source: Adapted from Michael E. Porter, *Competitive Strategy* (New York: Free Press, 1980), pp. 7–29.

Figure 2.4 Framework for Competitor Analysis

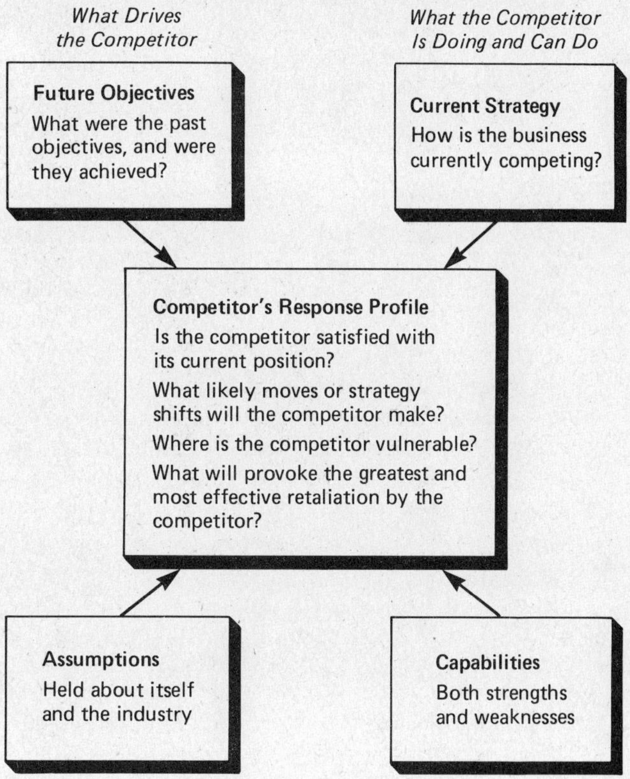

What Drives the Competitor	What the Competitor Is Doing and Can Do
Future Objectives What were the past objectives, and were they achieved?	**Current Strategy** How is the business currently competing?

Competitor's Response Profile

Is the competitor satisfied with its current position?

What likely moves or strategy shifts will the competitor make?

Where is the competitor vulnerable?

What will provoke the greatest and most effective retaliation by the competitor?

Assumptions Held about itself and the industry

Capabilities Both strengths and weaknesses

Source: Adapted from Michael Porter, *Competitive Strategy* (New York: Free Press, 1980), p. 49.

As can be seen, two factors must be analyzed to determine what drives the competitor. First, its future objectives must be identified. The answering of four key questions should help in this task:

1. What have the competitor's major objectives been in the relatively recent past?
2. Have these objectives been achieved?
3. What strategies has the competitor employed in the relatively recent past?
4. Have these strategies been successful?

Second, every business operates on a set of assumptions about itself and its industry. These assumptions significantly influence how the business operates in its environment. Answers to the following questions help identify a competitor's assumptions:

1. What does the competitor appear to *believe about its relative position*—in cost, product quality, technological sophistication, and other key aspects of its

business—on the basis of its public statements, claims of management and sales force, and other indications? What does it see as its strengths and weaknesses? Are these accurate?

2. Does the competitor have a strong *historical or emotional identification* with particular products or with particular functional policies, such as an approach to product design, desire for product quality, manufacturing location, selling approach or distribution arrangements?

3. Are there *cultural, regional, or national differences* that will affect the way in which competitors perceive and assign significance to events?

4. Are there *organizational values or canons* that have been strongly institutionalized and will affect the way events are viewed? Are there some policies that the company's founder believed in strongly that may still linger?

5. What does the competitor appear to believe about *future demand* for the product and about the *significance of industry trends?* Will it be hesitant to add capacity because of unfounded uncertainties about demand, or likely to overbuild for the opposite reason? Is it prone to over- or underestimate the importance of particular trends? Does it believe the industry is concentrating, for example, when it may not be?

6. What does the competitor appear to believe about the objectives and capabilities of its *competitors?* Will it over- or underestimate any of them?

7. Does the competitor seem to believe in industry *"conventional wisdom"* or historic rules of thumb and common industry approaches that do not reflect new market conditions?[3]

Although it is not shown in Figure 2.4, another good indicator of what drives a competitor is its history in the business. Answers to the following questions provide a historical basis for looking at what drives the competitor:

1. What is the competitor's current financial performance and market share, *compared to* that of the relatively recent past?

2. What has been the competitor's *history in the marketplace* over time? Where has it failed or been beaten, and thus perhaps not likely to tread again?

3. In what areas has the competitor *starred or succeeded* as a company? In new product introductions? Innovative marketing techniques? Others?

4. How has the competitor *reacted* to particular strategic moves or industry events in the past? Rationally? Emotionally? Slowly? Quickly? What approaches has it employed? To what sorts of events has the competitor reacted poorly, and why?[4]

As will be recalled from Figure 2.4, individual competitive analysis also requires an identification of what the competitor is doing and can do. First, the competitor's current strategy must be identified. Strategy options available to businesses are discussed in detail in Chapter 4. Then the competitor's capabilities—its strengths and weaknesses—must also be determined. Identifying strengths and weaknesses is described in more detail in Chapter 3.

After the competitor's future objectives, assumptions, current strategy, and capabilities are analyzed, a *competitor response profile* is developed. This profile, designed to indicate how a competitor is likely to respond in its competitive environment, is based on the answers to four questions:

1. Is the competitor satisfied with its current position?
2. What likely moves or strategy shifts will the competitor make?
3. Where is the competitor vulnerable?
4. What will provoke the greatest and most effective retaliation by the competitor?[5]

When completed, a competitive analysis should give management a comprehensive understanding of the competitive environment. This understanding should enable management to further assess its strengths and weaknesses and partially ascertain opportunities and threats from the environment. Example 2.1 shows the competitive analysis performed by a small business in the development of a business plan.

Sources of Competitive Information

Data on competitive information can come from many sources, either published or from the field. Sources of published data include annual reports, newspaper and trade publication articles, filings to government and regulatory agencies, speeches by management, patent records, and court records. Field data can be obtained from suppliers to the industry, advertising agencies, professional meetings, trade associations, personnel hired from competitors, investment bankers, and security analysts. One widely used source of field competitive data is an organization's sales force. Sales personnel should know the strengths and weaknesses of competitors' products, the competitors' prices, and a great deal of other information on the competition.

Once collected, the competitive data must be organized and disseminated to the strategy decision makers. Organizing the data on the basis of industry structure analysis and individual competitor analysis is a logical way of preparing it for dissemination.

ENVIRONMENTAL SCANNING

Organizations are influenced by forces outside their industry that may affect not only particular organizations within the industry but also the industry as a whole. *Environmental scanning is the systematic methods used by an organization to study and forecast external forces that are not under the direct control of the organization or its industry.* The basic purpose of environmental scanning is to study and interpret what is happening in an organization's current environment in order to forecast developments in its future environment.[6] Organizations generally categorize environmental scanning into four areas: economic, technological, political (including regulatory), and social. The focus of scanning in each area is on trends that have organization-wide relevance.

STRATEGY IN ACTION Example 2.1

Sieban's River North Brewery, Inc.

Sieban's River North Brewery, Inc., of Chicago is a new phenomenon known as a *brewpub*. A brewpub is a small brewery that combines manufacturing and retailing. In a brewpub, you can drink beer that is manufactured on-site and also eat at the on-site restaurant.

The brewpub is one alternative to regular retail channels for small brewers. Rather than battle for limited space on distributors' trucks and store shelves, a brewpub need only get people through the front door. Selling at the source keeps quality control in the hands of the manufacturer. With no kegging or bottling, line costs are low, and the brewer captures the retailer's, the distributor's, and the manufacturer's profit.

In drawing up its business plan, Sieban's management developed the following competitive analysis:

Competitive Analysis

Number of microbreweries in United States and Canada		115[a]
Number of "brewpubs" (subset of micro category)		32[a]
One-year growth in number of micros, 1987		65%[a]

	Typical Brewpub or Restaurant	Sieben's Actual
Size of facility	4,000 square feet[b]	20,000 square feet
Average brewing capacity	10 barrels[b]	30 barrels
Start-up costs	$350,000–$600,000[b, c]	$2 million
Annual sales (projected)	$700,000–$1 million[b]	$3.6 million
Beer price per glass	$2.15[a]	$2.25
Cost of sales, beer	3%[b]	3%
Average dinner check per person	$19[d]	$18
Cost of sales, food	35%[d]	49%

[a]Association of Brewers.
[b]Brewpub Manual.
[c]Brewing Systems Inc.
[d]National Restaurant Association.

Note also that Sieban's compared its actual results to the typical competitive brewpub.

Source: Adapted from Curtis Hartman, "New Brew," *Inc.*, April 1988, pp. 86–87.

Economic Forces

Of the four areas, scanning in the economic area is probably considered the most significant. The general state of the economy (e.g., depression, recession, recovery, or prosperity), the level of interest paid by corporations and individuals, the unemployment rate, and the level of consumer income are key economic variables in corporate investment, employment, and pricing decisions. The rate of inflation and the growth rate of the gross national product (GNP) are additional economic variables that must be considered in the strategy formulation process.

Technological Forces

Technology is the systematic application of scientific or other organized knowledge to practical purposes and includes new ideas, inventions, techniques, and materials. Technology has been traditionally associated with automated equipment or assembly lines, but this is an unnecessarily restrictive association. For example, a new method of planting trees could be considered new technology.

Technological forces influence organizations in several ways. First, technological developments can significantly alter the demand for an organization's or industry's products or services. Technological developments by an organization's competitors can make its products or services obsolete or overpriced. In international business, one country's use of new technological developments can make another country's products overpriced and noncompetitive. For example, the use of more sophisticated technology is one of the reasons that Japan is now a world leader in steel making while the U.S. steel industry languishes. Technology itself cannot save the U.S. steel industry, but it can be an essential ingredient. New technology can also reduce organizations' costs in ways ranging from better utilization of raw materials to energy conservation.

Political and Regulatory Forces

The political orientation (i.e., conservative versus liberal or Republican versus Democrat) of the U.S. House of Representatives, the Senate, and the presidency have an important influence on strategic planning decisions. For example, the Republican party has long been considered pro-business, and when it is in power both the legislative and executive branches of government are generally more favorably oriented toward business organizations.

In the regulatory environment, federal, state, and local governments have increasingly passed laws that affect the operation of businesses. Federal laws influence the hiring and firing of employees, compensation, working hours, and working conditions. Laws also influence advertising practices, the pricing of products, and corporate growth by mergers and acquisitions. In addition to these laws, governmental tax policies influence the financial structure and investment decisions of organizations.

Government agencies created by this legislation enforce most of the laws that make up the legal environment of organizations. Today, many federal agencies exercise some degree of control over business organizations. A brief examination of the function of just a few of these federal agencies illustrates this impact.

The Federal Trade Commission (FTC) monitors the entire area of business competition and unfair trade practices, including such important aspects of business as advertising, product pricing, and corporate growth by mergers and acquisitions. The Interstate Commerce Commission (ICC) licenses common carriers in interstate commerce and approves their rates. Similar agencies at the state level set rates and grant licenses for intrastate transportation and communication. Rates for telephone, water, gas, and electricity are set by these state agencies. The Federal Communications Commission (FCC) supervises all aspects of radio and TV broadcasting, and the Food and Drug Administration (FDA) oversees the food, drug, and cosmetic industries. The FDA, for example, requires drug companies to submit proof that a drug is effective before it can be marketed. The Securities and Exchange Commission (SEC) oversees the issue and sale of investment securities. And the Internal Revenue Service (IRS) is responsible for the interpretation and application of the tax laws.

Not all government actions are restrictive in nature; some affect organizations positively. For example, government purchases have a major influence in the aerospace, defense, and electronics industries. Government loans and subsidies have played a significant role in the farming industry and to companies such as Lockheed and Chrysler. The federal government can and does influence the level of foreign competition through the use of import quotas and tariffs.

During the 1990s, it is likely that greater emphasis will be placed on the deregulation of business organizations. Budget cuts during the 1980s for many of the previously mentioned agencies caused cutbacks in personnel, and these cutbacks have to some extent resulted in less government regulation. On the other hand, attempts have also been made to reduce federal subsidies for business by limiting Export-Import Bank funding, aid for synthetic-fuels development, and dairy industry price supports. These and other proposed initiatives make the assessment of political actions an essential element in strategic management.

In addition to the regulatory environment, a widening array of special-interest groups influence strategic decision making. The ethical-investor movement, public-interest groups, and the environmental protection movement are just a few of the groups that have brought public influence to bear on the strategic decision making of businesses.

Social Forces

Social forces include factors that relate to the values, attitudes, and demographic characteristics of an organization's customers. Dynamic social forces can significantly influence the demand for an organization's products or services and can alter its strategic decisions.

An organization, for example, can obtain a general picture of the U.S. consumer in the year 2000 by looking at some key demographic changes in the population. The median age in the United States is predicted to increase to 40 by the year 2000. Dual-income families will continue to increase. By the year 2000, 90 percent of women with children under the age of 6 will be employed outside the home. The number of households headed by a single person will increase to about 33 percent of all U.S. households. The middle class will decline in size, while the number of people in the affluent and poor classes will increase.[7] Also by the year 2000, 85 percent of the workers entering the work force will be women or minority men.[8] Obviously, these trends will have a significant impact on American businesses.

Determining the exact impact of social forces on an organization's objectives is difficult at best. Nevertheless, assessing the changing values, attitudes, and demographic characteristics of an organization's customers is an essential element in establishing organizational objectives.

ESTABLISHING AN ENVIRONMENTAL SCANNING PROGRAM

Three primary considerations in establishing an environmental scanning program are where the program should be located in the organizational structure, what sources of information should be scanned, and what system should be used in implementing the program. The location of the scanning program varies from organization to organization. Scanning programs have been placed in a separate corporate entity for scanning, the corporate strategic planning department, each individual strategic business unit, the legal department, the marketing research department, and the public affairs or public relations department.

Daily newspapers are considered the most important sources of environmental information.[9] Trade publications are also useful in the environmental scanning of an organization's competition. Four other important sources of information are publications of research organizations such as the Brookings Institute and the Conference Board; business periodicals such as *Business Week*, *Fortune*, and *Forbes;* publications of consulting organizations such as the Hudson Institute, SRI International, and Data Research, Inc.; and government publications.[10]

Finally, the following guidelines have been proposed for implementing an environmental scanning program:

1. Place a senior manager in charge of scanning.
2. Identify a list of about 100 relevant publications.
3. Assign one publication per person to volunteers within the organization. Extremely important publications should be reviewed by the scanning manager.
4. Have each scanner review items in the publication that meet predetermined criteria based on the organization's mission.
5. Assign a predetermined code or keyword to the scanned information and prepare an abstract on the information in a few lines.
6. Submit the code and abstract to a scanning committee consisting of several managers to determine its relevance in terms of effect on the organization. The scanning committee should also add a relevance code.

Environmental Scanning at Monsanto

Monsanto is engaged in the worldwide manufacture and sale of a widely diversified line of chemicals and agricultural products, prescription pharmaceuticals, low-calorie sweeteners, industrial-process control equipment, and synthetic fibers.

Monsanto was one of the first American corporations to establish an environmental scanning program. The company's management recognized the need for such a program because Monsanto often found itself reacting to situations after the fact: It reacted to the civil rights and women's movements by quickly establishing an affirmative action program; it reacted to environmental legislation and regulatory pressures by setting up an environmental policy committee and a variety of pollution abatement programs. In time, however, Monsanto got tired of merely reacting to situations. It felt a growing need to understand the total environment in which it operated.

Initially, Monsanto's environmental scanning was conducted in its public affairs department and focused on short-term issues. Later, the program was divided into two parts. One section remained in public affairs, focusing on short-term issues to alert the company to the daily actions of government, to continue to educate the public on Monsanto's practices, and to communicate Monsanto's responses to important issues to employees and the community.

The second section of environmental scanning was transferred to the corporate planning department. One person was made responsible for identifying critical issues and incorporating their potential effects into Monsanto's long-range planning process. Some of the environmental issues researched by the corporate planning department include the price of oil and its impact on production, public fears about biotechnology products, and the growth of the GNP.

Source: Adapted from Margaret A. Stroup, "Environmental Scanning at Monsanto," *Planning Review*, July/August 1988, pp. 24–27.

7. Computerize the codes and abstract.
8. Prepare a newsletter to disseminate the information organization-wide. Encourage managers who are directly affected by the information to contact the scanning department for further analysis.[11]

Example 2.2 describes how the environmental scanning program at Monsanto was created.

ENVIRONMENTAL FORECASTING METHODS

No one can deny that economic, technological, political, and social change are a part of organizational life. Given that fact, the obvious question is, how can these changes be forecast?

To say the least, forecasting is a most difficult process. At this point it may be consoling to recall some humorous forecasting rules:

1. It is very difficult to forecast, especially the future.
2. Those who live by the crystal ball soon learn to eat ground glass.
3. The moment you forecast you know you're going to be wrong—you just don't know when and in which direction.
4. If you're right, never let them forget it.[12]

Regardless of the possibility of error, to be successful, organizations must forecast their future environment.

Forecasting methods and levels of sophistication vary greatly. The methods employed may vary from educated guesses to computer projections using sophisticated statistical analyses. Several factors determine the most appropriate methods of forecasting, including the nature of the desired forecast, the available expertise, and the available financial resources.

All forecasting techniques can be classified as either qualitative or quantitative. *Qualitative techniques* are based primarily on opinions and judgments. *Quantitative techniques* are based primarily on the analysis of data and the use of statistical techniques. The following sections discuss several different qualitative and quantitative techniques.[13]

Qualitative Forecasting Techniques

Jury of Executive Opinion   With this method, several managers get together and devise a forecast based on their pooled opinions. Advantages of this method are simplicity and low cost. The major disadvantage is that the forecast is not necessarily based on facts.

Sales Force Composite   Under the sales force composite method, a forecast of sales is determined by combining the sales predictions of experienced salespeople. Because salespeople are in constant contact with customers, they are often in a position to accurately forecast sales. Advantages of this method are the relatively low cost and simplicity. The major disadvantage is that sales personnel are not always unbiased, especially if their sales quotas are based on sales forecasts.

Customer Evaluation   This method is similar to the sales force composite except that it goes to customers for estimates of what the customers expect to buy. Individual customer estimates are then pooled to obtain a total forecast. This method works best when a small number of customers make up a large percentage of total sales. Drawbacks are that the customer may not be interested enough to do a good job and that the method has no provisions for including new customers.

Delphi Technique   The Delphi technique is a method for developing a consensus of expert opinion. Under this method, a panel of experts is chosen to study a particular question. The panel members do not meet as a group and may not even know each other's identity. Panel members are then asked (usually by mailed questionnaire) to give their opinions about certain future events or forecasts. After the first round of opinions has been collected, the coordinator summarizes the opinions and sends this information to the panel members. Based on this information, panel members rethink their earlier responses and make a second forecast. This same procedure continues until a consensus is reached or until the responses do not change appreciably. The Delphi technique is relatively inexpensive and moderately complex.

Anticipatory Surveys   With this method, mailed questionnaires, telephone interviews, or personnel interviews are used to forecast customer intentions. Anticipatory surveys are a form of sampling, in that those surveyed are intended to represent some larger population. Potential drawbacks of this method are that stated intentions are not necessarily carried out and that the sample surveyed does not represent the population. This method is usually accompanied by medium costs and medium complexity.

Quantitative Forecasting Techniques

Time-Series Analysis   This technique forecasts future demand based on what has happened in the past. The basic idea of time-series analysis is to fit a trend line to past data and then to extrapolate this trend line into the future. Sophisticated mathematical procedures are used to derive this trend line and to identify any seasonal or cyclical fluctuations. Usually a computer program is used to do the calculations required by a time-series analysis. One advantage of this technique is that it is based on something other than opinion. This method works best when a significant amount of historical data is available and when the environmental forces are relatively stable. The disadvantage is that the future may not be like the past.

Regression Modeling   Regression modeling is a mathematical forecasting technique in which an equation with one or more input variables is derived to predict another variable. The variable being predicted is called the *dependent variable.* The input variables used to predict the dependent variable are called *independent variables.* The general idea of regression modeling is to determine how changes in the independent variables affect the dependent variable. Once the mathematical relationship between the independent variables and the dependent variable has been determined (in the form of an equation), future values for the dependent variable can be forecast based on known or predicted values of the independent variables. The mathematical calculations required to derive the equation are extremely complex and almost always require the use of a computer. Regression modeling is relatively complex and expensive.

Econometric Modeling   Econometric modeling is one of the most sophisticated methods of forecasting. In general, econometric models attempt to mathematically model an entire economy. Most econometric models are based on numerous regression equations that attempt to describe the relationships between the different sectors of the economy. Very few organizations are capable of developing their own econometric models. Those organizations that do use econometric models usually hire the services of consulting groups or companies that specialize in econometric modeling. Econometric modeling is very expensive and complex and is, therefore, primarily used only by very large organizations.[14]

FRAMEWORK FOR INTEGRATING COMPETITIVE ANALYSIS AND ENVIRONMENTAL SCANNING AND FORECASTING

The first part of this chapter dealt with suggestions for performing competitive analysis and environmental scanning and forecasting. This section offers a framework that ties all of these suggestions together, as shown in Figure 2.5.

Competitive analysis partially indicates the threats to and opportunities for an organization and also partially determines an organization's strengths and

Figure 2.5 Framework for Performing
Competitive Analysis and Environmental Scanning and Forecasting

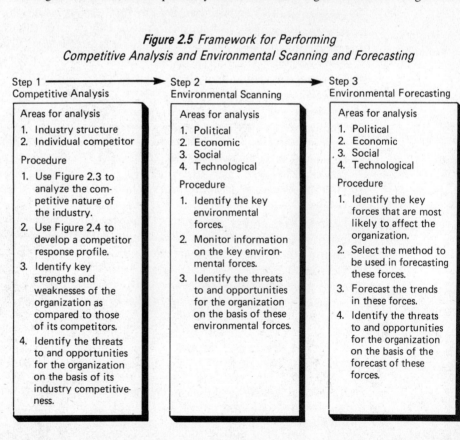

Step 1 → Competitive Analysis	Step 2 → Environmental Scanning	Step 3 Environmental Forecasting
Areas for analysis 1. Industry structure 2. Individual competitor **Procedure** 1. Use Figure 2.3 to analyze the competitive nature of the industry. 2. Use Figure 2.4 to develop a competitor response profile. 3. Identify key strengths and weaknesses of the organization as compared to those of its competitors. 4. Identify the threats to and opportunities for the organization on the basis of its industry competitiveness.	**Areas for analysis** 1. Political 2. Economic 3. Social 4. Technological **Procedure** 1. Identify the key environmental forces. 2. Monitor information on the key environmental forces. 3. Identify the threats to and opportunities for the organization on the basis of these environmental forces.	**Areas for analysis** 1. Political 2. Economic 3. Social 4. Technological **Procedure** 1. Identify the key forces that are most likely to affect the organization. 2. Select the method to be used in forecasting these forces. 3. Forecast the trends in these forces. 4. Identify the threats to and opportunities for the organization on the basis of the forecast of these forces.

weaknesses. Competitive analysis requires an examination of both the industry structure and individual competitors. Environmental scanning and forecasting identify the key environmental forces and their trends in order to indicate the threats and opportunities facing a business.

SUMMARY OF LEARNING OBJECTIVES

1. Explain the five forces that shape the intensity of competition in an industry.
   The five basic forces are the threat of new entrants into the industry, the bargaining power of suppliers to the industry, the threat of substitute products and services, the bargaining power of customers, and the maneuvering for position among current competitors.
2. Describe the purpose of individual competitor analysis.
   Individual competitor analysis is concerned with identifying what is driving the competitor.
3. Outline questions that must be answered in a competitor response profile.
   The questions that must be answered are: Is the competitor satisfied with its current position? What likely moves or strategy shifts will the competitor make? Where is the competitor vulnerable? What will provoke the greatest and most effective retaliation by the competitor?
4. Describe the two basic sources for collecting competitive data.
   The collecting of data on competitive information comes from published data and field data.
5. Define environmental scanning.
   Environmental scanning is the systematic methods used by an organization to monitor and forecast external forces that are not under the direct control of the organization or its industry.
6. Describe the four areas in which organizations should perform environmental scanning.
   Organizations generally categorize environmental scanning into four areas: economic, technological, political (including regulatory), and social.
7. Outline qualitative and quantitative techniques for forecasting.
   Qualitative techniques include jury of executive opinion, sales force composite, customer evaluation, Delphi technique, and anticipatory surveys. Quantitative techniques include time-series analysis, regression modeling, and econometric modeling.

REVIEW QUESTIONS

1. Outline the three questions management must answer in deciding about the future direction of a business.
2. What is an industry structure analysis?

3. Explain the five basic forces that influence an organization's industry competitive environment.
4. What is an individual competitor analysis?
5. Describe the four questions that must be answered in a competitive response profile.
6. Outline some sources of competitive information.
7. What is environmental scanning?
8. Describe the major forces that are normally scanned by businesses.
9. Outline techniques used in qualitative and quantitative forecasting.

DISCUSSION QUESTIONS

1. One of the sources for obtaining competitive information is through personnel hired from a competitor. Do you think it is ethical to obtain competitive information in this manner?
2. What environmental forces have changed over the past five years? Do you think these changes could have been forecast by an organization? Why or why not?
3. "You really don't need to worry about your competitors as long as you satisfy your customers." Do you agree or disagree?

REFERENCES AND ADDITIONAL READING

1. Michael Porter, *Competitive Strategy* (New York: Free Press, 1980), pp. 3–4.
2. Ibid., p. 49.
3. Ibid., pp. 59–60.
4. Ibid., p. 61.
5. Ibid., p. 49.
6. For additional discussion on the importance of environmental scanning, see Richard L. Daft, Juhani Sormanen, and Don Parks, "Chief Executive Scanning, Environmental Characteristics, and Company Performance: An Empirical Study," *Strategic Management Journal*, March–April 1988, pp. 123–139.
7. All of these forecasts come from Jagdish N. Sheth and Meryl Davids, "Search for Tomorrow," *Public Relations Journal*, December 1987, p. 22.
8. See Monica Gonzales, "White Men, Outnumbered," *American Demographics*, August 1988, p. 18.
9. Sabhash C. Jain, "Environmental Scanning in U.S. Corporations," *Long Range Planning*, April 1984, p. 122.
10. Ibid., p. 122.
11. Ibid., pp. 124–125.
12. Edgar R. Fiedler, "Fiedler's Forecasting Rules," *Reader's Digest*, March 1979, p. 100.
13. Material for the following sections is drawn from Leslie W. Rue and Lloyd L. Byars, *Management: Theory and Application*, 5th ed. (Homewood, Ill.: Irwin, 1989), pp. 211–213.
14. For a discussion of some newer approaches to environmental forecasting, see W. R. Huss, "A Move Toward Scenario Analysis," *International Journal of Forecasting* 4, no. 3 (1988): 377–388.

Chapter 2: Analyzing the External Environment

This case study presents an external environmental analysis of Ford Motor Company, including a competitive analysis and environmental scanning and forecasting. An overview of the competitive nature of the automobile industry is developed first, followed by a competitive response profile for six major firms in the industry. An environmental scanning and forecasting assessment is done, and finally an analysis of strengths, weaknesses, opportunities, and threats (SWOT) is developed for Ford on the basis of these external areas. Additional strengths and weaknesses at Ford will be examined in the following chapter through an internal organizational analysis.

MAJOR FORCES THAT GOVERN COMPETITION IN AN INDUSTRY

The major forces that govern competition in an industry are maneuvering for position among competitors, threat of new entrants, bargaining power of suppliers, bargaining power of customers, and threat of substitute products.

Maneuvering for Position Among Competitors

The following firms constitute the major competitors in the industry: three major American firms, the Big Three—Ford, General Motors (GM), Chrysler; and three major Japanese firms—Honda, Toyota, Nissan.

Company/Fiscal Year End	Auto Sales (millions)
General Motors/Dec. 88	97,777
Ford Motor Company/Dec. 88	82,193
Chrysler/Dec. 88	30,650 (units)
Toyota Motor/June 88	39,080
Nissan Motor/Mar. 89	29,717
Honda/Mar. 89	18,527

- Industry growth in the late 1980s and early 1990s is sluggish. Rebates and other dealer incentives are being used to attract a larger customer base.
- Many American consumers have been lost to Japanese companies whose products have an image of better quality and price.
- Japanese auto companies have employed high technology that has curbed production costs in comparison to the Big Three. However, the Big Three

are investing heavily in modernization of their production systems and joining forces with foreign companies to produce products (for example, Ford and Mazda are jointly producing the Probe; Chrysler and Renault of France will produce mini-utility vehicles; and Chrysler and Hyundai will build a new mid-size car) in order to become more efficient.

- American companies are taking steps to acquire smaller foreign-based companies in an effort to further diversify their product lines and take advantage of the smaller firms' independent spirit and creativity.
- Japanese firms are investing more money in American plants in an effort to skirt import restrictions. European companies are doing the same thing in order to avoid the tough new trade rules of the European Economic Community when it becomes a true common market in 1992.

Threat of New Entrants

- Economies of scale prevent any major competitor from entering the industry at this time.
- The capital requirements of auto production have increased dramatically, minimizing new entries into the market. Robotics and other automation developments are forecast to curb costs. However, the development and implementation of this automation requires huge up-front project costs, research and development costs, and state-of-the-art technical expertise.
- Government policy on emissions requirements and average miles per gallon of a firm's fleet will futher prevent the threat of a major competitor entering the market. The 1990 fuel economy average for American fleets is 27.5 miles per gallon.

Bargaining Power of Suppliers

There is a growing trend toward sole-sourcing and partnerships between the users and suppliers of manufacturing systems.

- The major Japanese, American, and European automotive parts suppliers have begun to build plants in other nations.
- Long-term contracts with suppliers are becoming more commonplace.
- General Motors and two of its capital equipment suppliers have signed long-term agreements without a termination date.
- Chrysler has established five-year contracts with major tooling firms.

Bargaining Power of Customers

The following trends are due to intensified competition, sluggish sales, and resultant high inventory levels:

- Rebates and price-cutting incentives are becoming prevalent as firms try to lure customers.
- Customers have been able to negotiate selling price, warranty coverage, and accessory packages to a greater extent.

- Service ratings by customers are increasingly used by company management to measure dealership performance. These ratings are used to determine dealership franchise opportunities, access to advertising funds, and other economic incentives.

Threat of Substitute Products or Services

- Major firms cannot provide the flair of a special niche market as well as a smaller specialized auto company.
- Residents of major cities have converted to public transportation in the face of increasing costs of vehicles, insurance, parking, maintenance, etc.

The level of competition in the auto industry has intensified in the last decade. The entry of Japanese firms into the U.S. market was the impetus for a reevaluation of market strategy and industry position among the Big Three. As a result, American and Japanese companies are both striving to become technologically competent. This competence will result in better-quality products produced at lower costs. The competition among the Big Three and the major foreign competitors will continue to result in benefits for the customer as the fight for market share continues to be based on a quality product for a fair price.

COMPETITIVE RESPONSE PROFILE

Summarized on pages 56–57 is a competitive response profile for Ford, GM, Chrysler, Toyota, Honda, and Nissan, based on Figure 2.4.

ENVIRONMENTAL SCANNING AND FORECASTING

Economic

Several economic factors will affect the growth of the automobile industry and Ford Motor Company including interest rates, rising gasoline prices, the value of the U.S. dollar, and the general condition of the U.S. economy.

Economists at Ford and other economic analysts look at many economic variables or "leading indicators" in order to forecast changes in the economy. Some of these indicators include the wholesale and consumer price indices, durable goods orders, consumer debt load, GNP growth, and interest rates. Often these variables are used as inputs in complex econometric forecasting models that seek to simulate the economy and accurately predict trends.

Ford's chief economist projected slow economic growth for 1990 of 1.5 percent, rising inflation and unemployment, declining interest rates for the first half of the year, and a weaker dollar against foreign currency. In the long term, gasoline prices are predicted to continue their rise, as will manufacturing costs attributed to mandated safety, pollution, and mileage standards.

The number of Japanese cars assembled in North America could soon reach 2 million annually and is forecast to contribute to an excess supply. This may threaten the pricing structure in the American car market and negatively impact the earnings of all participants in the U.S. market.

While most economists agree that the economy will take a downturn, there is less agreement about the prospect of a recession and when it is likely to occur. Finally, the U.S. Commerce Department predicts that new vehicle sales will decline 1.3 percent in 1990 but afterwards will improve steadily through 1994.

Political

The 1990s will mark a new era of increased regulatory and environmental pressure on automakers to improve fuel efficiency, safety standards, and pollution controls. The issues of clean air and global warming will continue to cloud Ford's future product plans, as will increased fuel efficiency standards. Some analysts forecast that by the year 2000, fuel efficiency standards will approach 40–50 miles per gallon.

Even greater changes will occur, however, on the global front with the anticipated 1992 European economic unification, the liberalization of Eastern Europe, the expanding economy of the Soviet Union, and the enormous potential of the infant economic market in China.

Ford has a strong market presence in Europe and Australia with its sales spread throughout both continents and assembly plants in the United Kingdom, Germany, Belgium, and Spain. The company also acquired Britain's Jaguar PLC in early 1990 and has an interest in acquiring a stake in Sweden's Saab Motor Company as it continues to prepare for Europe 1992.

Ford also owns 25 percent of Japan's Mazda Motor Corporation and will continue to forge joint ventures with foreign automobile manufacturers as the industry becomes truly global.

The recent political changes in Eastern Europe, which have liberalized many countries from strict Communist control, also may open up a vast underdeveloped economic market for automobiles. Labor markets are more favorable, and opportunities for trade, investment, and sales will improve. However, few believe that anything will happen quickly, for the political situation is still unstable, and inadequate infrastructures and lack of hard currency are still problems. Yet American, European, and Japanese firms are already staging talks with Eastern European and Soviet officials to negotiate their piece of the pie.

The outlook for industry development in China, however, is less clear since the government's crackdown on student protesters and the institution of stricter government controls in 1989. Ford did not have significant activity in

Competitive Response Profile of Six Auto Manufacturers

Company	Past and Present Objectives	Current Strategy	Satisfaction with Current Position	Likely Moves or Strategy Shifts
Ford	To continually improve product to meet customer needs, allowing reasonable return for stockholders.	Retaining auto production as primary business, with diversification into electronics, glass, automotive replacement parts, space technology, satellite communications, defense work, land development, equipment leasing, car rental, and financial services.	Placed first in overseas auto sales by U.S.-based manufacturer, but concerned that Japanese manufacturers continue to increase their share of market while reducing that of Ford.	(1) Growth through quality and value, and formation of partnerships with overseas companies (e.g., joint ventures with Mazda and Nissan). (2) Introduction of "centers of responsibility" (i.e., specific vehicle lines or components developed on a global basis by company activity best equipped for the assignment).
GM	To provide products and services of quality that customers will perceive as having superior value; employees and business partners will share in the business success; stockholders will receive a sustained superior return on investment.	(1) Production of high-quality, high-value products in the variety that customers demand. (2) Retaining position as significant force in key related industries such as robotics, data processing, communications, and computer controlled design and processing. (3) Exping. (3) Expansion of established capabilities as creative, innovative high-tech enterprise in 21st century. (4) Market responsiveness and flexibility.	Pleased with market share and on track with forecast. Has the highest sales volume in dollars.	(1) Manufacturing products that would set industry standards in quality, performance, styling, safety, and value. (2) Replacement of older, less efficient manufacturing facilities with new, modernized plants and equipment. (3) Development of new production system involving strengthened partnership with employees and greater participative management in order to achieve highest possible levels of productivity and improve market responsiveness. (4) Major cost reduction, which would include assuring the most competitive sources of components and parts, eliminating vertical integration where it impedes achievement of its objectives.
Chrysler	To produce and deliver high-value, "best-in-class" quality products that are safe, reliable, and known for outstanding design and performance.	(1) Launching a broad line of cars and trucks. (2) Extended warranty, 7/70, to match quality of products. (3) Investment in new products, facilities, and superior manufacturing technology.	Satisfied. Although room for improvement, has achieved its three objectives; also, had highest percentage improvement in U.S. retail sales of the Big Three—share of car market increased by 0.5%.	Advancement of processes; retraining of work force; keeping quality up and holding prices down.

Company	Past and Present Objectives	Current Strategy	Satisfaction with Current Position	Likely Moves or Strategy Shifts
Toyota	To produce products with quality as high as anywhere in the world while assuring that production costs are the most competitive of any manufacturer's.	*Kanban* system: design preventing overproduction and excess inventory. *Jidoka*: auto defect prevention system. Just-in-time production.	Not satisfied with position in industry; plans are in effect to increase overall position (i.e., market share and sales).	Change to introduce luxury sedan into international market and to penetrate European market by building plants and factories there to produce high-quality cars at minimum cost; flexible work force, lean inventory, and minimum defects.
Honda	To maintain international viewpoint by supplying products of the highest efficiency at a reasonable price for worldwide customer satisfaction.	Group responsibility instead of individual responsibility; building of plants overseas; internationalization and local community relations.	Satisfied, but would like to improve on market share and profit, both in Japan and abroad.	Building plants overseas; searching for new consumer markets and needs; ancillary firms producing a large percentage of machine parts and components.
Nissan	[Information not available.]	Competitiveness in the areas of production, price, promotion, and place-of-business logistics.	Satisfied; has had a 10% increase in worldwide sales despite down year for auto industry; regaining market share that had been lost between 1986 and 1988, although not comfortable with truck market.	Development and building of cars that are different enough to stand out from offerings of Toyota, Honda, and other Japanese makers while providing mainstream customers with basic transportation; development of ventures with other car companies.

China at the time of the political unrest; however, GM gave up its plans to participate in a joint venture in China with Fuji Motor Company. Most analysts still see China as a lucrative market for some industries, but the gains will probably be slower in the automobile industry since China's economy is underdeveloped.

Social

Studies of social and economic trends in the 1990s present the auto industry with an enormous population of buyers who are predisposed to purchase and will have the financial means to buy new cars on a regular basis. Three demographic groups that will be particularly significant to the industry are baby boomers, women, and the elderly.

Maturing baby boomers will have far more disposable income available for automobile purchases and a sizable upscale segment will favor luxury cars and sport-utility vehicles. Baby boomers and the elderly will also increase demand for recreational vehicles (RVs) while reducing the need for station wagons and minivans as their families mature. A large and growing blue-collar segment of the boomers, however, favor American cars and domestic minivans.

Women will increasingly become more involved in new-car purchases and are expected to exercise as much power in the automotive market as men. Automotive marketing successes of the nineties will be generated by advertising that prominently features women.

The final dominant group, which represents a "graying of America," is buyers 55 and older. They constitute 25 percent of new-car buyers, and this statistic will increase. Older buyers will look for features that make driving safer and easier, including electronic systems to warn drivers who are getting drowsy, nonglare instrument panels, and simplified electronic controls.

Technological

The cars of tomorrow will be loaded with convenience features and intelligent systems: smart computers that run the engine and transmission more efficiently, electronic suspension systems, radar obstacle detection to help drivers avoid accidents, and navigation systems that will help drivers avoid traffic jams while video screens indicate alternate routes. Self-tinting glass and infrared technology that enhances night vision will also be available. Antilock brakes, air bags, and traction control will become standard.

The use of space-age plastics will increase because they are lightweight, less expensive than steel, and noncorrosive. New techniques for making models and prototypes quickly and inexpensively using sophisticated computers are the wave of the future, and 10,000 electric cars are slated for use in Southern California in the next five years.

The extensive use of robotic technology in production will increase, and automobile manufacturers will develop cars for the nineties that will run on alternative fuels.

FORD MOTOR COMPANY SWOT ANALYSIS

On the basis of Ford's external environment, the following SWOT analysis can be developed.

Strengths

- Ford is the second largest car and truck producer in the world.
- Ford's 1988 earnings were at an all-time high—$5.3 billion, or $10.96 a share—the highest ever for any automotive company.
- Ford's mass production capabilities allow it to take advantage of economies of scale.
- Ford's portfolio is well balanced. Its diversification into financial services and diversified products operations allows it to offset any downward trend in auto sales.
- Ford is vertically integrated, with organizations such as Ford Glass Division, which produces virtually all of the glass for Ford's North American cars and trucks, and Ford Motor Credit Company, which provided financing for 1.6 million vehicles in 1988 and which also provided financial support to dealers and retail automotive customers.
- Ford has successfully joined forces with foreign companies to diversify product lines, update technology capabilities, and improve product quality.
- Ford has reduced production costs and improved the quality of products due to partnerships with Mazda and Nissan.
- Most of Ford's product design and manufacturing is linked to computer graphics via computer-aided design/computer-aided manufacturing (CAD/CAM).

Weaknesses

- Relative to Japanese competitors, Ford is spending more of its revenue on pensions, compensation benefits, and so on.
- Ford has not fully implemented robotics and other state-of-the-art technology in production.
- Ford had to export production in order to meet government regulations. It was not technically competent to meet the fuel efficiency standard of 27.5 miles per gallon. By law, cars with less than 75 percent domestic content are considered imports.

Opportunities

- Owning a manufacturing plant in Japan.
- Cost reduction methods for car building and distribution (Alpha Project).
- Alternate-fuel automobiles in compliance with the Clean Air Proposal.
- Capitalize on reestablished product quality, "Quality Is Job 1."
- Joint ventures hold possibility for maximizing quality of product via technology and integration efforts.

- Increased market potential for global sales due to European economic unification.

Threats

- Foreign car sales, which hold substantial market share.
- Sluggish auto industry sales.
- Value of the yen relative to the dollar.
- Entry of Japanese manufacturers into luxury car market (Nissan Infiniti, Acura Legend, Toyota Lexus).
- Increased government regulation.
- Downturn in the U.S. economy/possibility of a recession.

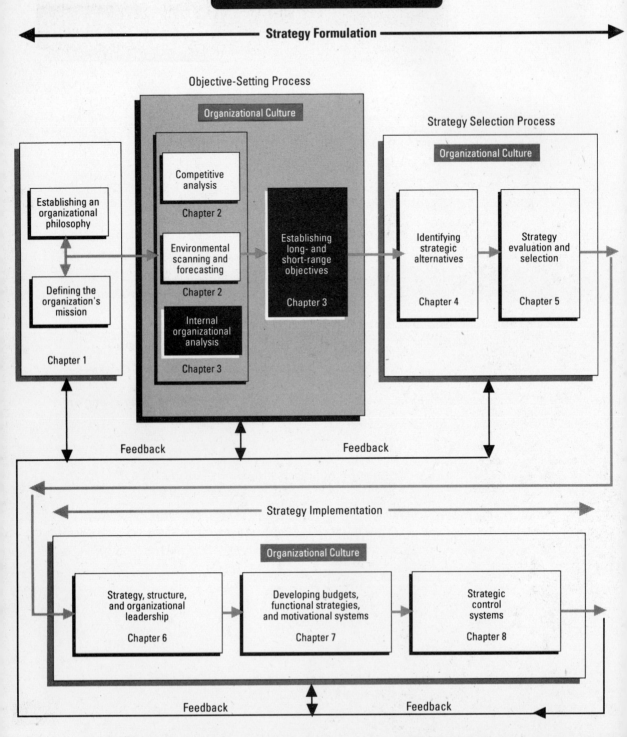

STRATEGIC MANAGEMENT PROCESS

Strategy Formulation

Objective-Setting Process

Organizational Culture

Competitive analysis

Chapter 2

Environmental scanning and forecasting

Chapter 2

Internal organizational analysis

Chapter 3

Establishing long- and short-range objectives

Chapter 3

Establishing an organizational philosophy

Defining the organization's mission

Chapter 1

Strategy Selection Process

Organizational Culture

Identifying strategic alternatives

Chapter 4

Strategy evaluation and selection

Chapter 5

Feedback

Feedback

Strategy Implementation

Organizational Culture

Strategy, structure, and organizational leadership

Chapter 6

Developing budgets, functional strategies, and motivational systems

Chapter 7

Strategic control systems

Chapter 8

Feedback

Feedback

CHAPTER 3
Analyzing the Internal Environment and Establishing Organizational Objectives

LEARNING OBJECTIVES

After studying this chapter, you should be able to

1. Define internal organizational analysis.

2. Outline the eight areas that businesses should analyze in performing an internal organizational analysis.

3. Describe questions that must be answered in assessing an organization's financial position.

4. Present questions that must be answered in assessing an organization's product position.

5. Outline questions that must be answered in assessing an organization's marketing capability.

6. Discuss questions that must be answered in assessing an organization's research and development capability.

7. Present questions that must be answered in assessing a firm's organizational structure.

8. Outline questions that must be answered in assessing an organization's human resources.

9. Describe questions that must be answered in assessing the condition of an organization's facilities and equipment.

10. Outline questions that must be answered in assessing an organization's past objectives and strategies.

11. Distinguish between long- and short-range objectives.

12. Describe 11 potential areas for establishing organizational objectives.

To answer the question "Where is the business now?" management must analyze the organization's internal and external environments. Both analyses must be completed before organizational objectives can be set. Whereas Chapter 2 discussed in detail how to analyze an organization's external environment, this chapter explains how to analyze the internal environment and describes the objective-setting process.

INTERNAL ORGANIZATIONAL ANALYSIS

An *internal organizational analysis* evaluates all relevant factors in an organization in order to determine its strengths and weaknesses. Typically, every area of the business that can significantly influence the long-term survival and success of the business should be analyzed. Some of the areas that most businesses should analyze include the following:

1. Financial position
2. Product position
3. Marketing capability
4. Research and development capability
5. Organizational structure
6. Human resources
7. Condition of facilities and equipment
8. Past objectives and strategies

Of course, the specific areas to be studied and the weight given to each area vary from business to business. For all businesses, however, the analysis should give management an understanding of the organization's major strengths, on which its future should be built, and major weaknesses, which should be corrected whenever possible. The following sections will describe questions that need to be addressed in the eight areas that should be analyzed in an internal organizational analysis.[1]

Financial Position

The financial position of a business plays a crucial role in determining what it can or cannot do in the future. Typical questions that need to be answered in assessing financial position include the following:

1. What are the trends in financial figures such as current ratio, acid-test ratio, inventory turnover, capitalization ratio, net working capital, earnings per share, earnings-sales ratio, earnings–tangible net worth ratio, and earnings–working capital ratio?
2. How do the trends in these financial figures compare to those of competitors?
3. What are the organization's sources and uses of funds, and how do they compare to those of its competitors?

4. What percentage of profits comes from each business unit or product?
5. What are the strengths and weaknesses in the financial position of the business?

Appendix B in Part Six explains in depth how to conduct financial analysis for understanding the financial position of an organization. Topics covered in Appendix B include ratio analysis, working capital analysis, capital budgeting, business acquisitions analysis, and pro forma financial statement analysis.

Product Position

For a business to be successful, it must be acutely aware of its product position in the marketplace. Without this type of information, no business can survive very long in today's competitive environment. Managers need to answer many questions in assessing an organization's product position; some of the more important ones are as follows:

1. What share of the market does the organization's product(s) currently hold? How firm is the hold on the market share? Is the market share increasing or decreasing? How do the present market share and trends in the market share compare to those of competitors? Is the share concentrated in a small number of customers, or is it diversified?
2. How do the organization's prices compare to those of its competitors? Is the firm a price leader or a price follower?
3. How do customers view the organization's product?
4. Are there any design, quality, or delivery problems with the organization's product?
5. Does the business hold any patents that give it a competitive edge? When do these patents expire?
6. Is the market for the organization's product expanding or contracting, and at what rate?
7. What is the product life cycle of the organization's product?
8. Is the organization's product vulnerable to business cycle changes?
9. What are the strengths and weaknesses in the organization's product position?

Marketing Capability

Closely allied with an organization's product position is its marketing capability (i.e., its ability to deliver the right product at the right place at the right time and at the right price). Typical questions that need to be answered in assessing an organization's marketing capability include the following:

1. What channels of distribution are used? How do they compare to the channels used by competitors?
2. How much of the total marketing job (research, sales, advertising, and promotion) does the business perform?

3. Is there a capability for developing and exploiting new products?
4. What are the strengths and weaknesses in the organization's marketing capability?

Research and Development Capability

Every organization, whether it has a formal research and development department or not, must be concerned about its ability to develop new products. For some industries, such as computers and medical technology, the research and development (R&D) capability of a business is critical if it is to survive. For those businesses in which research and development is crucial, some questions that need to be answered include the following:

1. What new products have been developed by R&D over the past years?
2. Are the new products developed by R&D first in the market, or are they a reaction to a competitor's new product?
3. What are the strengths and weaknesses in the organization's R&D capability?

Organizational Structure

All businesses produce and market their products through an organizational structure. This structure can either help or hinder an organization in achieving its objectives. The relationship between organizational strategy and structure is explored in more depth in Chapter 6. However, to assess a firm's strengths and weaknesses, managers need to answer several questions about its organizational structure:

1. What type of organizational structure currently exists?
2. Do all organizational units cooperate effectively in working toward organizational objectives?
3. Is there a formal organizational chart?
4. Are authority and responsibility relationships clearly established?
5. Are too many meetings required to make decisions?
6. What is the degree of centralization versus decentralization?
7. What style of management is used (e.g., autocratic or participative)?
8. Are people in the organization bogged down in paperwork?
9. What are the strengths and weaknesses of the present organizational structure?

Human Resources

All the activities of an organization are significantly influenced by the quality and quantity of its human resources. Training programs, compensation systems, performance appraisal systems, and management and employee development programs help determine not only the quantity and quality of current employees but also the type of employee that can be expected in the future. Effective human resource systems can give an organization a very real competitive edge in attracting and retaining high-quality personnel.

Thus, to accurately assess its strengths and weaknesses, an organization must make an objective evaluation of its human resources. This assessment must include not only operative personnel but also all levels of management. Some typical questions of interest in this area would include the following:

1. Was top management promoted from within or brought in from the outside?
2. How long has top management been with the organization?
3. What is the background of top management?
4. How old are the top managers, and how long are they expected to remain with the business?
5. What is the dominant value system of the managers?
6. What influence does the board of directors exercise, and what are the capabilities of the board members?
7. What is the quality of middle management and supervisory personnel?
8. What are the skills and abilities of the operative personnel? Are they adequate for meeting tomorrow's needs?
9. What are the general attitude and level of motivation of operative employees?
10. What are the strengths and weaknesses of the organization's human resources?

Condition of Facilities and Equipment

The condition of an organization's facilities and equipment can either enhance or hinder its competitiveness. For example, for years the U.S. steel industry has been at a competitive disadvantage with the Japanese steel industry largely because of the obsolete production facilities in the United States. Several questions that need to be answered in this area include the following:

1. Are the equipment and facilities the most modern, or are they obsolete?
2. Are production facilities efficient?
3. What type of production process is employed? What type of production process is employed by competitors?
4. Is there surplus capacity?
5. Is there room for expansion?
6. What are the strengths and weaknesses of the organization's facilities and equipment?

Past Objectives and Strategies

In assessing its internal environment, every business should attempt to explicitly describe its past objectives and strategies. In general, it can be said that past objectives and strategies are a strong indicator of future objectives and strategies. Four basic questions need to be answered in this area:

1. What have been the firm's major objectives in the relatively recent past?
2. Has it achieved these objectives?

3. What strategies has it employed in the relatively recent past?
4. Have these strategies been successful?

Example 3.1 illustrates a strengths-and-weaknesses analysis for a small business—Liberty Industries.

STRATEGY IN ACTION Example 3.1

Strengths-and-Weaknesses Analysis for Liberty Industries

Liberty Industries is a small industrial wholesale lumber firm in northeastern Ohio that specializes in wood packaging products. As part of its strategic planning process, Liberty formally identified its strengths and weaknesses, describing them as follows.

Strengths

- Nationwide market potential (regional sales offices in Virginia, Georgia, Ohio, Illinois, Texas, and California).
- Lumber products have historically been sold through wholesale channels.
- Strong reputation of providing quality and service.
- Wood products generate a reliable base of profit dollars.
- Strong regional-teams concept (two outside salespersons to one inside customer service representative).
- Ability to expand supply base to meet sales requirements.
- Commitment to success of all ventures.
- Product and market knowledge.
- Genuine concern for employees' well-being.
- Stress on professionalism and creativity.
- Competent inside staff working within excellent environment.
- New engineering and manufacturing capabilities generated through joint venture with established German packaging/machinery firm.
- Strong personal contacts through top management associations capable of providing potential opportunities.

Weaknesses

- Low profit margins of wood products.
- Cost of inventory in new venture with packaging systems ($250,000+).
- Need for strict budgetary controls in recessionary periods.
- Lack of market research to determine viability of current and proposed products.
- Sales staff too small, prohibiting maximum coverage.
- Lack of in-house design and engineering capabilities.
- Conflict of conservative versus aggressive management styles.
- Lack of consistent sales and middle management.
- Weak information transfer between corporate office and regional offices.

Source: Adapted from R. Henry Migliore and Ronald C. Ringness, "Nailing Down a Future for a Small Wood-Products Business," *Planning Review*, May/June 1987, pp. 30–37.

Responsibility for Performing an Internal Organizational Analysis

Who is responsible for performing internal organizational analyses? Some organizations assign this responsibility to their planning department. Others contract with outside consulting firms. Recently, however, the trend has been toward having a team of line managers in the organization develop the analysis with technical assistance and coordination from the planning department. The premises for this trend are that if line managers develop the analysis, they will understand it, perceive its implications for the future direction of the organization, and use it to guide their own strategic planning decisions.[2] For example, if an organization has several strategic business units, a group of managers in each SBU would be responsible for developing an internal organizational analysis for their unit. Each analysis would be reviewed and approved by the top management of the particular business unit and by the top management of the organization as a whole.

ESTABLISHING ORGANIZATIONAL OBJECTIVES

The purpose of management is to lead and motivate employees toward the accomplishment of an organization's objectives. *Long-range objectives specify the results desired in pursuing the organization's mission and normally extend beyond the current fiscal year of the organization.* Short-range objectives should follow logically from long-range objectives. *Short-range objectives are performance targets, normally of less than one year's duration, designed to achieve the organization's long-range objectives.*

Ideally, an organization's objectives should be compatible with its culture and should

1. Match its strengths to opportunities
2. Minimize threats to the organization
3. Eliminate weaknesses in the organization

They should also support the organization's mission and need to be established for every area of the organization where performance and results directly influence its survival and success.

American managers have been criticized for failing to look beyond the accomplishment of short-range objectives. However, the importance of establishing and achieving long-range objectives is extremely important. While extended planning horizons are critical to industries with large capital investments (e.g., utilities and automobiles), they are also important for most other industries. Even in the rapidly changing high-technology field the most savvy companies are, and have been for years, thinking about home robots, telecommunications, and electronic libraries, applications of which are now in existence. Without losing sight of short-range performance, top managers must be strategically planning for the future (5, 10, 15, or more years ahead) of their organization.

Mix of Organizational Objectives

No one mix or combination of objectives is applicable to all organizations. The type of objectives that are established depends on the nature of the particular organization. For example, the Boy Scouts of America would have a set of objectives different from the American Express Company.

The mix of organizational objectives is influenced by the mix of objectives from prior years. The degree of achievement of prior objectives influences the aspiration level of the management team and often serves as a starting point for determining the mix and exact nature of the objectives for a future time period.

The following items provide potential areas for establishing objectives for most organizations:

1. *Customer Service* Expressed in terms of delivery times or customer complaints. Example:
   a. To reduce the number of customer complaints by 40 percent over the next three years
2. *Financial Resources* Expressed in terms of the capital structure, new issues of common stock, cash flow, working capital, dividend payments, and collection periods. Examples:
   a. To increase working capital to $10 million within five years
   b. To reduce long-term debt to $8 million within three years
3. *Human Resources* Expressed in terms of rates of absenteeism, tardiness, turnover, or number of grievances. Also can be expressed in terms of number of people to be trained or number of training programs to be conducted. Examples:
   a. To reduce absenteeism by 8 percent within three years
   b. To conduct a 40-hour supervisory development program for 300 supervisors at a cost not to exceed $400 per participant over the next four years
4. *Markets* Expressed in terms of share of the market or dollar or unit volume of sales. Examples:
   a. To increase commercial sales to 85 percent of total sales and reduce military sales to 15 percent of total sales over the next three years
   b. To increase the number of units of product X sold by 500,000 units within four years
5. *Organizational Structure* Expressed in terms of changes to be made or projects to be undertaken. Example:
   a. To establish a decentralized organizational structure within three years
6. *Physical Facilities* Expressed in terms of square feet, fixed costs, or units of production. Examples:
   a. To increase storage capacity by 15 million units over the next three years
   b. To decrease production capacity in the West Coast plant by 20 percent within three years

7. *Product* Expressed in terms of sales and profitability by product line or product or target dates for development of new products. Example:
   a. To phase out the product with the lowest profit margin within two years
8. *Productivity* Expressed in terms of a ratio of input to output or cost per unit of production. Example:
   a. To increase the number of units produced per worker by 10 percent per eight-hour day over the next three years
9. *Profitability* Expressed in terms of profits, return on investment, earnings per share, or profit-to-sales ratios. Example:
   a. To increase return on investment to 15 percent after taxes within four years
10. *Research and Development* Expressed in terms of the amount of money to be spent on projects to be completed. Example:
    a. To develop an engine in the medium-price range within five years at a cost not to exceed $3 million
11. *Social Responsibility* Expressed in terms of types of activities, number of days of service, or financial contributions. Example:
    a. To increase our contribution to United Way by 30 percent over the next three years

Objectives can be expressed in both quantitative and qualitative terms. In both cases, they should be detailed enough so that personnel can clearly understand what the organization intends to achieve. Example 3.2 shows objectives set by the Tandy Corporation in its annual report to its stockholders.

Procedure for Establishing Objectives

An organization's objectives result from the interactions of the following factors:

1. Organizational culture
2. Competitive analysis
3. Environmental scanning and forecasting
4. Internal organizational analysis

Figure 3.1 shows the interrelationships between these factors. By identifying the key environmental forces and their trends, environmental scanning and forecasting indicate the threats to and opportunities for an organization. Competitive analysis partially indicates both threats and opportunities as well as strengths and weaknesses of the organization.

Internal organizational analysis identifies the organization's strengths and weaknesses. Figure 3.2 gives a step-by-step procedure that ties environmental scanning and forecasting, competitive analysis, and internal organizational analysis into a framework for analysis. This framework is useful in establishing organizational objectives.[3]

Strategic Objectives of Tandy Corporation

Tandy Corporation is a multifaceted multi-billion-dollar company. As a retail company, it is known for its nationwide chain of Radio Shack stores, Computer Centers, and dealer/franchise outlets and for the McDuff and VideoConcepts retail operations of its Tandy Name Brand Retail Group. As a manufacturer, it designs and produces almost a billion dollars of consumer electronics products and computers in 28 manufacturing operations and 2 manufacturing joint ventures.

In its annual report, Tandy spelled out its four strategic objectives as follows:

Accelerating the Growth in Cellular Telephones

By increasing awareness in the marketplace and by developing alternative channels of distribution. While cellular telephones have primarily been targeted to the business environment, we perceive a growth in their popularity as personal security and emergency devices. In addition to our traditional retail channels, this significant market potential is addressed by strategic alliances in technology, manufacturing, and service.

Capitalizing on World-Class Manufacturing

That produces innovative, quality products to be sold through an ever increasing number of retailers, dealers, resellers, and manufacturers. Supported by research and product development at seven locations in four countries, manufacturing plays a major role in stimulating market expansion. For example, the enormous potential of TANDY THOR-CD™ as the first CD-compatible record and erase optical disc technology could spawn a whole new segment of the electronics industry.

Continuing Growth in Sales Volume per Location

Through a multiyear plan of store renovation, expansion of merchandise offerings, aggressive promotional techniques, in-depth sales personnel training, and enhancements in productivity and distribution. Double-digit sales increases in Radio Shack consumer stores over the past three years indicate achievement in these important areas. These strategies enable us to better meet and serve customer needs and demands in sophisticated technology products.

Leveraging Our Computer Technology Base

Through the development of meaningful alternative channels of distribution and through opportune acquisitions. Outstanding design and manufacturing capabilities enable us to offer state-of-the-art computer products for home, education, and business use. Products like DeskMate®, our user-friendly software interface, continue to impact the computer industry and offer market-broadening potential. Additional growth is targeted through direct sales agreements with specialized resellers and through acquisitions like GRiD Systems Corporation which opens significant government and Fortune 1000 marketing opportunities.

Source: Annual Report, Tandy Corporation.

Figure 3.1 Establishing an Organization's Objectives

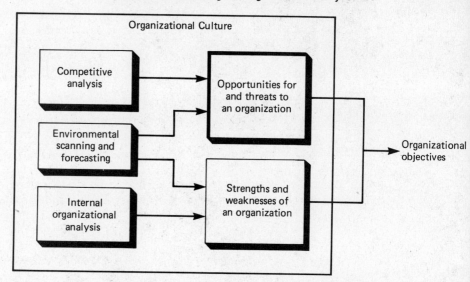

Figure 3.2 Step-by-Step Procedure for Performing Competitive Analysis, Environmental Scanning and Forecasting, and Internal Organization Analysis

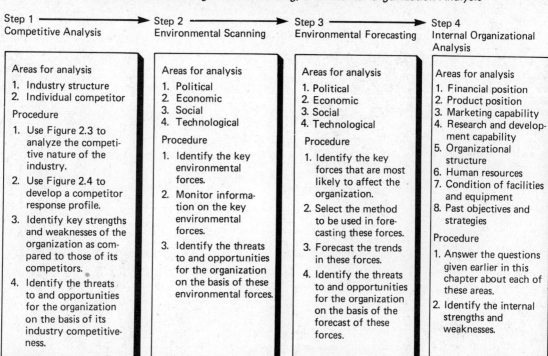

Step 1 ⟶ Competitive Analysis

Step 2 ⟶ Environmental Scanning

Step 3 ⟶ Environmental Forecasting

Step 4 Internal Organizational Analysis

Step 1 — Competitive Analysis

Areas for analysis
1. Industry structure
2. Individual competitor

Procedure
1. Use Figure 2.3 to analyze the competitive nature of the industry.
2. Use Figure 2.4 to develop a competitor response profile.
3. Identify key strengths and weaknesses of the organization as compared to those of its competitors.
4. Identify the threats to and opportunities for the organization on the basis of its industry competitiveness.

Step 2 — Environmental Scanning

Areas for analysis
1. Political
2. Economic
3. Social
4. Technological

Procedure
1. Identify the key environmental forces.
2. Monitor information on the key environmental forces.
3. Identify the threats to and opportunities for the organization on the basis of these environmental forces.

Step 3 — Environmental Forecasting

Areas for analysis
1. Political
2. Economic
3. Social
4. Technological

Procedure
1. Identify the key forces that are most likely to affect the organization.
2. Select the method to be used in forecasting these forces.
3. Forecast the trends in these forces.
4. Identify the threats to and opportunities for the organization on the basis of the forecast of these forces.

Step 4 — Internal Organizational Analysis

Areas for analysis
1. Financial position
2. Product position
3. Marketing capability
4. Research and development capability
5. Organizational structure
6. Human resources
7. Condition of facilities and equipment
8. Past objectives and strategies

Procedure
1. Answer the questions given earlier in this chapter about each of these areas.
2. Identify the internal strengths and weaknesses.

Setting Objectives in Strategic Business Units and Functional Areas

After top management has set objectives for the entire business, each strategic business unit (SBU) and/or functional area must establish its own objectives. Normally, the steps in this process are as follows:

1. The objective-setting process begins at the top of the organization with a statement of mission.
2. Long-range objectives are established to achieve this mission.
3. Long-range objectives lead to the setting of performance targets (short-range objectives) for the overall organization.
4. Long- and short-range objectives are established for each SBU, major division, or operating unit in the organization.
5. Long- and short-range objectives are established for the functional areas (marketing, finance, production) in each SBU, major division, or operating unit.

Figure 3.3 *Objective-Setting Process for SBUs and Other Organizational Units*

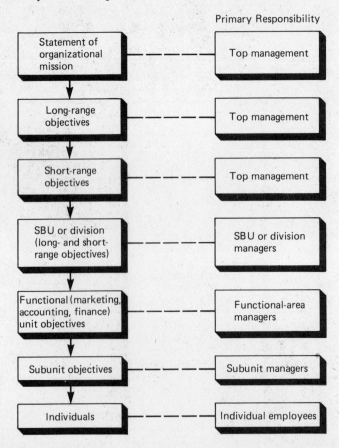

6. The same objective-setting process continues on down through the organizational hierarchy.

The entire process is shown in Figure 3.3. This cascade approach to objective setting does not imply "autocratic" or "top-down" management. It merely assures that the objectives of individual units are in phase with the objectives of the total organization. It coordinates the entire objective-setting process. Actually, participation in setting objectives by the managers responsible for achieving them facilitates their accomplishment and should be encouraged by senior management.

SUMMARY OF LEARNING OBJECTIVES

1. Define internal organizational analysis.
   An internal organizational analysis evaluates all relevant factors in an organization in order to determine its strengths and weaknesses.
2. Outline the eight areas that businesses should analyze in performing an internal organizational analysis.
   These areas are financial position, product position, marketing capability, research and development capability, organizational structure, human resources, condition of facilities and equipment, and past objectives and strategies.
3. Describe questions that must be answered in assessing an organization's financial position.
   The questions are as follows:

   - *What are the trends in financial figures such as current ratio, acid-test ratio, inventory turnover, capitalization ratio, net working capital, earnings per share, earnings–sales ratio, earnings–tangible net worth ratio, and earnings–working capital ratio?*
   - *How do the trends in these financial figures compare to those of competitors?*
   - *What are the organization's sources and uses of funds, and how do they compare to those of its competitors?*
   - *What percentage of profits comes from each business unit or product?*
   - *What are the strengths and weaknesses in the financial position of the business?*

4. Present questions that must be answered in assessing an organization's product position.
   The questions are as follows:

   - *What share of the market does the organization's product(s) currently hold? How firm is the hold on the market share? Is the market share increasing or decreasing? How do the present market share and trends in the market share compare to those of competitors? Is the share concentrated in a small number of customers, or is it diversified?*

- *How do the organization's prices compare to those of its competitors? Is the firm a price leader or a price follower?*
- *How do customers view the organization's product?*
- *Are there any design, quality, or delivery problems with the organization's product?*
- *Does the business hold any patents that give it a competitive edge? When do these patents expire?*
- *Is the market for the organization's product expanding or contracting, and at what rate?*
- *What is the product life cycle of the organization's product?*
- *Is the organization's product vulnerable to business cycle changes?*
- *What are the strengths and weaknesses in the organization's product position?*

5. Outline questions that must be answered in assessing an organization's marketing capability.
   The questions are as follows:

- *What channels of distribution are used? How do they compare to the channels used by competitors?*
- *How much of the total marketing job (research, sales, advertising, and promotion) does the business perform?*
- *Is there a capability for developing and exploiting new products?*
- *What are the strengths and weaknesses in the organization's marketing capability?*

6. Discuss questions that must be answered in assessing an organization's research and development capability.
   The questions are as follows:

- *What new products have been developed by R&D over the past years?*
- *Are the new products developed by R&D first in the market, or are they a reaction to a competitor's new product?*
- *What are the strengths and weaknesses in the organization's R&D capability?*

7. Present questions that must be answered in assessing a firm's organizational structure.
   The questions are as follows:

- *What type of organizational structure currently exists?*
- *Do all organizational units cooperate effectively in working toward organizational objectives?*
- *Is there a formal organizational chart?*
- *Are authority and responsibility relationships clearly established?*
- *Are too many meetings required to make decisions?*
- *What is the degree of centralization versus decentralization?*
- *What style of management is used (e.g., autocratic or participative)?*
- *Are people in the organization bogged down in paperwork?*
- *What are the strengths and weaknesses of the present organizational structure?*

8. Outline questions that must be answered in assessing an organization's human resources.
   The questions are as follows:

   - *Was top management promoted from within or brought in from the outside?*
   - *How long has top management been with the organization?*
   - *What is the background of top management?*
   - *How old are the top managers, and how long are they expected to remain with the business?*
   - *What is the dominant value system of the managers?*
   - *What influence does the board of directors exercise, and what are the capabilities of the board members?*
   - *What is the quality of middle management and supervisory personnel?*
   - *What are the skills and abilities of the operative personnel? Are they adequate for meeting tomorrow's needs?*
   - *What are the general attitude and level of motivation of operative employees?*
   - *What are the strengths and weaknesses of the organization's human resources?*

9. Describe questions that must be answered in assessing the condition of an organization's facilities and equipment.
   The questions are as follows:

   - *Are the equipment and facilities the most modern, or are they obsolete?*
   - *Are production facilities efficient?*
   - *What type of production process is employed? What type of production process is employed by competitors?*
   - *Is there surplus capacity?*
   - *Is there room for expansion?*
   - *What are the strengths and weaknesses of the organization's facilities and equipment?*

10. Outline questions that must be answered in assessing an organization's past objectives and strategies.
    The questions are as follows:

    - *What have been the firm's major objectives in the relatively recent past?*
    - *Has it achieved these objectives?*
    - *What strategies has it employed in the relatively recent past?*
    - *Have these strategies been successful?*

11. Distinguish between long- and short-range objectives.
    Long-range objectives specify the results desired in pursuing the organization's mission and normally extend beyond the current fiscal year of the organization. Short-range objectives are performance targets, normally of less than one year's duration, designed to achieve the organization's long-range objectives.

12. Describe 11 potential areas for establishing organizational objectives.
    Eleven potential areas for establishing organizational objectives are customer ser-
    vice, financial resources, human resources, markets, organizational structure, physi-
    cal facilities, product, productivity, profitability, research and development, and
    social responsibility.

REVIEW QUESTIONS

1. What is an internal organizational analysis?
2. Outline the eight areas that need to be analyzed in performing an internal organizational analysis.
3. Describe the questions that need to be answered in assessing the following areas:
   a. Financial position
   b. Product position
   c. Marketing capability
   d. Research and development capability
   e. Organizational structure
   f. Human resources
   g. Condition of facilities and equipment
   h. Past objectives and strategies
4. Distinguish between long-range and short-range objectives.
5. Outline the factors whose interaction determine an organization's objectives.
6. Describe 11 potential areas for establishing objectives.
7. Discuss the typical steps involved in setting objectives for SBUs and other functional areas of a business.

DISCUSSION QUESTIONS

1. A firm's own management cannot objectively evaluate its internal environment. Discuss your views on this statement.
2. Choose any business organization and see if you can identify its objectives by researching business publications or public documents of the organization.
3. The only objective of business organizations is to make a profit. Do you agree or disagree? Be prepared to defend your choice.

REFERENCES AND ADDITIONAL READING

1. Many of the questions in this and the following sections were taken from or adopted from Robert B. Buchele, "How to Evaluate a Firm," *Management Review,* Fall 1962,

pp. 5–17; and David E. Hussey, "The Corporate Appraisal: Assessing Company Strengths and Weaknesses," *Long Range Planning*, December 1968, pp. 19–25. For additional information on questions, see Stephen C. South, "A Competitive Advantage: The Cornerstone of Strategic Thinking," *Journal of Business Strategy*, Spring 1981, pp. 15–25; and Howard Stevenson, "Defining Strengths and Weaknesses," *Sloan Management Review*, Spring 1976, pp. 51–68.

2. William R. King, "Integrating Strength-Weakness Analysis into Strategic Planning," *Journal of Business Research*, December 1983, p. 479.

3. For an interesting discussion on strengths and weaknesses, see R. Duane Ireland, Michael A. Betts, Richard A. DePorras, and Deborah Auld, "Strategy Formulation Processes: Differences in Perceptions of Strengths and Weaknesses Indicators and Environmental Uncertainty by Managerial Level," *Strategic Management Journal*, September–October 1987, p. 469.

Strategy in Action Case Study: Ford Motor Company

Chapter 3: Analyzing the Internal Environment and Establishing Organizational Objectives

Ford Motor Company has enjoyed considerable success in the past decade. One significant reason is that Ford has made positive changes in its internal environment. An internal organization analysis helps a company determine its strengths and weaknesses and involves many areas of the company. Several areas of the Ford Motor Company are discussed in the internal organizational analysis that follows.

FINANCIAL POSITION

Exhibit 1 gives a five-year financial summary of Ford Motor Company. Exhibit 2 gives a consolidated balance sheet, and Exhibit 3 provides a consolidated statement of income. From this and other financial data, Exhibits 4 and 5 present a ratio analysis of Ford and its competitors.

As shown by the data, Ford's liquid position is below the industry average. Ford's current ratio for 1988 was below the industry average of 1.35, and its inventory turnover is slightly below the industry average of 13.2. Despite its below-average inventory turnover, Ford has actually improved in this area, running its plants with lower amounts of inventory and more just-in-time production. This confirms that Ford's manufacturing operations continue to improve every year. At the end of 1988, cash and marketable securities totaled $9.2 billion, down $933 million from 1987. Working capital was $2.5 billion at year-end 1988, which was $578 million lower than 1987. The decline in cash, marketable securities, and working capital may be attributed to record capital expenditures, higher dividend payments, continued purchases of Ford common stock, and reductions in debt.

Ford continues to maintain the most profitable position of all auto manufacturers. It maintained a profit margin higher than the industry and its sales

Exhibit 1
Five-Year Financial Summary
(dollars in millions, except per share amounts)

Summary of Operations	1988	1987	1986	1985	1984
Automotive					
Sales	$ 82,193.0	$ 71,797.2	$ 62,868.3	$ 52,915.4	$ 52,526.6
Operating income	6,611.9	6,255.9	4,142.2	2,902.4	3,527.5
Income before income taxes	7,312.0	6,499.3	4,299.5	3,153.7	3,909.1
Net income	4,608.8	3,767.4	2,512.1	2,011.6	2,528.0
Financial Services					
Revenues	10,252.6	8,095.8	8,826.3	4,700.3	3,796.6
Income before income taxes	1,030.5	1,385.4	1,320.9	860.8	629.4
Net income	691.4	857.8	773.0	503.8	378.8
Total Company					
Income before income taxes	8,342.5	7,884.7	5,620.4	4,014.5	4,538.5
Provision for income taxes	2,998.7	3,226.0	2,323.6	1,486.6	1,583.5
Minority interests	43.6	33.5	11.7	12.5	48.2
Net income	$ 5,300.2	$ 4,625.2	$ 3,285.1	$ 2,515.4	$ 2,906.8
Total Company per Share Data (in dollars)[a]					
Net income	10.96	9.05	6.16	4.54	5.26
Net income assuming full dilution	10.80	8.92	6.05	4.40	4.97
Cash dividends	2.30	1.58	1.11	0.80	0.67
Stockholders' equity at year end	43.87	36.44	27.68	21.97	17.62
Common stock price range (NYSE)	55	56⅜	31¾	19¾	17⅛
	38⅛	28½	18	13⅜	11
Average number of shares of capital stock outstanding (in millions)	483.8	511.0	533.1	553.6	552.4
Total Company Balance Sheet Data at Year End					
Assets					
Automotive	43,127.7	$ 39,734.4	$ 34,020.6	$ 29,297.4	$ 25,781.0
Financial Services	100,238.8	76,260.0	59,211.3	45,796.7	26,208.9
Total assets	$143,366.5	$115,994.4	$ 93,231.9	$ 75,094.1	$ 51,989.9
Long-term debt					
Automotive	1,335.7	2,057.8	2,467.0	2,458.7	2,347.2
Financial Services	30,777.1	26,008.9	19,127.8	13,752.7	8,833.0
Stockholders' equity	21,529.0	18,492.7	14,859.5	12,268.6	9,837.7
Total Company Facility and Tooling Data					
Capital expenditures for facilities (excluding special tools)	3,148.0	2,414.7	2,178.7	2,385.4	2,331.5
Depreciation	2,457.6	2,106.7	1,858.7	1,559.4	1,404.5

Continued

Exhibit 1

Five-Year Financial Summary

(dollars in millions, except per share amounts) *(Continued)*

Summary of Operations	1988	1987	1986	1985	1984
Expenditures for special tools	1,633.8	1,343.3	1,284.6	1,417.3	1,223.1
Amortization of special tools	1,334.7	1,353.2	1,293.2	948.4	979.2
Total Company Employee Data—Worldwide					
Payroll	13,010.4	11,682.9	11,289.7	10,175.1	10,018.1
Total labor costs	18,108.1	16,591.4	15,610.4	14,033.4	13,802.9
Average number of employees	358,939	351,711	382,274	369,314	389,917
Total Company Employee Data—U.S. Operations					
Payroll	8,473.0	7,761.6	7,703.6	7,212.9	6,875.3
Average number of employees	185,540	180,838	181,476	172,165	178,758
Average hourly labor costs[b]					
Earnings	17.39	16.50	16.12	15.70	15.06
Benefits	13.07	12.38	11.01	10.75	9.40
Total hourly labor costs	$ 30.46	$ 28.88	$ 27.13	$ 26.45	$ 24.46

[a]Share data have been adjusted to reflect stock dividends and stock split.
[b]Per hour worked (in dollars). Excludes data for subsidiary companies.

Source: Annual Report, Ford Motor Company.

Exhibit 2

Consolidated Balance Sheet

December 31, 1988 and 1987 (in millions)

	1988	1987
Assets		
Automotive		
Cash and cash equivalents	$ 5,490.8	$ 5,410.0
Marketable securities, at cost and accrued interest (approximates market)	3,751.7	4,765.1
Total cash, cash equivalents, and marketable securities	$ 9,242.5	$ 10,175.1
Receivables	4,395.7	3,095.8
Inventories	6,638.2	6,326.9
Other current assets	1,793.8	1,179.3
Total current assets	$ 22,070.2	$ 20,777.1

Continued

Exhibit 2
Consolidated Balance Sheet
December 31, 1988 and 1987 (in millions) *(Continued)*

	1988	1987
Equity in net assets of affiliated companies	2,102.7	2,001.2
Property, net	15,594.3	14,399.4
Other assets	2,350.0	1,389.9
Net receivable from Financial Services	1,010.5	1,166.8
Total Automotive assets	$ 43,127.7	$ 39,734.4
Financial Services		
Cash and cash equivalents	1,234.1	509.2
Investments in securities	4,293.4	2,797.2
Receivables and lease investments, net	91,290.9	70,608.7
Property, net	397.9	284.3
Other assets	3,022.5	2,060.6
Total Financial Services assets	$ 100,238.8	$ 76,260.0
Total assets	$143,366.5	$115,994.4
Liabilities and Stockholders' Equity		
Automotive		
Payables and accrued liabilities	16,787.8	15,139.7
Income taxes payable	1,007.3	654.7
Debt payable within one year	1,760.9	1,890.3
Total current liabilities	$ 19,556.0	$ 17,684.7
Long-term debt	1,335.7	2,057.8
Other liabilities	4,839.4	4,467.5
Deferred income taxes	2,297.9	2,312.5
Minority interests in net assets of consolidated subsidiaries	164.1	129.7
Total Automotive liabilities	$ 28,193.1	$ 26,652.2
Financial Services		
Payables	987.9	1,025.4
Income taxes currently payable	58.0	66.2
Debt	66,851.7	52,460.0
Deposit accounts	20,357.8	12,053.3
Deferred income taxes	1,635.2	1,485.7
Other liabilities and deferred income	2,743.3	2,592.1
Net payable to Automotive	1,010.5	1,166.8
Total Financial Services liabilities	$ 93,644.4	$ 70,849.5
Commitments	—	—
Stockholders' Equity		
Capital stock		
Preferred stock, par value $1.00 a share	—	—
Common stock, par value $1.00 a share (453.6 and 469.8 shares issued)	453.6	469.8
Class B stock, par value $1.00 a share (37.2 and 37.7 shares issued)	37.2	37.7
Capital in excess of par value of stock	586.7	595.1
Foreign-currency translation adjustments	325.0	672.6
Earnings retained for use in business	20,126.5	16,717.5
Total stockholders' equity	$ 21,529.0	$ 18,492.7
Total liabilities and stockholders' equity	$143,366.5	$115,994.4
Memo: stockholders' equity a share	$ 43.87	$ 36.44

Source: Annual Report, Ford Motor Company.

Exhibit 3
Consolidated Statement of Income
For the Years Ended December 31, 1988, 1987, and 1986 (in millions)

	1988	1987	1986
Automotive			
Sales	$82,193.0	$71,797.2	$62,868.3
Costs and expenses			
Costs, excluding items listed below	68,233.3	58,572.7	51,931.5
Depreciation	1,914.9	1,827.7	1,679.9
Amortization of special tools	1,334.7	1,353.2	1,293.2
Selling and administrative	3,452.0	3,289.3	3,109.8
Employee retirement plans	646.2	498.4	711.7
Total costs and expenses	$75,581.1	$65,541.3	$58,726.1
Operating income	6,611.9	6,255.9	4,142.2
Interest income	885.2	823.5	671.7
Interest expense	354.0	452.9	490.1
Net interest income	$ 531.2	$ 370.6	$ 181.6
Equity in net income/(loss) of affiliated companies	147.8	(136.6)	11.6
Net revenue/(expense) from transactions with Financial Services	21.1	9.4	(35.9)
Income before income taxes—Automotive	7,312.0	6,499.3	4,299.5
Financial Services			
Revenues	10,252.6	8,095.8	6,826.3
Costs and expenses			
Interest expense	5,784.0	4,298.1	3,650.1
Operating and other expenses	1,625.4	1,259.6	985.7
Provision for credit and insurance losses	1,248.9	864.3	726.7
Depreciation	542.7	279.0	178.8
Total costs and expenses	$ 9,201.0	$ 6,701.0	$ 5,541.3
Net revenue/(expense) from transactions with Automotive	(21.1)	(9.4)	35.9
Income before income taxes—Financial Services	1,030.5	1,385.4	1,320.9
Total Company			
Income before income taxes	8,342.5	7,884.7	5,620.4
Provision for income taxes	2,998.7	3,226.0	2,323.6
Income before minority interests	$ 5,343.8	$ 4,658.7	$ 3,296.8
Minority interests in net income of consolidated subsidiaries	43.6	33.5	11.7
Net income	$ 5,300.2	$ 4,625.2	$ 3,285.1
Average number of shares of capital stock outstanding	483.8	511.0	533.1
Net income a share	10.96	9.05	6.16
Cash dividends a share	2.30	1.58	1.11

Source: Annual Report, Ford Motor Company.

Exhibit 4 *Highlights of Ford's Financial Position Compared to Its Competitors (1988)*

	Ford	GM	Chrysler	Honda	Toyota	Nissan	Industry
Current ratio	1.13	1.7	1.01	1.21	1.7	NI[a]	1.35
Acid-test ratio	0.79	1.4	0.624	0.758	1.59	NI	1.03
Invent. turnover	13.9	15.0	11.9	7.3	27.56	NI	13.2
EPS ($)	10.96	6.82	5.08	1.49	1.54	0.70	4.19
Profit margin (%)	5.7	3.8	3.2	2.8	4.9	2.4	4.50
Return on equity (%)	24	13.0	15.1	10.8	9.5	6.9	17.10
Sales ($ billions)	82.2	120.4	35.5	26.4	54.3	36.5	393.0
Market share (domestic) (%)	26.5	48.2	14.3	NA[b]	NA	NA	

[a]NI—no information available.
[b]NA—not applicable.

Exhibit 5 *Historical Trends in Ford's Ratios from 1984 to 1988*

	1984	1985	1986	1987	1988
Current ratio	1.10	1.10	1.19	1.22	1.13
Acid-test ratio	NI[a]	0.74	0.81	0.88	0.79
Invent. turnover	NI	11.4	10.8	11.3	12.4
EPS ($)	9.94	8.81	12.11	9.05	10.96
Profit margin (%)	5.6	4.8	5.2	6.5	5.7
Return on equity (%)	29.5	20.5	22.1	27.2	26.5
Sales ($ billions)	52.3	52.7	62.7	71.8	82.2
Net income ($ billions)	2.9	2.5	3.3	3.8	4.6
Market share (%)	21.1	21.4	22.5	25.8	26.5

[a]NI—no information available.

Source: Annual Report, Ford Motor Company.

continued to increase. Ford's automotive sales were $82.2 billion for 1988, an increase of 14 percent from 1987. The company's profit margin is 5.7 percent, which is above the industry average of 4.5 percent.

During 1988, Ford spent a record $4.8 billion for new products and facilities and reduced debt in the automotive business by $851 million. The company also purchased $816 million of Ford common stock. Also during 1988, the company increased dividends by 46 percent, to $2.30 a share, and paid total cash dividends of $1.1 billion. Earnings per share were at an all-time high of $9.53 compared to an industry low of $4.19. Stockholders earned about 26 percent on their investment. Ford's stock is expected to keep pace with the market, protected from most downside risk by a secure dividend that provides an attractive yield. The stock has been projected to provide above-average returns over the next five years.

PRODUCT POSITION

As of the first quarter of 1989, Ford's market share was 23.4 percent, an increase of 1.6 percentage points over the previous quarter. The rest of the market breaks down with GM as leader holding approximately 37 percent, the Japanese with another 26 percent, Chrysler at 10 percent, and the remaining 4 percent going to everyone else. Although this news is encouraging for Ford, company officials cannot afford to celebrate. In the spring of 1989, Ford announced that it would temporarily close two U.S. assembly plants, its first shutdowns since 1983. Additionally, market share is precarious for all American companies in the auto industry.

There are more models, styles, and manufacturers of cars and trucks than ever, which makes it increasingly difficult for any one brand to pull away from the pack. Imports continue to capture more of the domestic market, as the Big Three stumbled in the latter years of the decade. However, there is some good news for Ford and other domestic car makers. A 1988 survey revealed that consumers perceive the quality and styling of U.S. cars to be steadily improving.

Ford has had great success with its Taurus models and seems to be ahead of its domestic competition in terms of styling and quality. In fact, Ford had the number two and three best-selling cars for 1989 in the Taurus and Escort, respectively. The most shocking signal to the Big Three, however, was that for the first time in the history of the industry, the best-selling car was an import: the Honda Accord.

MARKETING CAPABILITIES

When it comes to the basics of marketing such as advertising, promotion, selling, and distribution, the Big Three have perennially lagged behind their foreign counterparts. Only twice in the last nine years has a television ad for a U.S. car been ranked among the top 25 in viewer surveys. This occurred in 1986–1987 when Chevrolet's "Heartbeat of America" campaign came in eleventh and nineteenth, respectively, for those two years.

To combat this problem domestic companies have turned to ad agencies and consumer packaged-goods companies such as General Mills to add some punch to their marketing efforts. Ford hopes that these actions will lead to advertising that competes with the sleek, eye-catching, and memorable ads produced by companies such as Toyota and Nissan. One reason that the Japanese have been so successful is that they have been so consistent. Toyota has changed its theme only twice since 1976.

One quick fix that seems to have lost its luster is the use of incentives or rebates. Consumer response to rebate offers has been declining for the past five quarters. In addition, this approach is costly for the manufacturer. Despite stronger sales and the company's highest market share since 1978, Ford's profits for the first quarter of 1989 fell 5.5 percent.

Instead, Ford is pursuing other avenues to better its marketing impact. Consumers have long held negative feelings about car salespersons. Ford is attempting to improve this image and also take a more active role in the behavior of dealers. The emergence of superdealers—those who offer dozens of car lines at many outlets—has aided in the blurring of brand images. Additionally, dealers are often reluctant to support new brands and would rather stay with the tried and true. Only through more creative marketing and more effective advertising can Ford hope to foster dealer support for its new car models and designs.

CONDITION OF FACILITIES AND EQUIPMENT

Japanese automakers have continuously invested in their manufacturing facilities to remain competitive. Ford, in turn, has done the same. By comparison, Ford's and GM's manufacturing facilities on average are about 10 years old. Chrysler plants have an average age of 12 years. To remain competitive, Ford has invested over $4.8 billion in new plants over the past year, and it has budgeted even more for the 1990s.

Presently, Ford's production facilities require fewer people to build more vehicles. The latest figures show that in 1987 Ford's worldwide productivity increased by 11.3 percent. Furthermore, Ford's hourly employees were able to share in its improvements by earning an average of $3700 in profit sharing. However, even more improvements are needed. Ford must work even harder to reduce its total manufacturing cost. For example, Ford's labor cost per sale is about 20 percent, fifth among its competitors:

Chrysler:	17%
Honda:	18%
Nissan:	18%
Toyota:	18%
Ford:	20%
GM:	22%

To overcome inefficiencies, Ford is planning to run its facilities and equipment with lower amounts of inventory and more just-in-time production. In addition, Ford plans to use the computer-driven robot to aid in the manufacturing process along with infrared and ultrasonic technologies for precision inspections.

STATEMENT OF STRENGTHS AND WEAKNESSES BASED ON INTERNAL ORGANIZATIONAL ANALYSIS

Strengths

- Financial position—profitability, return on equity, and market share
- Product line—Taurus and Escort
- Facilities and equipment—state-of-the-art technology in manufacturing
- Past objectives and strategies—participatory management program

Weaknesses

- Financial position—working capital position
- Marketing—inability to reach consumer through advertising
- Facilities and equipment—inability to implement technology in a timely matter

FORD'S OBJECTIVES

As a result of the strengths, weaknesses, threats, and opportunities described in the analysis of Ford Motor Company in Chapters 2 and 3, Ford's objectives, as stated in its 1988 annual report, are as follows:

1. Provide high-quality products and services that meet its customers' needs and exceed their expectations at a cost that represents superior value.
2. Continue its efforts to instill a people-oriented culture throughout the company.
3. Identify, implement, and refine the most cost-efficient operating and business processes while carrying out the most ambitious worldwide investment actions it has ever undertaken.
4. Continue to strengthen its partnerships with its dealers and suppliers. Each employee acts as a partner in assuring the levels of customer satisfaction needed for individual and collective success.

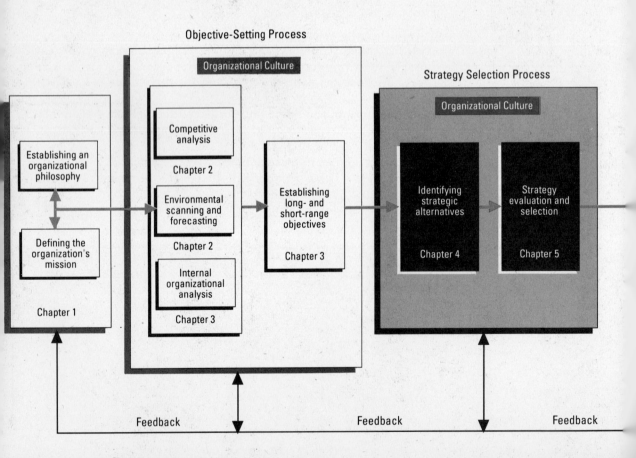

STRATEGIC MANAGEMENT PROCESS

Strategy Formulation

Objective-Setting Process

Organizational Culture

Strategy Selection Process

Organizational Culture

Establishing an organizational philosophy

Defining the organization's mission

Chapter 1

Competitive analysis

Chapter 2

Environmental scanning and forecasting

Chapter 2

Internal organizational analysis

Chapter 3

Establishing long- and short-range objectives

Chapter 3

Identifying strategic alternatives

Chapter 4

Strategy evaluation and selection

Chapter 5

Feedback   Feedback   Feedback

PART THREE
THE STRATEGY SELECTION PROCESS

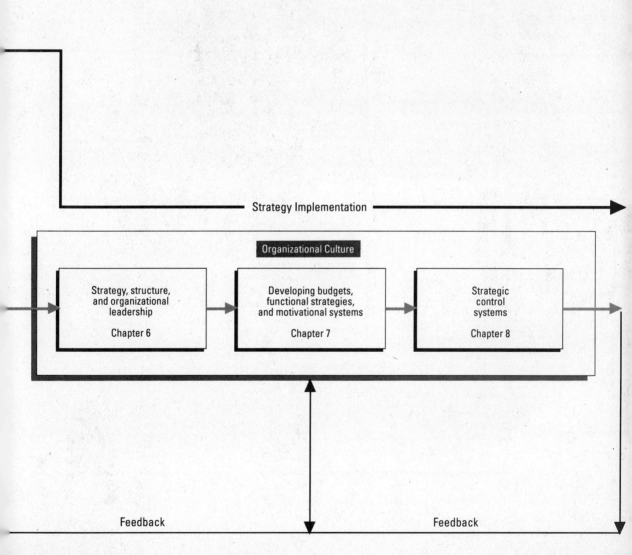

Strategy Implementation

Organizational Culture

Strategy, structure, and organizational leadership	Developing budgets, functional strategies, and motivational systems	Strategic control systems
Chapter 6	Chapter 7	Chapter 8

Feedback

Feedback

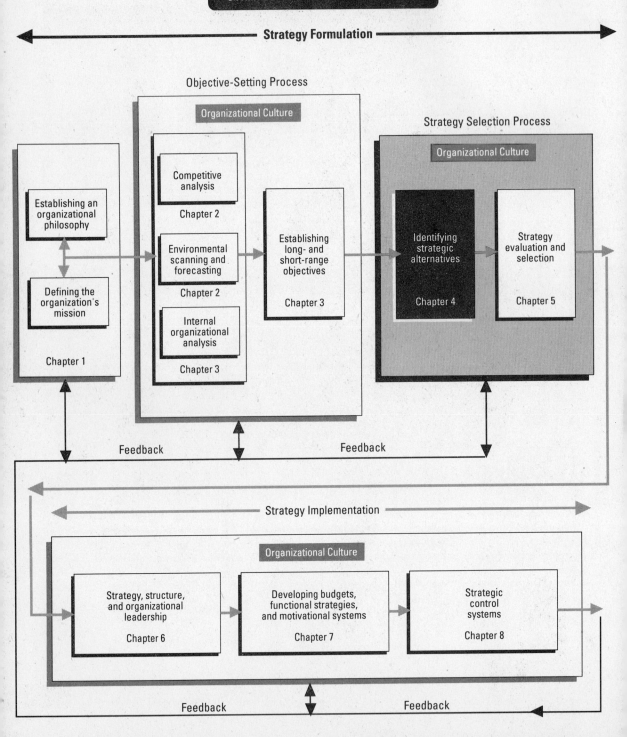

STRATEGIC MANAGEMENT PROCESS

Strategy Formulation

Objective-Setting Process

Organizational Culture

Establishing an organizational philosophy

Defining the organization's mission

Chapter 1

Competitive analysis

Chapter 2

Environmental scanning and forecasting

Chapter 2

Internal organizational analysis

Chapter 3

Establishing long- and short-range objectives

Chapter 3

Strategy Selection Process

Organizational Culture

Identifying strategic alternatives

Chapter 4

Strategy evaluation and selection

Chapter 5

Feedback

Feedback

Strategy Implementation

Organizational Culture

Strategy, structure, and organizational leadership

Chapter 6

Developing budgets, functional strategies, and motivational systems

Chapter 7

Strategic control systems

Chapter 8

Feedback

Feedback

CHAPTER 4
Identifying Strategic Alternatives

LEARNING OBJECTIVES

After studying this chapter, you should be able to

1. Define corporate, business unit, and functional strategies.
2. Describe stable growth strategy.
3. Describe growth strategy.
4. Define concentric diversification.
5. Define vertical integration.
6. Describe horizontal integration.
7. Discuss conglomerate diversification.
8. Explain endgame strategies.
9. Present three retrenchment strategies.
10. Explain three major types of generic competitive strategies.
11. Define mergers and acquisitions.
12. Explain joint ventures.

Strategy outlines the fundamental steps an organization intends to take in order to achieve a set of objectives. Management develops a strategy by evaluating options available to the organization and choosing one or more of the options.

As you will recall from Chapter 1, strategies exist at different levels in an organization and are classified according to the scope of their coverage. Strategies that address what businesses a multibusiness organization will be in and how resources will be allocated among those businesses are called *corporate strategies*. Corporate strategies are established at the highest levels of the organization and involve a long-range time horizon. *Business unit strategies* focus on how to compete in a given business. The scope of a business strategy is narrower than a corporate strategy and generally applies to a single business unit or SBU. A third level of strategy is functional strategies, which are narrower in scope than business strategies. Functional strategies are concerned with the activities of the different functional areas such as production, finance, marketing, and personnel. Usually functional strategies are for a relatively short period of time—normally one year or less. Although functional strategies must support corporate and business unit strategies, they are primarily concerned with "how-to" issues. Corporate and business unit strategies are described in this chapter, and functional strategies will be described in Chapter 7.

In choosing corporate and business unit strategies, most organizations have a wide variety of options. Figure 4.1 summarizes the options available to most organizations. These options are described in greater detail in the following sections.

Stable Growth Strategy

A *stable growth strategy* can be characterized as follows:

- The organization is satisfied with its past performance and decides to continue to pursue the same or similar objectives.
- Each year the level of achievement expected is increased by approximately the same percentage.
- The organization continues to serve its customers with basically the same products or services.

A stable growth strategy is a relatively low-risk strategy and is quite effective for successful organizations in an industry that is growing and in an environment that is not volatile. For many organizations, stable growth is probably the most effective strategy. Some of the reasons for the use of a stable growth strategy follow:

- Management may not wish to take the risk of greatly modifying its present strategy. Change threatens those people who employ previously

Figure 4.1 Corporate and Business Unit Strategy Options

I. Corporate Strategies
   A. Stable Growth Strategy
   B. Growth Strategy
      • Concentration on a Single Product or Service
      • Concentric Diversification
      • Vertical Integration
      • Horizontal Diversification
      • Conglomerate Diversification
   C. Endgame Strategies
   D. Retrenchment Strategies
      • Turnaround
      • Divestment
      • Liquidation
   E. Combination Strategies
      • Simultaneous
      • Sequential
II. Generic Competitive (or Business Unit) Strategies
   A. Overall Cost Leadership
   B. Differentiation
   C. Focus

learned skills when new skills are required. It also threatens old positions of influence. Furthermore, the management of a successful organization quite frequently assumes that strategies that have proved to be successful in the past will continue to be successful in the future.

• Changes in strategy require changes in resource allocations. Changes in patterns of resource allocation in an established organization are difficult to achieve and frequently require long periods of time.

• Too-rapid growth can lead to situations in which the organization's scale of operations outpaces its administrative resources. Inefficiencies can quickly occur.

• The organization may not keep up with or be aware of changes that may affect its product and market.

Generally, organizations that pursue a stable growth strategy concentrate on one product or service. They grow by maintaining their share of the steadily increasing market, by slowly increasing their share of the market, by adding new product(s) or service(s) (but only after extensive marketing research), or by expanding their market coverage geographically. Many organizations in the public utility, transportation, banking, and insurance industries follow a stable growth strategy. In fact, for many industries and for many organizations, stable growth is the most logical and appropriate strategy. Ex-

STRATEGY IN ACTION Example 4.1

Stable Growth at McIlhenny Company

Tabasco sauce, first produced commercially in 1868 by E. L. McIlhenny & Company, has been manufactured and marketed in much the same way since the company's first factory opened in 1905. The overall strategy taken by the family firm has been one of stable growth. In fact, the second factory was not added until 1980. Between 1918 and 1928 McIlhenny consolidated its position through various legal actions fighting the use of its name, Tabasco, and its label by rivals. By 1931, the name and label were patented and remain uniquely their own. The sauce's ingredients and recipe, the way the sauce is manufactured (bottling, labeling, packaging, and materials handling), and distribution have remained stable. The company controls production of the basic ingredients and the formula, so quality control is no problem. McIlhenny has operated in international markets since its beginning. As a result of this stable growth strategy, Tabasco sauce has a 95 percent share of the market.

Source: Public company documents.

ample 4.1 describes the stable growth strategy pursued by the McIlhenny Company, the maker of Tabasco sauce.

Growth Strategies

Organizations pursuing a *growth strategy* can be described as follows:

- They do not necessarily grow faster than the economy as a whole but do grow faster than the markets in which their products are sold.
- They tend to have larger-than-average profit margins.
- They attempt to postpone or even eliminate the danger of price competition in their industry.
- They regularly develop new products, new markets, new processes, and new uses for old products.
- Instead of adapting to changes in the outside world, they tend to adapt the outside world to themselves by creating something or a demand for something that did not exist before.

Organizations pursuing growth strategies, however, are not confined to growth industries. They can be found in industries with relatively fixed markets and long-established product lines.

Why does an organization decide to pursue a growth strategy? One of the most important reasons is the values held by either the top manager or the top-management team. Many top managers equate growth with their own personal effectiveness. In other words, growth of their business indicates their effectiveness as managers. Furthermore, many top executives have stock options as part of their compensation package. They know that if growth of the business leads to growth in the price of their organization's stock, then they will benefit directly through an increase in their own net worth.

Although growth strategies are often appealing to many managers, stockholders, and investment analysts, a word of caution seems appropriate at this point. Peter Drucker phrased it as follows:

> The securities market would be well advised to put a discount on growth stocks and growth industries rather than a premium. For growth is a risk.
> . . . There is no virtue in a company's getting bigger. The right goal is to become better. Growth to be sound, should be the result of doing the right things. By itself, growth is vanity and little else.[1]

In fact, too much growth in the short run can result in inefficiencies that can prove disastrous in the long run. It is for these reasons that management should answer the following three questions before embarking on a growth strategy:

1. Are company financial resources adequate?
2. If the company is stopped short in its strategy for any reason, will its position be competitively viable?
3. Will government regulators permit the company to follow the strategy it has chosen?

Regardless of the cautions and potential problems, many companies have successfully implemented growth strategies. In fact, when a growth strategy is selected and properly implemented, it can be very effective for the stakeholders of the organization. In the following sections, several growth strategy options are described.

Concentration on a Single Product or Service   Concentration on a single product or service entails increasing sales, profits, or market share faster than it has increased in the past. One approach is to determine why an organization's sales, profits, or market share are falling short of their potential. Reasons might include

- Lack of a full product line in the relevant market (product line gap)
- Absent or inadequate distribution system to or within the relevant market (distribution gap)
- Less than full usage in the market (usage gap)
- Competitors' sales (competitive gap)

Some of the options available to an organization in filling these gaps include the following:

- Filling out the existing product line (e.g., new sizes, options, styles, or colors could be offered for the existing product line)

- Developing new products in the existing product line (e.g., Cherry Coke was a new product in an existing product line)
- Expanding distribution into new geographic areas either nationally or internationally
- Expanding the number of distribution outlets in a geographic area
- Expanding shelf space and improving the location and displays of the product in present distribution outlets
- Encouraging nonusers to use the product and light users to use it more frequently through the use of advertising, promotions, and special pricing campaigns
- Penetrating competitors' positions through pricing strategies, product differentiation, and advertising

An organization faces one major risk by adopting a growth strategy of concentrating on a single product or service. If the market for the organization's product or service declines, then the organization is in trouble. This is an especially important concern when one considers that it has been estimated that 80 percent of today's products will have disappeared from the market ten years from now, while an estimated 80 percent of the products that will be sold in the next decade are as yet unknown. Several factors outside the control of

STRATEGY IN ACTION Example 4.2

McDonald's Growth Strategy

Contrary to popular belief, McDonald's was not created by Ray Kroc. McDonald's was founded in 1948 by Dick and Maurice McDonald, two brothers from San Bernardino, California. At that time, Kroc was selling Multimixers, a machine that could make five milk shakes at one time. The McDonald brothers had purchased eight Multimixers for their hamburger drive-in restaurant. Kroc was amazed that a small hamburger drive-in had enough business to make 40 milk shakes at a time.

Upon reaching the restaurant, Kroc became more bewildered because he could see nothing obvious to attest to the attraction. The place was spotlessly clean, but it had no particular angle. The menu was basic—hamburgers, french fries, and something to drink—and people were practically running to get in line. All of this piqued Kroc's curiosity, so he got in line and began to talk to the people around him. He questioned the excitement for what was basically a hamburger joint. The answers were pretty much the same. Although there wasn't much variety, the food was the best you could get anywhere.

At the time, Ray Kroc had no vision of a billion-dollar business. However, he thought that if he could talk the McDonald brothers into opening a few more restaurants he could sell more Multimixers. The brothers had little ambition and were not particularly interested in opening other restaurants (they didn't want to leave their home). Kroc next suggested allowing other people to open more of these drive-ins. The McDonald brothers said they had already tried selling the rights to any single organization can cause a decline in the demand for a product or service. The increasing instability of consumer preferences, the growing intensity and sophistication of competition, technological change, and changes in government policy pose a major risk for an organization concentrating on a single product or service. Example 4.2 shows how McDonald's has followed a growth strategy of concentrating on a single service.

Concentric Diversification   *Concentric diversification* is a growth strategy that involves adding new products or services that are similar to the organization's present products or services. In order for the strategy to be considered concentric diversification, the products or services that are added must lie within the organization's know-how and experience in technology, product line, distribution channels, or customer base. When an organization's industry is growing, concentric diversification is a viable strategy for strengthening its position in a field where it has knowledge and experience.

Many organizations have successfully adopted the concentric diversification strategy. After reviewing what they described as America's excellent companies, Thomas Peters and Robert Waterman concluded that organizations that do branch out but stick very close to their knitting outperform the others.[2]

other people and had failed. There were about ten McDonald-like drive-ins scattered around California and Arizona that had been licensed to operate like the San Bernardino McDonald's. However, not all of these drive-ins had the same high quality as the original, and anything lower in quality tended to reflect on the brothers' San Bernardino drive-in.

Exasperated, Kroc gave it one more try. He suggested finding one person who would run the whole operation. This person would maintain the high quality, find the operators, find places for the operators to set up business, build the drive-ins, and make sure all the operators adhered to standards. The McDonald brothers liked this idea and questioned where to find such a man. Ray Kroc volunteered, and McDonald's Corporation was founded. The year was 1954.

The company has flourished. Today, it holds a 7 percent share of the U.S. restaurant market, an 18 percent share of the domestic fast-food market, and a 45 percent share of the fast-food hamburger market. McDonald's attracts about 10 million Americans per day. The International Division alone is large enough to qualify as one of the United States' ten largest restaurant systems.

McDonald's main product is the hamburger, complemented by french fries and a soft drink or shake. Over the years, it has added breakfast items, McRib, McChicken, and other fast-food items. However, it has grown by expanding geographically and maintaining its quality, service, and reputation for cleanliness.

Vertical Integration   *Vertical integration* is a growth strategy that involves extending an organization's present business in two possible directions. *Forward integration* moves the organization into distributing its own products or services. *Backward integration* moves an organization into supplying some or all of the products or services used in producing its present products or services.[3]

Several factors, including the following, might cause an organization to pursue either forward or backward integration:

- Backward integration gives an organization more control over the cost, availability, and quality of the raw materials it uses.
- When suppliers of an organization's products or services have large profit margins, the organization can convert a cost into a profit by integrating backward.
- Forward integration gives an organization control over sales and distribution channels, which can help in eliminating inventory buildups and production slowdowns.
- When the distributors of an organization's products or services have large markups, the organization may increase its own profits by integrating forward.
- Some organizations use either forward or backward integration in hopes of benefiting from the economies of scale available from the creation of nationwide sales and marketing organizations and the construction of larger manufacturing plants. These economies of scale may result in lower overall costs and thus increased profits.
- Some organizations use either backward or forward integration to increase their size and power in a particular market or industry in order to gain some degree of monopolistic control.

Vertical integration is a reasonable and rational strategy in certain situations. However, organizations should adopt a vertical integration strategy with caution because integrated organizations have become associated with mature and less profitable industries. At the same time, escape from these industries is particularly difficult for a large, vertically integrated organization.

Regardless of these cautions, organizations have made use of and will continue making use of vertical integration. The characteristics of the most profitable (as measured in pretax return on investment) businesses with high vertical integration have been described as follows:

- The corporations to which the businesses belong are highly diverse (i.e., involved in many unrelated fields of business endeavor).
- The businesses belong to medium-size corporations (sales between $1 billion and $2 billion).
- The ratio of gross book value of plant and equipment to sales is low (below 37 percent). Integration should be accomplished with a minimum of investment. Investment per employee of highly profitable, highly integrated businesses is not more than $17,000.

- The products these businesses sell are deemed relatively unimportant to the immediate customer. To use an extreme example, most manufacturing operations would consider the purchase of light bulbs unimportant compared to the purchase of tooling or fixtures. Important products require customer scrutiny, adherence to strict specifications, and special or customized end products, all of which are costly.
- The degree of customer fragmentation is low. That is, 40 or fewer customers equal 50 percent of the sales of this business. Selling expenses are reduced with repeat business, and a lack of a variety of customers enables more product standardization.
- The ratio of new products as a percent of sales is low (less than 1 percent). Here again, standardization and repetition pay off for highly integrated businesses.[4]

Backward integration also seems to be more helpful in improving return on investment than forward integration because it enables a business to take advantage of production economies without having to tackle new marketing problems.

Horizontal Diversification   *Horizontal diversification* is a growth strategy in which an organization buys one of its competitors. Horizontal diversification and concentric diversification are similar strategies in that the new products or services added to the organization under both approaches are closely related to the organization's present products or services. However, under concentric diversification new products or services are added either through internal development or by the acquisition of an organization that is producing a product or service that is closely related to, but not directly competitive with, the acquiring organization's product or service. On the other hand, under horizontal diversification new products or services are added by the purchase of a competitive organization. As can be seen, there is little difference between these two strategies.

Horizontal diversification can be accomplished by the acquisition of a competitor's common stock, by the purchase of a competitor's assets, or by a pooling of interest of the two organizations. Horizontal diversification is normally accomplished through mergers, which are described later in this chapter.

The primary problem with employing horizontal diversification is that such a strategy eliminates the competition that has existed between the two organizations and may result in legal ramifications. In the 1950 Celler-Kefauver amendment to Section 7 of the Clayton Act, Congress prohibited mergers that substantially lessened competition or that tended to create a monopoly in any field of business in any section of the country. Some of the factors that are examined by the Antitrust Division of the U.S. Department of Justice in determining the legality of a merger are (1) the level of concentration in the industry (e.g., the market shares of the leading organizations and the increase in concentration that will be caused by the proposed merger), (2) whether the merger will give the resulting organization a competitive advantage over other organizations in the industry, (3) whether entry into the industry is difficult, (4) whether there has been a trend of mergers within the industry, (5) the economic power of the merged organizations, (6) whether demand for the industry's products is growing, and finally (7) whether there is danger that the merger will trigger others.

Conglomerate Diversification   *Conglomerate diversification* is a growth strategy that involves adding new products or services that are significantly different from the organization's present products or services. Conglomerate diversification can be pursued internally or externally. Most frequently, however, it is achieved through mergers and joint ventures, which are described later in this chapter.

A great many organizations prefer the conglomerate diversification strategy. In fact, the names of organizations employing this strategy would read like a Who's Who of American business. American Express, ITT, and others too numerous to mention are examples. The reasons for following such a strategy are also numerous. Some of the more important ones follow:

- Supporting some strategic business units (SBUs) with the cash flow from other SBUs during a period of development or temporary difficulties.
- Using the profits of one SBU to cover expenses in another SBU without paying taxes on the profits from the first SBU.
- Encouraging growth for its own sake or to satisfy the values and ambitions of management or the owners.
- Taking advantage of unusually attractive growth opportunities.
- Distributing risk by serving several different markets.
- Improving the overall profitability and flexibility of the organization by moving into industries that have better economic characteristics than those of the acquiring organization.
- Gaining better access to capital markets and better stability or growth in earnings.
- Increasing the price of an organization's stock.
- Reaping the benefits of synergy. *Synergy* results from a conglomerate merger when the combined organization is more profitable than the two organizations operating independently.

In choosing a conglomerate diversification strategy, an organization should proceed with caution and not diversify merely to be diversified. Conglomerate diversification brings with it bigness and the difficult management problems associated with bigness.

The basic elements in employing a successful conglomerate diversification strategy seem to be as follows:

1. A clear definition of organizational objectives
2. A determination of the organization's ability to diversify, which includes an analysis of its present operations (internal organizational analysis) and the resources available for diversification
3. Establishment of specific criteria for purchasing other organizations in line with points 1 and 2
4. A comprehensive search for organizations and their evaluation against the criteria

Example 4.3 shows how Philip Morris has pursued a conglomerate diversification strategy.

Endgame Strategies

Endgame strategies are used by organizations in an environment of declining product demand where it is unlikely that all the plant capacity and competitors put in place during the industry's heyday will ever be needed.[5] This condition can develop in a strategic business unit (SBU) of an organization or with a product line or separate product or brand.

Industry conditions in a declining industry influence the strategic options available to a company. Favorable industry characteristics include relatively low exit barriers, few "maverick" competitors who lapse into periods of cut-throat competition, or a low rate of technological change by users. Unfavorable industry characteristics include relatively high fixed costs, capital-intensive technologies, high exit barriers, many "maverick" competitors, and rapid standardization of the product. In a particular industry, individual organizations can have relative competitive strengths or weaknesses. Organizations with relative competitive strengths are described as being cost-efficient in producing the endgame product or are clearly identified as the industry leader. Figure 4.2 illustrates which strategies are most likely to be appropriate given endgame industry conditions and the individual organization's relative competitive strengths.

Basically, four strategic options exist for an organization in a declining industry. An organization using a *leadership strategy* tries to achieve above-average profitability by becoming one of the few companies remaining in the industry. The *niche strategy* attempts to identify a segment of the declining industry that will either maintain stable demand or decline slowly and that has favorable industry characteristics. Under a *harvest strategy* management decreases investments, cuts maintenance, and reduces advertising and research in order to cut costs and improve cash flow. Sales volume and/or market share are generally expected to decline, but the lost revenue is anticipated to be more than offset by reduced costs. Organizations following a harvest strategy ultimately sell or liquidate the business. *Quick divestment* involves selling the busi-

---

STRATEGY IN ACTION Example 4.3

Philip Morris Companies, Inc.: Conglomerate Diversification

Philip Morris is best known as a cigarette company, but it is much more than just that. Over the years, it has pursued a conglomerate diversification strategy that has positioned the company in the domestic and international tobacco business, the food business, the beer business, and the financial services and real estate businesses.

Although the company is faced with a stagnant market in its domestic tobacco business, its Marlboro and Virginia Slims brands continue to be the number one brands in their target markets. In the international tobacco business, growth continues to be strong, and Marlboro remains the top-selling cigarette.

Philip Morris conducts its food business through its subsidiary, the General Foods Corporation. Some of its better-known brand names include Jell-o, Kool-Aid, Crystal Light, Country Time, and Oscar Mayer.

Miller Brewing Company is the second leading brewer in the United States. Some of its products include Miller Lite, Miller High Life, Meister Brau, and Matilda Bay Wine Cooler.

Philip Morris Credit Corporation (PMCC) provides equipment-leasing services and financing to support customers of Philip Morris's operating companies. Mission Viejo Realty Group is concerned with residential housing, land, and business properties, primarily in California and Colorado.

Summarized below are the operating revenues and income for each of the operating divisions of Philip Morris:

	Revenues[a]	Income[a]
Domestic tobacco	$ 8,501	$3,087
International tobacco	8,085	774
Food	11,265	849
Beer	3,262	190
Financial services and real estate	629	163

[a]Figures are in thousands.

---

ness in the early stages of the decline rather than harvesting and selling it later. Divestment is discussed more fully later in this chapter.

Retrenchment Strategies

Retrenchment strategies are most frequently used during economic recessions and during times when the organization is having poor financial performance. Generally, organizations intend to pursue a retrenchment strategy only on a short-run basis. Three alternative retrenchment strategies employed by organizations are turnaround, divestment, and liquidation.

Turnaround Strategy   A *turnaround strategy* is an attempt to improve efficiency of operations during a decline in an organization's financial situation. Some of the more important reasons for declines in an organization's financial situation are as follows:

- Higher costs of wages and raw materials
- Decreased demand that results from temporary demand dips (such as a lost government contract) or economic recessions
- Strikes
- Increased competitive pressures
- Management problems

Of course, the purpose of the turnaround strategy is to weather the bad times in hopes that the situation will change, and then a new strategy can be adopted during the upturn. Below are some of the actions that can be taken in a turnaround strategy:

- Change management personnel, both top and lower levels.
- Cut back on capital expenditures.
- Centralize decision making in an attempt to control costs.
- Cut back on hiring.
- Reduce advertising and promotion expenditures.
- Engage in general belt-tightening, including a reduction in the number of employees.
- Increase emphasis on cost control and budgeting.
- Sell off some assets.
- Tighten inventory control.
- Improve the collection of accounts receivable.

Figure 4.2 *Strategies for Declining Industries*

	Has competitive strengths	Lacks competitive strengths
Favorable industry conditions	Leadership or niche	Harvest or divest quickly
Unfavorable industry conditions	Niche or harvest	Divest quickly

Source: Kathryn Rudie Harrigan and Michael E. Porter, "End-game Strategies for Declining Industries," *Harvard Business Review* 61 (July–August 1983):119.

Another action that can be taken in a turnaround strategy is the use of Chapter 11 of the federal bankruptcy laws. Chapter 11 outlines the legal requirements for restructuring the financial affairs of an organization. Both voluntary and involuntary bankruptcy are permitted. Creditors can force a company into bankruptcy if it is not paying its debts when they come due. Chapter 11 gives an organization time to use some of the previously outlined strategies in an attempt to return the organization to a sound financial condition.

Almost every organization, at one time or another, must use a turnaround strategy.[6] Obviously, one of the keys to a successful turnaround strategy is having a good strategic plan.

Divestment Strategy   Divestment is a frequently used strategy when either endgame or turnaround strategies are not successful. *Divestment* involves selling off a major part of the business, which can be an SBU, a product line, or a division.

Divestment is a difficult decision for management to make. The barriers that impede an organization from following a divestment strategy have been described as follows:

1. *Structural (or Economic)* Characteristics of a business's technology and its fixed and working capital impede exit.
2. *Interdependence* Relationships between the various business units in an organization may deter divestment of a particular business unit.
3. *Managerial* Aspects of a company's decision-making process inhibit exit from an unprofitable business. Such aspects may include the following:
   a. Company does not know that it is making an unsatisfactory return on its investment
   b. Exit is a blow to management's pride
   c. Exit is taken externally as a sign of failure
   d. Exit threatens manager's careers
   e. Exit conflicts with social goals
   f. Managerial incentive systems work against exit

Special suggestions on overcoming exit barriers include the following:

- Make someone in the top-management team responsible for encouraging management to consider the divestment option.
- Design compensation and incentive systems so that they do not discourage sound exit decisions.
- Design management information systems that provide meaningful data to assist in the exit decision.
- Carefully plan answers to the questions of job security and easier progression for the middle managers affected by the divestment decision.
- Change top management periodically to overcome the commitments built up over time by incumbents.[7]

Liquidation Strategy *Liquidation* involves terminating an organization's existence either by selling off its assets or by shutting down the entire operation. Obviously, liquidation is a most unattractive strategy, and it is normally used only when all else fails. However, early liquidation may be a more appropriate strategy for an organization than pursuing a lost cause. The latter leads inevitably to bankruptcy, which in turn leaves less to liquidate.

Combination Strategies

Most multibusiness organizations use some type of combination strategy, especially when they are serving several different markets. Certain types of strategies lend themselves to combination with other strategies. For example, a divestment strategy in one area of an organization is normally used in combination with one or more strategies in other areas. Combination strategies, which can be either simultaneous or sequential, are the norm. The following are just a few of the possible combination strategies:

Simultaneous
1. Divesting an SBU, product line, or division while adding other SBUs, product lines, or divisions
2. Retrenching in certain areas or products while pursuing a growth strategy in other areas or products
3. Using an endgame strategy on certain products and growth strategies on other products

Sequential
1. Employing a growth strategy for a specified time and then using stable growth for a specified time
2. Using a turnaround strategy and then employing a growth strategy when conditions improve

Example 4.4 shows how Avon Products has pursued several different strategies over time.

GENERIC COMPETITIVE (OR BUSINESS UNIT) STRATEGIES

As you will recall from Chapter 2, Michael Porter has postulated that the intensity of competition in an industry is determined by the threat of new entrants into the industry, the bargaining power of suppliers to the industry, the threat of substitute products or services, the bargaining power of customers, and the maneuvering for position among the current competitors. Porter has suggested three generic or general strategies that organizations can use to outperform other firms in an industry:

1. Overall cost leadership
2. Differentiation
3. Focus[8]

STRATEGY IN ACTION Example 4.4

Avon's Turnaround Strategy

Avon has gone through several different strategies over time. A household name in the United States, it grew from a small family-run operation in Brooklyn, New York, into the world's leading manufacturer of beauty products, health care items, and fashion jewelry. The secret to Avon's success was adding on sales representatives. In the early 1980s, however, something happened. Avon continued to throw investment and managerial energy into increasing the sales representative count. Corporate revenues rose every year from 1980 on, but profits began to sink. Twice Avon had to slash its dividend. Avon stock lost two-thirds of its market value, and the credit-rating agencies downgraded Avon debt severely. A turnaround strategy was required, and Avon responded. Some of the actions the firm took were to boost the pay of sales representatives, which reduced turnover; to dismantle the top-heavy administrative structure in field sales; to examine alternative means of distribution; and to decentralize its foreign operations.

In May 1989, Avon's turnaround strategy had been so successful that it was facing a hostile takeover bid by Amway. Avon rejected the offer. Since that bid, however, Avon has been slimming down and reducing debt in preparation for the possibility of other takeover battles. In November 1989, Avon announced that it was selling its Oscar de la Renta, Cher, Perry Ellis, and Deneuve fragrance brands to Sanofi SA of France for $210 million in cash. It also sold its Valentino fragrance brand to the Valentino group for $12.3 million.

Each of these generic strategies can be used in pursuing any of the previously described strategic alternatives. For example, a firm that is employing a stable growth strategy can also be using the generic strategy of overall cost leadership.[9] In addition, recall that business unit strategies focus on how to compete in a given business. Thus, the three generic strategies can also be viewed as describing business unit strategies.

Overall Cost Leadership Strategy

The overall cost leadership strategy emphasizes producing and delivering the product or service at a low cost relative to competitors while not neglecting quality and service. This strategy requires construction of efficient-scale facilities, vigorous pursuit of cost reductions, avoidance of marginal customer accounts, and cost minimization in areas such as R&D, service, sales force, and advertising.

Differentiation Strategy

A differentiation strategy requires that an organization create a product or service that is recognized industry-wide as being unique, thus permitting the organization to charge higher-than-average prices. Differentiation can take many forms, such as design or brand image, technology, customer service, or dealer network. The basic purpose of a differentiation strategy is to gain the brand loyalty of customers and a resulting lower sensitivity to price.

Focus Strategy

An organization using a focus strategy concentrates on a particular group of customers, geographic markets, or product line segments in order to serve a well-defined but narrow market better than competitors who serve a broader market.

The implementation of any of the generic strategies entails different skills, resources, and organizational requirements. Some implications for organizations using one of these strategies are summarized in Figure 4.3.

Figure 4.3 *Organizational Requirements for Generic Strategies*

Strategy	Commonly Required Skills and Resources	Common Organizational Requirements
Overall cost leadership	Substantial capital investment and access to capital Process engineering skills Intense supervision of labor Products designed for ease in manufacture Low-cost distribution systems	Tight cost control Frequent, detailed control reports Structured organization and responsibilities Incentives based on meeting strict quantitative targets
Differentiation	Strong marketing abilities Product engineering Creative flair Strong capability in basic research Corporate reputation for quality or technological leadership Long tradition in the industry or unique combination of skills drawn from other businesses Strong cooperation from channels	Strong coordination among functions in R&D, product development, and marketing Subjective measurement and incentives instead of quantitative measures Amenities to attract highly skilled labor, scientists, or creative people
Focus	Combination of the above practices directed at the particular strategic target	Combination of the above practices directed at the particular strategic target

Source: Michael E. Porter, *Competitive Strategy* (New York: Free Press, 1980), pp. 40–41.

IMPLEMENTING STRATEGIES THROUGH MERGERS AND ACQUISITIONS

Mergers and acquisitions are two frequently used methods for implementing diversification strategies. A *merger* takes place when two companies combine their operations, creating, in effect, a third company. An *acquisition* is a situation in which one company buys, and controls, another company.

Horizontal mergers or acquisitions are the combining of two or more organizations that are direct competitors. *Concentric mergers or acquisitions* are the combining of two or more organizations that have similar products or services in terms of technology, product line, distribution channels, or customer base. *Vertical mergers or acquisitions* are the combining of two or more organizations to extend an organization into either supplying products or services required in producing its present products or services or into distributing or selling its own products or services. Finally, *conglomerate mergers or acquisitions* involve the combining of two or more organizations that are producing products or services that are significantly different from each other. Of course, it is entirely possible for mergers and acquisitions to take place between organizations in different countries.

Reasons for Mergers and Acquisitions

Organizations seek mergers and acquisitions for many reasons. One of the primary reasons is the potential benefit that can accrue to the stockholders of both companies. For example, if the earnings of two companies are valued differently in the stock market (i.e., they have different price-earnings ratios), a merger or acquisition can increase the market value of the stock of both organizations. This result is achieved if the acquiring company reports an increase in its earnings per share and if the multiple applied to its earnings rises as a result of the merger or acquisition.

Other reasons for mergers and acquisitions include the following:

- Providing a better utilization of existing manufacturing facilities.
- Selling in the same channels as existing channels to make the existing sales organization more productive.
- Getting the services of a proven management team to strengthen or succeed the existing staff.
- Smoothing out cyclical trends in present products or services.
- Evening out seasonal trends in present products or services.
- Providing new volume to replace static or shrinking volume in present products or services.
- Providing new products or services and better margins of profit in order to supplement older products or services still selling in good demand but at increasingly competitive levels.
- Entering a new and growing field.
- Securing or protecting sources of raw materials or components used in its manufacturing process (vertical integration).

- Effecting savings in income and excess-profits taxes.
- Broadening the opportunities for using the managerial ability of the acquiring organization's personnel or its resources.
- Providing an avenue for the selling of the organization's stock. This is an especially important reason for an organization whose stock is not publicly traded and is held by a small number of individuals. Selling out to a publicly owned organization facilitates the sale of the acquired company's stock.
- Providing resources for expanding the organization.
- Reducing tax obligations. In many situations the owner of a business may sell it and make substantial savings both in income taxes and in estate and inheritance taxes.
- Providing for management succession and the perpetuation or continuation of the business. Frequently, family-owned businesses or smaller businesses have few people capable of carrying on the business if the principal manager dies or is incapacitated. Merging with or being acquired by a larger organization helps to ensure the continuity of the organization.

Still, the primary reason for large mergers and acquisitions is the potential benefits that can accrue to the stockholders of both companies. Furthermore, mergers continue to be a popular technique for corporate growth strategies.

Carrying Out Mergers and Acquisitions

Mergers and acquisitions can be carried out in either a friendly or a hostile environment. *Friendly mergers and acquisitions* are accomplished when the stockholders and management of both organizations agree that the combination will benefit both firms and then work together to ensure its success. On the other hand, *hostile* (or, as they are frequently called, *takeover) mergers and acquisitions* result when the organization to be acquired (also sometimes called the *target company)* resists the attempt. Takeover attempts are often bitterly resisted by the management of the target organization, because if the takeover attempt is successful, the acquiring organization normally replaces the management of the target company. Takeover mergers and acquisitions usually come as a surprise to the target company. Generally, three conditions can make an organization a likely candidate for a takeover. First, the organization's stock may be selling for less than book value. Second, the organization may have a large cash surplus. Finally, the organization may be performing poorly compared to its competitors. In recent years, many companies have been installing antitakeover devices in corporate charters and bylaws and taking other defensive measures against hostile takeovers. Some of these measures include staggered terms for board members and stipulations requiring approval by two-thirds of the stockholders for a merger that is not approved by the board of directors.

Several methods are available for carrying out mergers and acquisitions. One, the *tender offer,* is a well-publicized bid made by a corporation for all or a prescribed amount of the stock of another organization. Tender offers are generally higher than the current trading price of the target company's stock. Another option is for one company to purchase stock of the target organization in the open market. The acquiring company can also purchase the assets of the target company. Finally, the two firms may agree to an exchange of stock. In agreeing to an exchange of stock, organizations use one of the following four yardsticks for determining the value of the stock: (1) book value per share, (2) earnings per share, (3) market price per share, or (4) dividends per share.

Because so many terms are used in describing activities involved in mergers and acquisitions, Figure 4.4 is provided as a summary of the definitions of many of these terms.

Guidelines for Successfully Implementing Mergers and Acquisitions

The following ten guidelines are proposed for successfully implementing mergers and acquisitions. The first four guidelines are critical and apply to any and all mergers and acquisitions. If any one of them is violated, then the chances of a successful merger or acquisition are very small.

1. Pinpoint and spell out the objectives.
2. Specify the gains for the stockholders of both organizations.
3. Ensure that the management of the acquired company is or at least can be made competent.
4. Seek to ensure that the acquiring company's resources fit or mesh with the resources of the target company. This results in synergy.
5. Involve the chief executive officers of both the acquiring and the target organization in the entire merger program.
6. Clearly define the business of the acquiring company (organizational purpose).
7. Determine the strengths, weaknesses, and other key performance factors of both the acquiring and target organizations.
8. Create a climate of mutual trust by anticipating problems and discussing them early with the target company.
9. Make the right advances. Avoid clumsy overtures, thoughtless actions, and carelessly voiced sentiments.
10. In assimilating a newly acquired company, exercise a minimum of control over it. Maintain, and if possible improve, the status of the newly acquired management team.

On the other hand, several factors need to be avoided to ensure a successful merger or acquisition. These factors include

- Paying too much
- Straying too far afield
- Marrying disparate corporate cultures
- Counting on key managers staying
- Assuming that a boom market will not crash
- Leaping before looking
- Swallowing too large a company[10]

Figure 4.4 *Terms of Business*

Acquisition: Situation in which one company buys, and controls, another company.

Arb or arbitrageur: Professional stock trader who invests in stocks of companies that are takeover candidates, or rumored takeover candidates, hoping to make profits on price movements.

Bear hug: Offer for a company at so large a premium over the market price for the stock and with such favorable terms—such as all cash, with the financing in place—that the company has no choice but to accept it.

Creeping tender offer: Gradual accumulation of a company's stock through purchases on the open market. Law doesn't require disclosing holdings of a company's stock until 5% is acquired, then disclosure of each change in the holding is required.

Friendly takeover: Situation in which the management and directors of the target company support the takeover.

Golden parachute: Provisions in executives' employment contracts with their companies that guarantee substantial severance benefits if they lose their jobs or authority in a takeover.

Greenmail: Putting a company in the position of having to purchase its own shares from a suitor for more than the going market price to stop the threat of a hostile takeover.

In play: Term used by Wall Street deal makers to indicate a company is on the auction block and will be acquired, whether it wants to be or not.

Junk bond: Nickname derived years ago for bonds of corporations down on their luck. Now the name describes very high-yield, below-investment-grade bonds issued by many corporations to finance acquisitions and other activities. Corporate raiders have used them to finance hostile takeovers, but the Federal Reserve Board has limited their use.

Leveraged buy-out: Acquisition of a public company by a small group of investors, typically including the company's management, which then takes the company private. Most of the purchase price is borrowed, with the debt repaid from the company's profits or by selling assets.

Lockup: Agreement between two companies in a merger or acquisition designed to thwart a third-party suitor. A common lockup involves the acquirer receiving an option to buy the target's most valuable operations.

Merger: Situation in which two companies combine their operations, creating, in effect, a third company.

Pac-man defense: Tactic by which the target company in a hostile takeover bid becomes the aggressor and tries to take over the would-be acquirer.

Poison pill: Issue of securities by a target company, often preferred stock granted to holders of common stock, designed to thwart a hostile takeover. The shares are initially worthless, but their venom comes when a hostile bidder acquires a specified percentage of the target company's stock. Then the preferred shares can be converted into the target's common stock, forcing the bidder to extend an offer to a much larger number of shares and increasing the cost of the takeover so much that the bidder ends the takeover try.

Continued

Figure 4.4 (*Continued*)

Raider: Investor, often using his or her own money and that of other investors, who buys a big block of a company's stock in a hostile takeover attempt. He or she may want to take the company over or to be bought out by the target company at a premium—a practice called greenmail.

Self-tender offer: Company offer to buy back its own shares, a move often used to keep the shares out of unfriendly hands.

Shark repellent: Measures taken in a company's bylaws to reduce the odds of a hostile takeover bid. These include staggering the terms of directors so a proxy fight cannot result in taking over an entire board and requiring "super-majorities": approval by 75% or 80% of stockholders for takeovers.

Standstill agreement: Agreement between the bidder and the target company for the bidder to stop buying the target's stock or simply to leave the target alone for a specified period of time.

Stock buy-back: Company repurchase of its own stock, which reduces the number of shares outstanding. With earnings spread over fewer shares, the earnings per share increase, and so should the price of the company's stock. The move can deter a hostile takeover.

Target company: The company that is the takeover candidate.

Ten-day window: Federal law and Securities and Exchange Commission requirement that if 5% or more of a company's stock is bought by an individual or a company, the purchase must be made public within ten working days after the stock changes hands. Reason: to inform the company and investors of a possible change in control of the company.

Tender offer: Public offer to buy a company's stock. Usually priced at a premium above the market price to get shareholders to sell their shares to the bidder, the offer must remain open for 20 working days.

Two-tiered tender offer: Offer to pay cash for part of a company's shares, usually enough to give the bidder control. The bidder then offers a lower price, often in bonds, for the rest. The idea is to get shareholders to stampede their holdings into the cash offer.

White knight: Third party that takes over a hostile takeover target on a friendly basis, usually at the target's invitation, to avoid a hostile bid from another suitor.

Source: Adapted from Charley Blaine, "Terms of Business," *USA Today*, January 27, 1986, p. 3E. Used with permission.

Lessons learned from corporate mergers and acquisitions are that they work under the right circumstances. The ability to understand those circumstances and choose the correct conditions for a merger or acquisition is a skill greatly needed by top management.

IMPLEMENTING STRATEGIES THROUGH JOINT VENTURES

Another method used in carrying out diversification strategies is the joint venture. A *joint venture* is a separate corporate entity jointly owned by two or more parent organizations. It combines the features of a partnership (which corporations cannot create) with those of a corporation (limited liability, indefinite life, and a familiar framework for funding and control). Thus, joint ventures represent one organizational form for achieving organizational objectives that neither organization could normally attain acting alone.

Joint ventures can take place between organizations within national boundaries or between private enterprise and government or not-for-profit organizations. Another frequent form of joint venture takes place between organizations in different countries.

Reasons for Entering Joint Ventures

The major reasons for entering joint ventures include the following:

- Many countries have imposed formal and/or informal restrictions on foreigners doing business in their country. To deal with such restrictions, foreign organizations form a joint venture with a local company.
- In many industries there are advantages connected with size of operations. Economies of scale can pertain to manufacturing, sales, and research and development. A joint venture can allow an organization to benefit from these economies of scale.
- Because of the tremendous risk involved in certain projects, many organizations find it appropriate to enter a joint venture in these situations.
- Certain resources and markets may not be available to an organization, and in such cases the need for access to these resources and markets can only be satisfied through a joint venture. A typical case occurs when one organization possesses a product that it wants to sell abroad. A joint venture with a partner abroad offers access to a distribution system together with a knowledge of local business practices, customs, and institutions.

Strategies Used in Joint Ventures

Three basic strategies have been proposed for use in joint ventures. They are called the spider's web, go together–split, and successive integration.

The *spider's web strategy* is employed in an industry with a few large organizations and several smaller ones. One strategy for a smaller organization would be to enter a joint venture with one large organization and then, in order to avoid being absorbed, enter a new joint venture as quickly as possible with one or more of the remaining organizations. These different linkages thus form counterbalancing forces.

Go together–split is a strategy in which two or more organizations cooperate for an extended time and then separate. This strategy is particularly appropriate on projects that have a definite life span, such as construction projects.

Successive integration starts with a weak joint venture relationship between the organizations, becomes stronger, and ultimately may result in a merger—either friendly or hostile.

Considerations in Forming a Joint Venture

Three major considerations seem to be particularly important in forming a joint venture. The first is choosing a partner. The issue of cultural difference arises almost immediately in that different approaches frequently are taken in selecting and appraising a joint venture partner. For example, an American organization's objective may be to enter a new market, whereas the objective of its joint venture partner (especially if it is in a developing country) may be to gain access to American technology.

A second consideration is the question of control over the joint venture. An organization can have a majority, an equal, or a minority participation in the equity capital of a joint venture. A foreign country may have legal restrictions (in its constitution, specific laws, or government policy) on the degree of control that organizations from other countries can hold in joint ventures. Negotiations between prospective joint ventures over the control issue have often resulted in failure. The major control consideration in a joint venture is to what extent control will contribute to the success of the venture.

A final consideration involves the management of the joint venture. Both parties to the joint venture should be interested in having the quality of management necessary to ensure its success. However, this can become a difficult problem, especially in joint ventures in foreign countries. One approach has been to allow staffing of all key positions in the joint venture to be limited to citizens of the country where the joint venture is located. Another approach involves requiring managers from the parent companies in joint ventures to become familiar with the language and culture of their partner. This approach helps the managers adapt to cross-cultural management decisions.

SUMMARY OF LEARNING OBJECTIVES

1. Define corporate, business unit, and functional strategies.
   Corporate strategies are established at the highest levels of the organization and involve a long-range time horizon. Business unit strategies focus on how to compete in a given business. Functional strategies are concerned with the activities of the different functional areas such as production, finance, and marketing.

2. Describe stable growth strategy.
   Stable growth strategy occurs when the organization is satisfied with its past performance and decides to continue to pursue the same or similar objectives, when the level of achievement expected each year is increased by approximately the same percentage, and when the organization continues to serve its customers with basically the same products or services.

3. Describe growth strategy.
   Organizations pursuing a growth strategy do not necessarily grow faster than the economy as a whole but do grow faster than the markets in which their products are sold; tend to have larger-than-average profit margins; attempt to postpone or even eliminate the danger of price competition in their industry; regularly develop new

products, new markets, new processes, and new uses for old products; and tend to adapt the outside world to themselves by creating something or a demand for something that did not exist before.

4. Define concentric diversification.

   Concentric diversification is a growth strategy that involves adding new products or services that are similar to the organization's present products or services.

5. Define vertical integration.

   Vertical integration is a growth strategy that involves extending an organization's present business in two possible directions. Forward integration moves the organization into distributing its own products or services. Backward integration moves it into supplying some or all of the products or services that are used in producing its present products or services.

6. Describe horizontal diversification.

   Horizontal diversification is a growth strategy in which an organization buys one of its competitors.

7. Discuss conglomerate diversification.

   Conglomerate diversification is a growth strategy that involves adding new products or services that are significantly different from the organization's present products or services.

8. Explain endgame strategies.

   Endgame strategies are used by organizations in an environment of declining product demand where it is unlikely that all the plant capacity and competitors put in place during the industry's heyday will ever be needed.

9. Present three retrenchment strategies.

   Three alternative retrenchment strategies employed by organizations are turnaround, divestment, and liquidation. A turnaround strategy is an attempt to improve efficiency of operations during a decline in an organization's financial situation. Divestment involves selling off a major part of the business, which can be an SBU, a product line, or a division. Liquidation involves terminating an organization's existence either by selling off its assets or by shutting down the entire operation.

10. Explain three major types of generic competitive strategies.

    The overall cost leadership strategy emphasizes producing and delivering the product or service at a low cost relative to competitors while not neglecting quality and service. A differentiation strategy requires that an organization create a product or service that is recognized industry-wide as being unique, thus permitting the organization to charge higher-than-average prices. A focus strategy involves concentrating on a particular group of customers, geographic markets, or product line segments in order to serve a well-defined but narrow market better than competitors who serve a broader market.

11. Define mergers and acquisitions.

    A merger takes place when two companies combine their operations, creating, in effect, a third company. An acquisition is a situation in which one company buys, and controls, another company.

12. Explain joint ventures.

    Joint ventures are separate corporate entities jointly owned by two or more parent organizations.

REVIEW QUESTIONS

1. Describe the characteristics of a stable growth strategy.
2. Outline the characteristics of a growth strategy.
3. What three questions should an organization's management answer before embarking on a growth strategy?
4. Define the following strategies:
   a. Concentric diversification
   b. Vertical integration
   c. Horizontal diversification
   d. Conglomerate diversification
5. Describe four endgame strategies.
6. Define the following strategies:
   a. Turnaround
   b. Divestment
   c. Liquidation
7. Describe the following generic competitive strategies:
   a. Overall cost leadership
   b. Differentiation
   c. Focus
8. What is a joint venture?

DISCUSSION QUESTIONS

1. Select an organization in which you have been employed or with which you have some familiarity and identify the strategic alternatives available to it.
2. Many large companies have chosen conglomerate diversification as a strategy. Identify one of these companies and explain why you think the company selected this strategy.
3. Identify a company that has used a growth strategy by concentrating on a single product or service. What are the risks to this company in using this strategy?
4. Select a merger that has recently occurred and identify the reasons for it.

REFERENCES AND ADDITIONAL READING

1. Peter Drucker, *Management: Task, Responsibilities and Practices* (New York: Harper & Row, 1974), p. 772.
2. Thomas Peters and Robert Waterman, Jr., *In Search of Excellence* (New York: Harper & Row, 1982), p. 15.
3. For an in-depth look at vertical integration strategies, see Kathryn Rudie Harrigan, "Formulating Vertical Integration Strategies," *Academy of Management Review* 9 (October 1984):638–652.
4. Joseph Vesey, "Vertical Integration: Its Effect on Business Performance," *Managerial Planning* 25–26 (May–June 1978):12.

5. Kathryn Rudie Harrigan and Michael E. Porter, "End-game Strategies for Declining Industries," *Harvard Business Review* 61 (July–August 1983):111.
6. For a discussion of turnaround strategies, see Donald C. Hambrick and Steven M. Schecter, "Turnaround Strategies for Mature-Industrial-Product Business Units," *Academy of Management Journal* 26 (June 1983):231–248.
7. See also Surendra S. Singhvi, "Divestment as a Corporate Strategy," *Journal of Business Strategy* 4 (Spring 1984):85–88.
8. Michael E. Porter, *Corporate Strategy* (New York: Free Press, 1980), pp. 34–46.
9. For an in-depth analysis of the effectiveness of these strategies, see Gregory G. Dess and Peter S. Davis, "Porter's (1980) Generic Strategies as Determinants of Strategic Group Membership and Organizational Performance," *Academy of Management Journal* 27 (September 1984):467–488.
10. Steven E. Prokesch and William J. Powell, Jr., "Do Mergers Really Work?" *Business Week*, June 3, 1985, p. 90.

Strategy in Action Case Study: Ford Motor Company

Chapter 4: Identifying Strategic Alternatives

Ford Motor Company vividly illustrates how a large company moves in many strategic directions.

THE EARLY YEARS—GROWTH BY CONCENTRATING ON A SINGLE PRODUCT

Ford grew during its early years by improving its only product—the car. The Model T, which was built in 1908, was a considerable improvement over all previous models. It sold over 10,000 units during its first year of production. In 1927, the Model T began to lose ground to its competitors. Ford responded by introducing the Model A, which came in several body styles and a wide variety of colors. When the Model A began to lose ground to its competitors, the Ford V-8 was introduced in 1932. Six years later, in 1938, the Mercury became Ford's entry in the growing medium-priced automobile market.

Ford also grew by expanding its geographic coverage. This is illustrated by its move into Canada during 1904. Also during its early years, Ford employed a concentric diversification strategy when it began to produce trucks and tractors in 1917 and purchased the Lincoln Motor Company in 1922.

VERTICAL INTEGRATION STRATEGIES

The Diversified Products Division of Ford is an excellent example of backward vertical integration. A brief description of the role of several of Ford's businesses in this area follows:

- Plastic Products Division—supplies 30 percent of Ford's plastics requirements and 50 percent of its vinyl needs.
- Ford Glass Division—provides virtually all of the glass for Ford's North American cars and trucks and also supplies glass to other auto manufacturers. This division is also a major supplier to the construction, specialty glass, and mirror industries and the automotive aftermarket.
- Electrical and Fuel Handling Division—provides starters, alternators, small motors, fuel senders, and other parts for Ford vehicles.

FORD NEW HOLLAND, INC.—CONCENTRIC DIVERSIFICATION

As was mentioned earlier, Ford employed concentric diversification by beginning to produce tractors in 1917. Ford New Holland, Inc., is now one of the world's largest tractor and farm equipment manufacturers. A relatively new subsidiary, formed on January 1, 1987, Ford New Holland consolidated Ford's tractor operations with New Holland, a farm equipment manufacturer acquired from the Sperry Corporation in 1986.

Ford New Holland subsequently acquired Versatile Equipment, Ltd., North America's largest manufacturer of four-wheel-drive tractors. Both of these transactions are examples of Ford implementing its concentric diversification strategy through acquisitions.

FINANCIAL SERVICES DIVISION—CONGLOMERATE DIVERSIFICATION

Ford Motor Credit Company was created to loan money to dealers and retail automobile customers. This is probably best described as being a concentric diversification strategy.

However, in the 1980s Ford used this business unit to aggressively pursue conglomerate diversification. First Nationwide Financial Corporation, acquired in 1985, is North America's second largest savings and loan operation. U.S. Leasing, acquired in late 1987, is involved in business and commercial equipment financing, leveraged lease financing, commercial fleet leasing, transportation equipment, and corporate and real estate financing.

OTHER CONGLOMERATE DIVERSIFICATION STRATEGIES

Ford Motor Land Development Corporation, a business unit of Diversified Products Operations, is an example of conglomerate diversification. Since

1972, this unit has built 59 commercial structures surrounding Ford world headquarters in Dearborn, Michigan. The market value of land and facilities owned and managed by this business unit is estimated at over $1 billion.

Ford Aerospace Corporation and Hertz Corporation are also examples of conglomerate diversification.

TURNAROUND STRATEGIES

During its history, Ford has been forced to pursue turnaround strategies several times. After World War II, Ford was losing money at the rate of several million dollars a month. Henry Ford II reorganized and decentralized the company, which rapidly restored its health.

Perhaps the most dramatic turnaround strategy employed by any American business was accomplished by Ford in the early 1980s. From 1979 to 1982, Ford lost more than $511 million in profits. Sales declined from $42 million in 1978 to $38 million in 1981. Needless to say, Ford was in deep trouble.

One of the causes of this decline was aggressive foreign competition, but perhaps more importantly, much of the decline was a result of how Ford did business. New models looked like the previous year's models, there was very little communication between divisions (i.e., design and engineering), management was doing a poor job of managing its people, and there was little upward communication.

What did Ford management do to turn around this situation? First, they reduced operating costs significantly, taking $4.5 billion out of ongoing operating expenses from 1979 to 1983. Secondly, quality became the number one priority. Management also changed Ford's process of designing cars. Previously, each unit worked independently; now, design, engineering, and assembly work together in this process.

However, the most important change implemented by Ford was a new corporate culture. Starting with CEO Philip Caldwell and President Don Petersen, priorities were changed. A new style of management, which emphasized joint action and the participation of all employees in working toward common goals, was established. Closer relationships developed among the people at Ford, and a stronger emphasis on employees, dealers, and suppliers emerged. There was a new spirit of teamwork.

DIVESTMENTS

Over the years, Ford has not been reluctant to divest business units. For example, in October 1989, Ford signed a memorandum of understanding with a group of investors to sell its Rouge Steel Company. Ford sold the operation because it did not want to pay modernization costs, which it estimated would total $100 million annually for several years. Other divestments made by Ford include the selling of a chemical operation in 1987 and a paint operation unit to du Pont in 1986.

ACQUISITIONS AND JOINT VENTURES

On November 2, 1989, Ford acquired Jaguar PLC for $2.5 billion as a way to eliminate one of its weaknesses in the auto market: the lack of a product to compete in the luxury car market. Some of the competing cars in the luxury category are the Toyota Lexus LS 400, Honda Acura Legend, and BMW 3 series. The demand for luxury cars in 1989 was $25 billion, and it is forecast to grow to $40 billion by 1994. This growth is much greater than the overall auto market. Ford sees Jaguar as an opportunity to move into the luxury car market in both the United States and Europe.

Ford has also used joint ventures—two of the more significant ones are with Mazda and Nissan. Ford and Mazda have worked together to produce five vehicles. The Probe, for example, is produced at a Mazda plant, has the exterior and interior design done by Ford, and has detailed engineering done by Mazda.

Nissan and Ford are cooperating on a front-wheel-drive minivan that Ford will build at its Ohio truck plant. The minivan will be marketed by both companies. In Australia, Ford's Maverick, a version of the Nissan Patrol four-wheel-drive vehicle, is sold by Ford dealers, while Nissan dealers sell versions of the Ford Falcon pickup and van.

As can be seen from these examples, Ford has pursued a combination of strategies. Obviously, the firm has used many other strategies than the ones discussed. The strategies presented here, however, illustrate many of the strategic alternatives discussed this chapter.

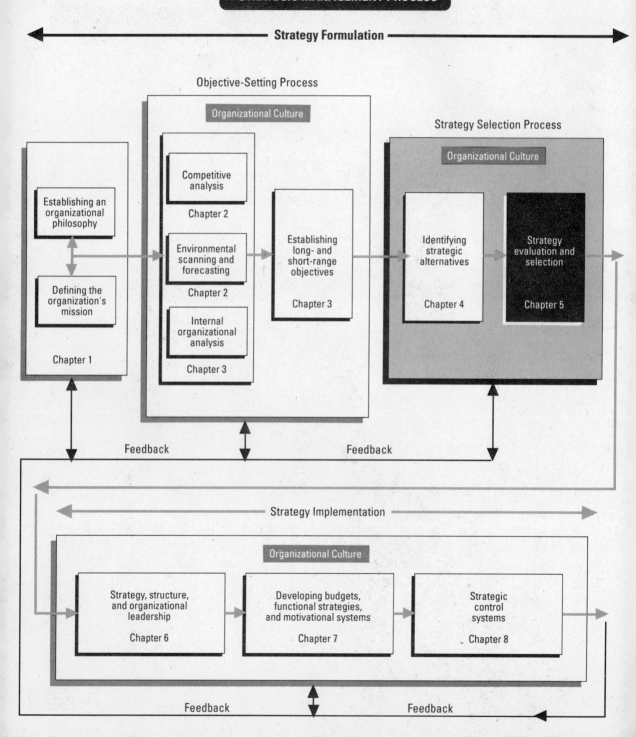

STRATEGIC MANAGEMENT PROCESS

Strategy Formulation

Objective-Setting Process

Organizational Culture

Strategy Selection Process

Organizational Culture

Establishing an
organizational
philosophy

Defining the
organization's
mission

Chapter 1

Competitive
analysis

Chapter 2

Environmental
scanning and
forecasting

Chapter 2

Internal
organizational
analysis

Chapter 3

Establishing
long- and
short-range
objectives

Chapter 3

Identifying
strategic
alternatives

Chapter 4

Strategy
evaluation and
selection

Chapter 5

Feedback

Feedback

Strategy Implementation

Organizational Culture

Strategy, structure,
and organizational
leadership

Chapter 6

Developing budgets,
functional strategies,
and motivational systems

Chapter 7

Strategic
control
systems

Chapter 8

Feedback

Feedback

CHAPTER 5
Strategy Evaluation and Selection

LEARNING OBJECTIVES

After studying this chapter, you should be able to

1. Describe the growth-share matrix.
2. Define cash cows, dogs, problem children, and stars.
3. Discuss the industry attractiveness–business unit strength matrix.
4. Describe the life-cycle approach to strategy evaluation.
5. Describe the product-market evolution matrix.
6. Discuss PIMS.
7. Define value-based planning.
8. Describe qualitative factors that influence the strategy evaluation and selection process.

In what direction should an organization go? Ideally, an organization's strategy should be designed to take advantage of market opportunities and neutralize adverse environmental impacts. At the same time, it should reinforce internal strengths and improve on perceived weaknesses relative to the competition. Given these characteristics of an ideal strategy and considering the options available to most organizations, one can begin to see why strategy selection is such a complex and difficult decision. Fortunately, several methodologies have been developed to help organizations make these decisions.

BUSINESS PORTFOLIO ANALYSIS

One methodology developed to assist in the strategy evaluation and selection process is known as business portfolio analysis. Among the various approaches of this type, the most popular seem to be the growth-share matrix, the industry attractiveness–business strength matrix, and the life-cycle approach.

Growth-Share Matrix

Originally developed by the Boston Consulting Group (BCG), the *growth-share matrix* approach postulates that all except the smallest and simplest organizations are composed of more than one business.[1] These *businesses* in an organization are called its *business portfolio*. The BCG approach proposes that a separate strategy be developed for each of these largely independent units.

In order to visually display an organization's business portfolio, BCG developed a four-quadrant grid as shown in Figure 5.1. The horizontal axis indicates the market share of the business relative to its major competitor and characterizes the strength of the organization in that business. The market share for any particular year is calculated as follows:

$$\text{Relative market share (current year)} = \frac{\text{Business unit sales (current year)}}{\text{Leading competitor's sales (current year)}}$$

The vertical axis indicates the percent of growth in the market in the current year and characterizes the attractiveness of the market for the business unit. The market growth rate is calculated as follows:

$$\text{Market growth rate (current year)} = \frac{\text{Total market (current year)} - \text{Total market (previous year)}}{\text{Total market (previous year)}} \times 100$$

The lines that divide the matrix into four quadrants are somewhat arbitrarily set. A high market growth rate is taken to be over 10 percent. The demarcation between high and low relative market share is set at 1.5. This means that if a particular business unit's current sales are 1.5 times or greater than its leading

Figure 5.1 *Growth-Share Matrix*

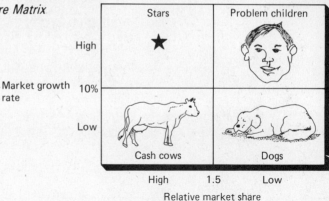

competitor's sales, then it is considered to have a high relative market share. These lines of demarcation are not absolutes and can be modified to fit the particular needs of an organization. Furthermore, in actual practice the market growth rate axis is plotted on a linear scale, whereas the relative market share is plotted on a logarithmic scale.

BCG describes the four quadrants of the growth-share matrix as follows:

1. *Cash cows* have low market growth and high market share. Because of high market share, profits and cash generation should be high. The low rate of growth means that the cash demands should be low. Thus, large cash surpluses are normally generated by cash cows. They provide the cash to meet company needs and are thus the foundation of the company.

2. *Dogs* have low market share and low market growth. The former normally implies poor profits. Because the growth rate is low, investments to increase market share are often prohibitive. Unfortunately, the cash required to maintain a competitive position often exceeds the cash generated. Thus, dogs often become cash traps. Generally, dogs are harvested or divested.

3. *Problem children* have low market share and high market growth rate. Their cash needs are high because of their growth, and the cash generated is low because of their market share. Because growth is high, one strategy for a problem child is to make the necessary investments to gain market share and become a star. When the market growth rate slows, the unit can then become a cash cow. Another strategy is to divest the problem children that management feels cannot be developed into stars.

4. *Stars* have high growth and high market share. Because of the high growth and high market share, stars use and generate large amounts of cash. Stars generally represent the best profit and investment opportunities. Obviously, the best strategy for stars is to make the necessary investments to maintain or improve their competitive position.

The labels used by BCG to classify the quadrants have often been criticized. After all, who would want to be known as the manager in charge of a dog? However, despite what some people feel are derogatory connotations, the terms have become widely accepted.

The following steps are generally followed in using the growth-share matrix in strategy evaluation and selection:

1. Divide the company into its business units. Many organizations perform this step when they establish strategic business units (SBUs). On the matrix, a circle is used to depict individual business units.
2. Determine the business unit's relative size within the total organization. Relative size can be measured in terms of assets employed in the business unit as a percentage of the total assets or in terms of sales of the business unit as a percentage of total sales. On the matrix, the area in the circle indicates the business unit's relative size.
3. Determine the market growth rate for each business unit.
4. Determine the relative market share of each business unit.
5. Develop a graphical picture of the company's overall portfolio of businesses.
6. Select a strategy for each business unit based on its position in the company's overall portfolio of businesses.

Strategy Selection   Strategy selection using the growth-share matrix assumes that the primary objectives of the organization are growth and profitability.[2] The advantage of multibusiness organizations is that they can transfer cash from business units that are highly profitable but have low growth potential to other units that have high growth and high profit potential. Strategy selection among the various business units is designed to produce a balanced portfolio in terms of the generation and uses of cash.

Thus, relative market share and the market growth rate are the two fundamental parameters that influence strategy selection. Relative market share determines the rate at which the business unit generates cash. A business unit with a relatively high share of the market compared to its competitors should have higher profit margins and thus higher cash flows. On the other hand, the market growth rate has a twofold influence on strategy selection. First, the market growth rate influences the ease of gaining market share. In slow-growth markets, increases in market share generally come from decreases in a competitor's market share. Second, the market growth rate determines the level of opportunity for investment. Growth markets provide an opportunity for plowing cash back into the business unit and compounding the return on investment. This opportunity can also present problems because the faster a business unit grows, the more cash it needs to finance the growth. Of course, businesses do have external sources of cash such as debt and equity financing, but the BCG approach assumes that external debt would have to be met ultimately through internal cash flows.

BCG uses market share to determine the strategic choice for individual business units. The four major strategic choices identified are

1. To increase market share
2. To hold market share

Figure 5.2 Strategic Choices Using Growth-Share Matrix

Quadrant	Strategic Choice	Business Unit Profitability	Investment Required	Cash Flow
Star	Hold or increase market share	High	High	Around zero or slightly negative
Cash cows	Add market share	High	Low	Highly positive
Problem children	Increase market share	None or negative	Very high	Highly negative
	Harvest/divest	Low or negative	Disinvest	Positive
Dogs	Harvest/divest /liquidate	Low or negative	Disinvest	Positive

Source: Adapted from Arnoldo C. Hax and Nicholas S. Majiluk, "The Use of the Growth-Share Matrix in Strategic Planning," *Interfaces* 13 (February 1983):51.

3. To harvest
4. To divest

Figure 5.2 identifies the strategic choices for business units in each quadrant of the growth-share matrix. It would also seem that business units that have holding or increasing market share as their strategic choice would likely use an overall cost leadership strategy or a differentiation strategy.

The growth-share matrix can also be used to prepare a portfolio display for the organization at different times (present, three to five years ago, and forecast in three to five years). This gives management a picture of what the results of its strategic choices have been and might be.

Criticisms of the Growth-Share Matrix   Several potential problems and difficulties with the use of the growth-share matrix have been widely described.[3] One difficulty is in determining market share in complex industries. Another area of concern involves the concept of "shared experience." Under the BCG approach, dogs are generally harvested, divested, or liquidated. However, it has been pointed out that valuable experience may be gained in a low-profit business unit (dog) that can help lower costs in a related but more profitable business unit (star or cash cow).[4]

Furthermore, some research has indicated that well-managed dogs can become cash generators.[5] One study of 87 organizations that had low-market-share positions in slow-growth industries classified 40 of these organizations as being ineffective (i.e., a return on investment of less than 5 percent).[6] This research concluded that effective organizations tended to pursue a high-quality, medium-price strategy complemented by careful spending on marketing and R&D. On the other hand, ineffective dogs must still be considered candidates for harvesting, divestment, or liquidation.

Industry Attractiveness–Business Strength Matrix

General Electric (GE) found the visual display of the growth-share matrix appealing but felt that using only two dimensions—market growth rate and relative market share—was inadequate for describing its portfolio of businesses. GE felt that a wider variety of factors needed to be identified and assessed in order to develop an effective display of its business units. Thus, GE asked McKinsey and Company to develop the portfolio approach that is now called the industry attractiveness–business strength matrix.

The industry attractiveness–business strength matrix is illustrated in Figure 5.3. The use of the matrix first requires an identification and/assessment of both critical external factors and critical internal factors. Critical external factors are not directly controllable by the organization and determine the overall attractiveness of the industry in which the business unit operates. After identifying and assessing these critical external factors, top management makes a qualitative decision on whether the industry has a low, medium, or high attractiveness. Critical internal factors, or *critical success factors* as they are frequently called, are generally controllable by the organization and determine the business unit's strengths. Again, a qualitative decision is made on whether the business unit's strengths are low, medium, or high.

Identifying and assessing industry attractiveness and business unit strengths allows each business unit to be positioned on the nine-cell matrix.

Figure 5.3 *Industry Attractiveness–Business Strength Matrix*

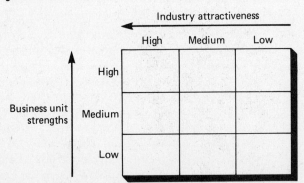

The following sections outline a methodology for using the industry attractiveness–business strength matrix.[7]

Defining and Assessing Critical External Factors Critical external factors include the competitive characteristics of the industry and the economic, technological, political, and social forces that influence the industry. Industry structure analysis, which was described in Chapter 2, can be helpful in defining and assessing critical external factors.

Defining and Assessing Critical Success Factors *Critical success factors* (CSF) have a significant impact on the success of the particular business unit that is competing in an industry.[8] Some of the critical success factors that have been identified are market share, strength of sales force, manufacturing capability, corporate image, breadth of product line, strength of financial resources, product quality and reliability, and managerial competence. The position that a particular business unit achieves on these factors, relative to its competition, determines its strength.[9]

Forecasting Critical External Factors Several techniques for forecasting external factors were described in Chapter 2. Any of those techniques can be used to assess the future trends of the critical external factors.

Specifying the Desired Position on Critical Success Factors After forecasting the critical external factors, management must decide where it would like the business unit to be at a future time in relation to the critical success factors.

Corporate-Level Strategies Management can obtain an overall view of the corporate portfolio by placing the present and desired positions of all business units on the matrix. Because of the scarcity of money and other resources, the top management of most organizations must become selective and limit their investments to those business units that can provide an attractive payoff and in which they are strong. In addition, they must use some business units to finance the growth of others. Figure 5.4 illustrates the general corporate-level strategies available to an organization. Generally, when a business unit is high on industry attractiveness and business strengths, the natural corporate-level strategy is to invest heavily and pursue a growth strategy. When attractiveness and business strengths are low, the strategy is normally to harvest or divest. In the intermediate positions, the strategy generally involves concentrating resources on the most attractive business units or in business units that have a unique competence. Obviously the choice of what units to fund is influenced by the organizational culture and other nonquantifiable factors which are discussed later in this chapter. Furthermore, changes in the external factors that can make the industry attractiveness of a business unit either high, medium, or low also influence the decision process.

Figure 5.4 Strategies Available to Organizations

Industry attractiveness

		High	Medium	Low
Business unit strengths	High	Growth	Growth	Selective investment
	Medium	Growth	Selective investment	Harvest or divest
	Low	Selective investment	Harvest or divest	Harvest, divest, or liquidate

Business Unit Strategies   Obviously, the strategy of a particular business unit depends on the corporate-level strategy and the funding and resources provided to the business unit by corporate-level management. Nevertheless, after these decisions are made, the industry attractiveness–business strength matrix can be used to examine the performance of each of the product lines in the business unit and to identify those product lines that deserve either more or less support. It also can help identify the particular strategy—overall cost leadership, differentiation, or focus—that could be used for each product line.

Functional-Area Strategies   As will be recalled, use of the industry attractiveness–business strength matrix requires an assessment and specification of the desired future position of the business unit on critical success factors; generally this provides a basis for the development of functional strategies. Most of the critical success factors fall either within functional areas of the business unit or across multifunctional areas. The development of functional strategies involves determining the actions that need to be taken within each functional area in order to move the functional area from its present position to its desired position. Of course, each functional-area strategy is totally dependent on the strategies developed at the corporate and business unit levels and the resources provided from these levels. Functional-area strategies are described in more detail in Chapter 7.

Criticisms of Industry Attractiveness–Business Strength Matrix   Several problems or difficulties with the use of the industry attractiveness–business strength matrix have been identified and discussed. First, because it is often difficult to identify and agree upon standard lists of external and internal factors to be used by all business units in an organization, inconsistencies in the classification of business units can develop. It has also been argued that when applying the matrix, managers often do not agree and many categorize a business unit as medium because they cannot reconcile diverging opinions. Regardless of these difficulties, however, the industry attractiveness–business strength matrix is widely used in strategy evaluation and selection.

Life-Cycle Approach

The life-cycle approach, developed by Arthur D. Little, Inc., classifies business units in an organization by (1) industry maturity and (2) strategic competitive position, resulting in the matrix shown in Figure 5.5.

The life-cycle approach postulates that industries can be grouped into the following stages of maturity:

- Embryonic—characterized by rapid growth, rapid changes in technology, pursuit of new customers, and fragmented and changing shares of market.
- Growth—characterized by rapid growth, but customers, market share, and technology are better known and entry into the industry is more difficult.
- Mature—characterized by stability in known customers, technology, and market shares. The industry can, however, still be competitive.
- Aging—characterized by falling demand, declining number of competitors, and in many such industries, a narrowing of the product line.

Example 5.1 shows how Quaker Oats classifies its products according to a modified life-cycle analysis.

The determination of a business unit's strategic competitive position using the life-cycle approach calls for a qualitative decision based on multiple criteria such as breadth of product line, market share, movement in market share, and changes in technology. The life-cycle approach maintains that as these criteria

Figure 5.5 Life-Cycle Matrix

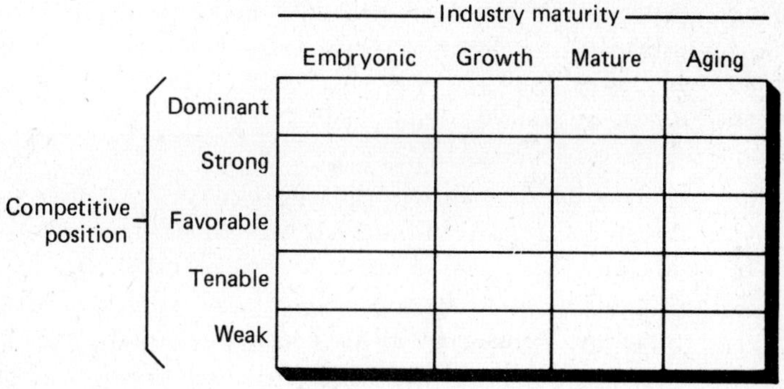

The Value-Driven Portfolio at Quaker Oats

Quaker Oats is one of America's best-known companies. Its products include Aunt Jemima mixes and syrups, Gatorade, Rice-A-Roni, Ken-L Ration, Gaines, Savory Classics, Van Camp's, and Quaker Rice Cakes. It also owns Fisher-Price.

Quaker's strategic plan recognizes that all businesses go through a natural evolution of investment, growth, and cash flows. Each phase overlaps the next, and, if properly managed, the process repeats and renews itself as established brands fund investments in new products. At any time, Quaker's brands go through the following three phases of the cash flow cycle:

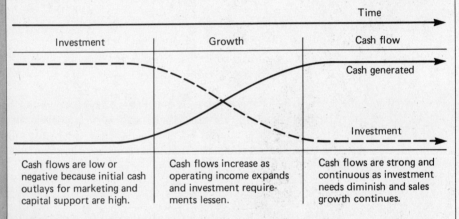

Investment	Growth	Cash flow
Cash flows are low or negative because initial cash outlays for marketing and capital support are high.	Cash flows increase as operating income expands and investment requirements lessen.	Cash flows are strong and continuous as investment needs diminish and sales growth continues.

Quaker gauges the cash flow generation potential of a new project by looking at three key factors: the brand's prospective sales growth, its profit margin and the amount of investment cash needed to support sales growth, and the projected profit margin. Quaker uses the term *value drivers* to describe these factors because sales growth, margin levels, investment, and cost of capital do determine a company's "value." Quaker's assumptions about these key factors let it assess the relative desirability of future investment in terms of today's dollars. This process is known as discounted cash flow (DCF) analysis. After Quaker weighs the strategic business issues, it uses the DCF analysis to choose investments producing a profitable return—equal to or better than its minimum required rate of return—which is also known as its cost of capital.

Source: Annual report.

---

change over time, a business unit either gains or loses competitive advantage and can be classified as being dominant, strong, favorable, tenable, or weak.

Strategy Selection   After a business unit has been positioned in the matrix, a strategy can be formulated for each business unit. At the corporate level, resources are normally allocated among business units on a competitive basis. Business units are screened or ranked on criteria such as desirability of certain maturities, strength of competitive position, ability to produce positive cash flows in the short or long term, rates of return on investment or net assets, and degree of risk. This screening enables top management to decide which business units are to receive what resources.

Product-Market Evolution Matrix

Very closely allied with the life-cycle approach and only slightly different is the product-market evolution matrix.[10] Figure 5.6 illustrates the matrix, in which business units are plotted in terms of their stage of product-market evolution and their competitive position. The circles represent the relative sizes of the industries. The wedges in the circles represent the market share of the business unit.

Several useful ideas concerning the strategic alternatives available to each business unit emerge from an analysis of Figure 5.6:

1. Business unit A appears to be a potential star. Its relatively large share of the market combined with its being at the development stage of product-market evolution and its potential for being in a strong competitive position make it a good candidate for receiving more corporate resources.

Figure 5.6 *Product-Market Evolution Portfolio Matrix*

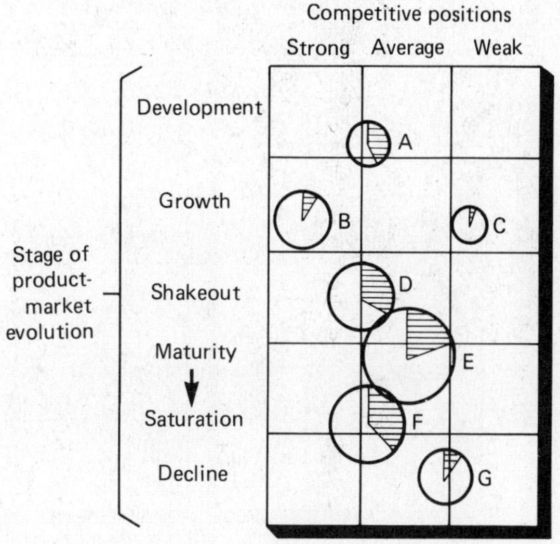

Source: Adapted from C. W. Hofer, *Conceptual Constructs for Formulating Corporate and Business Strategies* (Boston: Intercollegiate Case Clearing House, 9-378-754, 1977), p. 3.

2. Business unit B is somewhat similar to A. However, investments in B would be contingent on determining why B has such a relatively small share of the market given its strong competitive position. A strategy would have to be developed to overcome this low market share in order to justify more investments.

3. Business unit C has a small market share in a relatively small but growing industry and has a weak competitive position. A strategy must be developed to overcome the low market share and weak competitive position in order to justify future investments. This might be a good candidate to divest in order to use the resources in either A or B.

4. Business unit D is in a shakeout period, has a relatively large share of the market, and is in a relatively strong competitive position. Investments should be made to maintain that position. In the long run, D should become a cash cow.

5. Business units E and F are cash cows and should be used for cash generation.

6. Business unit G appears to be a dog in the corporate portfolio. It should be managed to generate cash in the short run, if possible; however, the long-run strategy will more than likely be divestment or liquidation.

Organizations can have a variety of mixes in their business portfolios. It has been suggested that most portfolios are variations of one of three ideal types: (1) growth, (2) profit, and (3) balanced.[11]

Figure 5.7 *Three Ideal Types of Corporate Portfolios*

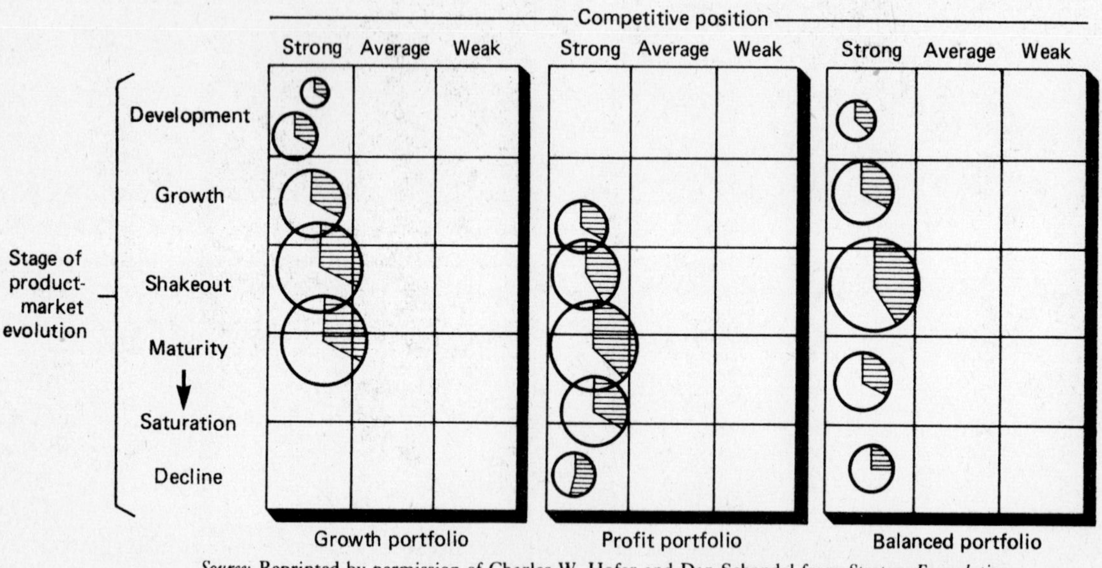

Source: Reprinted by permission of Charles W. Hofer and Dan Schendel from *Strategy Formulation: Analytical Concepts* (St. Paul, Minn.: West Publishing Company, 1978), p. 183. All rights reserved.

Figure 5.7 illustrates these ideal portfolios. Each type of portfolio represents different objectives an organization might pursue in its allocation of resources.

COMPETITIVE STRATEGY ANALYSIS

One approach to evaluating and selecting both corporate-level and business unit strategies has been proposed by Michael E. Porter and is referred to as competitive strategy formulation.[12] Porter contends that competitive strategies are built on four key factors: (1) company strengths and weaknesses; (2) industry opportunities and threats; (3) personal values of the key managers; and (4) broader societal expectations such as government policy, social concerns, and evolving mores. These four factors determine an organization's objectives. As you will recall, policies are general guides to action and should flow logically from the corporate philosophy. Porter postulates that the appropriateness of a competitive strategy can be determined by testing the objectives and policies for consistency. Figure 5.8 provides questions that when answered determine the consistency between objectives and policies.

Porter's approach to selecting the optimal competitive strategy is summarized in Figure 5.9. Porter further contends that businesses and business units pursue basically three generic strategies, which can be used singly or in combination. These strategies—overall cost leadership, differentiation, and focus—were discussed earlier in Chapter 4. Performing the analysis required in answering the questions shown in Figure 5.9 enables an organization to choose the most effective strategy or strategies not only for each business unit but also for the organization as a whole.

PIMS ANALYSIS

The profit impact of market strategies (PIMS) project was initially developed at General Electric and later transferred to the Strategic Planning Institute (SPI). The basic idea behind PIMS is to provide insights and information on the expected profit performance of different kinds of businesses and business units under different competitive conditions using different strategies. About 200 organizations submit data annually on a total of about 2000 of their business units.[13] A business unit for the purposes of PIMS analysis is an operating unit that sells a distinct set of products to an identifiable set of customers in competition with a well-defined set of competitors. Data submitted to PIMS include factors such as market share, total marketing expenditures, product quality, and R&D expenditures.

The submitted data are analyzed and several reports, including the following, are regularly generated:

Figure 5.8 Tests of Consistency for Objectives and Policies

Internal Consistency

- Are the objectives mutually achievable?
- Do the key operating policies address the objectives?
- Do the key operating policies reinforce each other?

Environmental Fit

- Do the objectives and policies exploit industry opportunities?
- Do the objectives and policies deal with industry threats (including the risk of competitive response) to the degree possible with available resources?
- Does the timing of the objectives and policies reflect the ability of the environment to absorb the actions?
- Are the objectives and policies responsive to broader societal concerns?

Resource Fit

- Do the objectives and policies match the resources available to the company relative to competitors?
- Does the timing of the objectives and policies reflect the organization's ability to change?

Communication and Implementation

- Are the objectives well understood by the key implementers?
- Is there enough congruence between the objectives and policies and the values of the key implementers to ensure commitment?
- Is there enough of a managerial capability to allow for effective implementation?

Source: Adapted from Michael E. Porter, *Competitive Strategy* (New York: Free Press, 1980), p. xix.

- The *par ROI report* is concerned with return on investment (ROI) and cash flow that is normal for the combination of circumstances a particular business unit faces (market share, competition, market position, production process, capital/cost structure). The generated ROI figure is based on the past performance of real business units under "comparable" conditions and assumes that managerial skills and decision abilities are at "average" levels. Example 5.2 describes the PIMS par ROI report in more detail.
- The *strategy report* analyzes short- and long-term effects of strategic changes on ROI. Usual strategic changes analyzed include changes in market share, changes in degree of vertical integration, and changes in capital intensity. The report summarizes the effects of these changes in several financial areas, including ROI.
- The *optimum strategy report* isolates a particular combination of strategic moves that optimize a particular criterion (including profit, cash, or growth), again judging by the past experiences of others in similar situations.[14]

Figure 5.9 Process for Formulating a Competitive Strategy

A. What is the business (or business unit) doing now?
  1. Identification
      What is the implicit or explicit current strategy?
  2. Implied assumptions
      What assumptions about the company's relative position, strengths and weaknesses, competitors, and industry trends must be made for the current strategy to make sense?
B. What is happening in the environment?
  1. Industry analysis
      What are the key factors for competitive success and the important industry opportunities and threats?
  2. Competitor analysis
      What are the capabilities and limitations of existing and potential competitors and their probable future moves?
  3. Societal analysis
      What important governmental, social, and political factors will present opportunities or threats?
  4. Strengths and weaknesses
      Given an analysis of industry and competitors, what are the company's strengths and weaknesses relative to present and future competitors?
C. What should the business be doing?
  1. Tests of assumptions and strategy
      How do the assumptions embodied in the current strategy compare with the analysis in B above? How does the strategy meet the tests in Figure 5.8?
  2. Strategic alternatives
      What are the feasible strategic alternatives given the analysis above? (Is the current strategy one of these?)
  3. Strategic choice
      Which alternative best relates the company's situation to external opportunities and threats?

Source: Adapted from Michael E. Porter, *Competitive Strategy* (New York: Free Press, 1980), pp. xix and xx.

Companies pay a great deal of money to participate in PIMS. The data they submit and reports they receive give them reliable information for strategy evaluation and selection. Obviously, however, merely because a strategy has worked for another business in similar situations does not mean that the strategy is appropriate for all businesses in that same situation.

VALUE-BASED PLANNING

The rash of corporate buy-outs by "raiders" during the 1980s was at least partially triggered by an undervaluing of the target company's stock price by the market. *Value-based planning* (VPB) is aimed at structuring and managing

PIMS Par ROI

The PIMS Par ROI Report

The PIMS model gives an expected value of the returns for a business unit, given its strategic position and market/industry situation. This expected performance is based on a complex statistical regression analysis of all the businesses in the PIMS data base. This model explains over 70% of the variance in ROI among these businesses. A par ROI report lists the 28 most important factors from the PIMS data and their relative impact on profitability. It also summarizes the impact on the par ROI of the 4 major categories of these 28 factors. A sample of such a summary for a hypothetical business is reproduced below:

Par ROI Summary for Business ABC	Factor Impact (pct. points)
Competitive position (market share, quality, etc.)	−0.7
Life-cycle stage (growth rate, R&D, new products, etc.)	+0.5
Marketing environment (concentration, mktg. intensity, etc.)	+1.2
Capital & production structure (investment, productivity, etc.)	−2.8
	−1.8
Total impact + average ROI (PIMS businesses)	20.2%
Par return on investment for this business	18.4%

PIMS as a Guide to Management Action

The PIMS par ROI report can give some clues for management actions to be taken for improving profitability. The PIMS variables reflect four categories of factors found to be important to business profitability:

- Competitive position
- Stage of life cycle
- Marketing environment
- Capital and production structure

The most serious strategic problem of the hypothetical business unit illustrated above is its relatively poor capital and production structure. This weakness, combined with its slightly inferior competitive position, are "costing" this business a total of 3.5 percentage points (− 2.8 and − 0.7%) in profitability relative to the PIMS mean. On the other hand, this business is above the PIMS average in the attractiveness of its market environment (+1.2%) and life-cycle stage (+0.5%). These positive factors partially offset its internal weaknesses to give a net negative impact of 1.8 percentage points.

Source: Adapted from Bernard C. Reimann, "Managing for the Shareholders: An Overview of Value-Based Planning," *Planning Review*, January/February 1988, p. 21.

a corporation in a way that will create more value for its shareholders.[15] Proponents of value-based planning argue that traditional performance indicators such as EPS, ROE, or ROI have little to do with the market valuation of a company's stock.

Value-based planning seeks to increase the value investors put on all the strategic business units of a company. Since the individual SBUs do not have markets for their own stock, value-based planning attempts to determine how investors would assign value to an SBU if it were a freestanding company. Several approaches have been proposed for making this evaluation for each SBU. One approach focuses on the spread between return on equity and the cost of capital of the SBU. Another approach postulates that investors are only interested in the cash generated by the SBU before financing charges and bookkeeping entries that have no effect on cash. Finally, PIMS can be used in value-based planning. For example an SBU's par ROI can provide a benchmark value for the SBU's performance. Example 5.3 shows how value-based planning was used at Coca-Cola.

QUALITATIVE FACTORS IN THE STRATEGY EVALUATION AND SELECTION PROCESS

In practice, the strategy evaluation and selection process requires the decision makers to constantly reassess the future, find new congruencies as they unfold, and blend the organization's resources into new balances to meet the constantly changing conditions. The decision process is totally dynamic, with no real beginning or end. The methods discussed earlier in this chapter provide considerable guidance in the strategy evaluation and selection process, but ultimately several qualitative factors play a key role in this stream-of-decisions process.[16] Some of these are

1. Managerial attitudes toward risk
2. Environment of the organization
3. Organizational culture and power relationships
4. Competitive actions and reactions
5. Influence of previous organizational strategies
6. Timing considerations

These factors are discussed in the following sections.

Managerial Attitudes Toward Risk

A common definition of risk is the chance of incurring loss or damage. Risk generally refers to those factors that can negatively influence planned results. In organizations, this translates into questions such as the following:

- What risks are involved in acquiring a new company?
- What risks are there in entering foreign markets?

STRATEGY IN ACTION Example 5.3

Value-Based Planning at the Coca-Cola Company

Some recent actions of the Coca-Cola Company provide good illustrations of the VBP approach. A value-based portfolio analysis revealed that its Entertainment Business Sector was not contributing its fair share to corporate value. A key reason was that the business was very different in nature from Coke's other endeavors. In particular, its performance was much more volatile, resulting in greater risk and, therefore, a relatively high cost of capital. Top management decided to spin the entertainment business off as a separate unit, by combining it with its 38.6 percent-owned Tri-Star Pictures, Inc. Coca-Cola will keep only a minority financial interest in the new company, to be called Columbia Pictures Entertainment, Inc. Since this move will reduce the Coca-Cola Company's risk considerably, the stock market reacted very favorably to the news.

However, Coca-Cola has used the VBP approach not only for deciding which businesses to divest or acquire but also for fixing poorly performing individual businesses. The VBP analysis uncovered a rather surprising fact: Its mainstay soda fountain business was actually destroying shareholder value at a worrisome rate. This discovery came as quite a shock, since the business had always been regarded as highly profitable. After all, there weren't a lot of bottles or cans to fill, transport, and store. What management had not realized was that, over time, the business had become quite capital intensive. The return on capital was only 12.5 percent, while the company's cost of capital was estimated to be 16 percent. Thus, every dollar invested in this business was dissipating shareholder value.

The main culprit turned out to be an expensive five-gallon stainless steel container used to transport the Coke syrup. The business switched to disposable bag-in-a-box containers and to 50-gallon containers for large customers. Its return on capital rose to 17 percent, and by increasing its leverage, the company was able to reduce its cost of capital to 14 percent. Suddenly the business was turned into a strong contributor to shareholder value.

Source: Adapted from Bernard C. Reimann, "Managing for the Shareholders: An Overview of Value-Based Planning," *Planning Review*, January/February 1988, p. 16.

- What risks are faced in enlarging plant capacity by 50 percent?

No amount of strategy evaluation can eliminate risk in the final strategy selection decision. Investing resources today in expectation of future conditions is in and of itself a risk-taking adventure.

Organizations and managers develop attitudes toward risk that influence the strategic choice decision. Some organizations seem to be eager to assume risk whereas others have a strong aversion to risk. Risk assumers generally adopt an offensive strategy in that they react to environmental change before they are forced to react. Risk avoiders generally adopt a defensive strategy in that they only react to environmental change when forced to do so by circumstances. Risk avoiders rely heavily on past strategies. Risk assumers look at a wider variety of options.

Many large organizations attempt to balance their business by having some risk-assuming business units and some risk-avoiding business units. In summary, the risk attitudes of management reduce or expand the number of strategic alternatives considered and increase or decrease the likelihood that certain strategic options will be adopted.

Environment of the Organization

Organizations exist in an environment that is influenced by stockholders, competitors, customers, government, unions, and society in general. The degree of dependence that an organization has on one or more of these environmental forces also influences the strategic choice process. A higher degree of dependence reduces the organization's flexibility in its strategic choices.

Organizational Culture and Power Relationships

Organizational culture is a term used to describe the the collective assumptions and beliefs of an organization's employees which shape the behavior of individuals and groups in the organization. *Power* is a relationship between people that consists of one individual's capacity to influence another individual or group of individuals to do something they would not otherwise do. Both organizational culture and power relationships significantly influence the strategy evaluation and selection process.

As stated in Chapter 1, all organizations have a culture. An organization's culture can contribute significantly to its success or can be an obstacle to future success. Matching an organization's culture to its environment and ensuring that it is a positive force is one of top management's key concerns in strategy evaluation and selection.

The power of the chief executive officer (CEO) is also a major influence on both the organization's culture and its strategic choices. Among large organizations, Henry Ford, Jr., at Ford Motor Company, Thomas Watson, Sr., at IBM, and Harold Geneen of ITT are just a few of the powerful CEOs who have dramatically influenced the culture and strategic choices of their organizations. In most organizations, when a powerful CEO favors a particular strategy, it generally becomes the strategy that is selected. Of course, if a powerful CEO selects a strategy that clashes with the present organizational culture, significant problems are likely to develop in the implementation of the strategy. In most highly successful organizations, however, the CEO and/or other top managers recognize and create the culture that is needed to implement the strategy.

Competitive Actions and Reactions

Another factor that influences strategy selection is the external coalition of competitive actions and reactions. This factor is of critical importance, especially in certain industries. For example, the actions and reactions of IBM strongly influence the strategic choices of all firms in the computer industry. Changes in product line, pricing, or organizational structure by IBM cause all firms in this industry to reexamine their strategic position. Another example is the pricing structure in the U.S. automobile industry. Pricing decisions made by General Motors almost always lead to changes by other automobile manufacturers.

Influence of Previous Organizational Strategies

For most organizations, past strategies serve as a beginning point in the strategy selection process. A natural result is that the number of strategic alternatives considered is limited based on past organizational strategies. Generally, managers commit the greatest amount of resources to a previously chosen course of action when they are personally responsible for the negative consequences of the chosen course of action. This may partially explain why changes in top management are often necessary to change strategy. The new management is less likely to be bound by the previous strategies.

Timing Considerations

Another factor influencing the strategy selection process is the amount of time available for making the decisions. Time pressures limit the number of alternatives that can be considered and also reduce the amount of information that can be gathered in evaluating the alternatives. When managers are placed under time pressures, they tend to place greater weight on negative rather than positive factors and consider fewer factors in making their decision.

On the other hand, determining the exact time to implement the strategy is also of critical importance. Waiting too long can be just as disastrous as jumping in too quickly.

SUMMARY OF LEARNING OBJECTIVES

1. Describe the growth-share matrix.
   The growth-share matrix plots each business in an organization on a four-quadrant grid. The vertical axis of the matrix indicates the percent of growth in the market, and the horizontal axis indicates the market share of the business.
2. Define cash cows, dogs, problem children, and stars.
   Cash cows have low market growth and high market share. Dogs have low market share and low market growth. Problem children have low market share and high market growth rate. Stars have high growth and high market share.
3. Discuss the industry attractiveness–business strength matrix.
   The industry attractiveness–business strength matrix plots each business unit on a

nine-cell grid. *The vertical axis is a qualitative analysis of the business unit's strengths, and the horizontal axis is a qualitative analysis of the industry attractiveness.*

4. Describe the life-cycle approach to strategy evaluation.
   The life-cycle approach classifies business units in an organization by industry maturity and strategic competitive position. The stages of industry maturity are embryonic, growth, mature, and aging.
5. Describe the product-market evolution matrix.
   This matrix classifies business units in an organization by stage of product-market evolution and competitive position. The stages of product-market evolution are development, growth, shakeout, maturity/saturation, and decline. Circles on the matrix represent the relative size of the industries of the business unit. The wedges in the circles represent the market share of the business unit.
6. Discuss PIMS.
   PIMS is a data base on about 200 companies. It provides insights and information on the expected profit performance of different kinds of businesses and business units under different competitive conditions using different strategies.
7. Define value-based planning.
   Value-based planning is the structuring and managing of a corporation in a way that will create more value for its shareholders.
8. Describe qualitative factors that influence the strategy evaluation and selection process.
   Some of the key qualitative factors that influence the strategy evaluation and selection process are managerial attitudes toward risk, environment of the organization, organizational culture and power relationships, competitive actions and reactions, influence of previous organizational strategies, and timing considerations.

REVIEW QUESTIONS

1. What is a business portfolio?
2. Describe the four quadrants in the growth-share matrix.
3. Outline the steps followed in strategy evaluation and selection using the growth-share matrix.
4. Discuss the variables used in developing the industry attractiveness–business strength matrix.
5. Describe the variables used in developing the life-cycle approach.
6. What are growth, profit, and balanced portfolios?
7. What tests are used for determining the consistency of objectives and policies?
8. Outline the process for formulating a competitive strategy.
9. What is PIMS?
10. Describe the following reports:
    a. Par report
    b. Strategy report
    c. Optimum strategy report

11. What is value-based planning?
12. Describe the influence of each of the following factors on the strategy evaluation and selection process:
    a. Managerial attitudes toward risk
    b. Environment of the organization
    c. Organizational culture and power relationships
    d. Competitive actions and reactions
    e. Previous organizational strategies
    f. Timing

DISCUSSION QUESTIONS

1. Which variable or variables do you think have the most influence in an organization's strategy evaluation and selection process? Why?
2. Which of the techniques discussed in this chapter do you think is the most useful? Why?
3. Choose an organization with which you have some familiarity and describe its business using the business portfolio matrix.
4. Do you think that most small organizations have a large number of strategic options? Why or why not?

REFERENCES AND ADDITIONAL READING

1. For a discussion of the application of the growth-share matrix, see Bruce D. Henderson and Alan J. Zakon, "Corporate Growth Strategy: How to Develop and Implement It," in *Handbook of Business Problem Solving*, Kenneth J. Albert (ed.) (New York: McGraw-Hill, 1980), pp. 1.3–1.19.
2. See Arnoldo C. Hax and Nicholas S. Majluk, "The Use of Growth-Share Matrix in Strategic Planning," *Interfaces* 13 (February 1983):46–60.
3. See, for instance, Richard A. Bettis and William K. Hall, "The Business Portfolio Approach—Where It Falls Down in Practice," *Long Range Planning* 16 (April 1983):95–104.
4. Richard Rumelt, "Evaluation of Strategy: Theory and Models," in *Strategic Management: A New View of Business Policy Planning*, Dan E. Schendel and Charles W. Hofer (eds.) (Boston: Little, Brown, 1979), p. 210.
5. For a discussion of effectively managing dog businesses, see H. Kurt Christensen, Arnold C. Cooper, and Cornelis A. DeKluyver, "The Dog Business: A Re-examination," *Business Horizons* 25 (November–December, 1982):12–18.
6. Carolyn Y. Y. Woo and Arnold C. Cooper, "Strategies of Effective Low Market Share Businesses," *Academy of Management Proceedings*, August 1980, pp. 21–25.
7. Much of the material in the following sections is adapted from Arnoldo C. Hax and Nicholas S. Majluk, "The Use of the Industry Attractiveness–Business Strength Matrix in Strategic Planning," *Interfaces* 13 (April 1983):34–71.
8. For other definitions, see Joel K. Leidecker and Albert V. Brano, "Identifying and Using Critical Success Factors," *Long Range Planning* 17 (February 1984):23–32.

9. For a more detailed description of critical success factors, see York P. Freund, "Critical Success Factors," *Planning Review,* July/August 1988, pp. 20–23.

10. C. W. Hofer, *Conceptual Constructs for Formulating Corporate and Business Strategies* (Boston: Intercollegiate Case Clearing House, 9-378-754, 1977).

11. C. W. Hofer and Dan Schendel, *Strategy Formulation: Analytical Concepts* (St. Paul, Minn.: West Publishing Company, 1978), p. 182.

12. See Michael E. Porter, *Competitive Strategy* (New York: Free Press, 1980).

13. Donald C. Hambrick, Ian C. MacMillan, and Diana L. Day, "Strategic Attributes and Performance in the BCG Matrix—A PIMS-Based Analysis of Industrial Product Businesses," *Academy of Management Journal* 25 (September 1982):515.

14. Carl R. Anderson and Frank T. Paine, "PIMS—A Reexamination," *Academy of Management Review* 3 (July 1978):603.

15. Bernard C. Reimann, "Managing for the Shareholders: An Overview of Value-Based Planning," *Planning Review,* January/February 1988, p. 10.

16. For a discussion of other qualitative factors in the strategy evaluation and selection process, see Michael A. McGinnis, "The Key to Strategic Planning: Integrating Analysis and Interaction," *Sloan Management Review* 26 (Fall 1984):45–52.

Strategy in Action Case Study: Ford Motor Company

Chapter 5: Strategy Evaluation and Selection

The use of two methodologies—the growth-share matrix and the industry attractiveness–business strength matrix—are described in relation to Ford Motor Company in this case study.

GROWTH-SHARE MATRIX

Ford Motor Company has diversified into three main business units. They are Automotive, Financial Services, and Diversified Products Operations (DPO). Ford Financial Services Group consists of Ford Motor Credit Company, First Nationwide Financial Corporation, United States Leasing International Inc., and Ford's international credit affiliates. DPO consists of ten automotive and nonautomotive businesses, including Ford New Holland, a major producer of agricultural equipment, and Climate Control, which produces heaters and air-conditioning systems. Ford Automotive is the core business of Ford, and it has two main components—North American Automotive Operations and International Automotive Operations.

One of the first problems encountered in using the growth-share matrix for Ford is that Ford does not report separate financial data for its DPO business unit. Thus, it is impossible to make the necessary calculations for locating it on the matrix.

Another problem is determining market share and market growth rate in complex industries. For example, it is difficult to compare Ford's financial services business unit with industry financial service organizations. The financial services industry is complex itself, with companies such as mutual savings banks, bank holding companies, savings and loan institutions, insurance companies, and other credit institutions.

So, in trying to compare Ford's financial services business unit with the industry, one encounters major problems trying to decide exactly who Ford's competitors are. Therefore, the growth-share matrix will be analyzed using only Ford's automotive division.

Exhibit 1 shows the calculations necessary to determine relative market share and market growth rate for Ford's automotive operations. Exhibit 2 shows the location of automotive services on the growth-share matrix. From Exhibit 1, automotive operations would have a circle eight times greater than financial services. The Ford automotive operations SBU is a dog because its market share is 0.75 and its market growth rate is 6.14 percent. (These figures are based on Ford and GM automotive operations worldwide, not just the United States.) As can be seen from the calculations, Ford's automotive operations have a low relative market share and a low market growth rate.

The major problem in applying the growth-share matrix to a worldwide organization such as Ford is that this matrix would lead one to believe that Ford's automotive division should be harvested, divested, or liquidated, which is usually what happens to dogs according to the Boston Consulting Group. As can clearly be seen, Ford's automotive operations unit is not a dog since it represents 89 percent of Ford's total company sales and earned over $4 billion

Exhibit 1 *Ford Worldwide Automotive Operations (Car and Truck)*

$$\text{Relative market share (1988)} = \frac{\text{Business unit sales (current Ford)}}{\text{Leading competitor's sales (current GM)}}$$

$$= \frac{82,193}{110,228.5}$$

$$= 0.7457$$

$$\text{Market growth rate (1988)} = \frac{\text{(Total market 1988)} - \text{(total market 1987)}}{\text{Total market 1987}}$$

$$= \frac{31,673,748 - 29,842,348}{29,842,348}$$

$$= 0.0614$$

$$\text{Size of circle} = \frac{\text{Sales of automotive operations (1988)}}{\text{Total sales (1988)}}$$

$$= \frac{82,193}{92,445}$$

$$= 0.89$$

Exhibit 2 *Location of Automotive Services on Growth-Share Matrix*

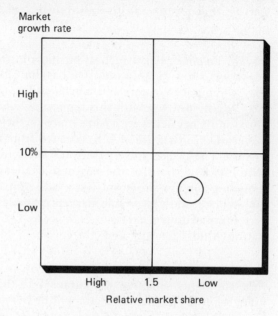

in 1988. It is by far the most profitable business unit in Ford's portfolio. Thus, instead of harvesting, divesting, or liquidating the automotive unit, Ford has continued to pursue a growth strategy.

INDUSTRY ATTRACTIVENESS–BUSINESS STRENGTH MATRIX

A wider variety of factors need to be identified and assessed to develop an industry attractiveness–business strength matrix. The use of the matrix first requires an identification of both critical external factors and critical success factors. Critical external factors are not directly controllable by the organization and determine the overall attractiveness of the industry in which the business unit operates. The critical success factors are generally controllable by the organization and determine the business unit's strength. Both of these factors will be used to determine the overall industry attractiveness and business strength of the U.S. automotive industry and Ford Motor Company.

Defining and Assessing Critical External Factors

In defining and assessing the critical external factors for the U.S. automotive industry, some of the primary factors that are examined are market volume, pricing, and technology. Each factor will be given a rating of extremely attractive, mildly attractive, even or neutral, mildly unattractive, or extremely unattractive to determine an overall industry attractiveness of low, medium, or high.

Market Volume For a cyclical business in the seventh year of an economic expansion, the U.S. auto industry has done surprisingly well. In model year 1989, the number of cars and trucks sold in the United States was estimated at 15.9 million. Even with this high sales volume, however, General Motors, Ford, and Chrysler were losing more of their home market to Japanese car makers. Detroit's share of U.S. sales fell from 84 percent in 1978 to 68 percent in 1989. The projections of Detroit's declining market share actually understate the dimensions of the Japanese challenge in the 1990s. Instead of just scrapping for low-profit small-car sales, Japan's automakers are making an assault on the most profitable markets in the auto industry: mid-size and luxury cars and pickup trucks.
Rating: Mildly unattractive.

Pricing Automaking is a business with very high fixed costs. Profits, therefore, are highly sensitive to volume. With the projected shrinkage of overall sales, the Big Three automakers will be hurting. Currently their margins are about 2.2 percent for profit after taxes.
Rating: Extremely unattractive.

Technology Successful companies must target their customers with precision and then speed their products to dealers. Shorter cycles reduce the odds of guessing wrong because the interval between planning and execution is shorter. Japanese automakers traditionally redesign 80 percent of their models in five-year intervals, whereas American automakers change only 40 percent.

Despite some of the challenges facing the U.S. automakers, they have made progress in productivity, quality, and technology that might have seemed impossible a few years ago. They dominate in market segments where the Japanese do not compete, including full-size sedans and station wagons. Pickup trucks built by American manufacturers enjoy overwhelming market shares.
Rating: Mildly attractive.

- *Overall attractiveness for the U.S. auto industry is in the medium-low range.*

Defining and Assessing Critical Success Factors

Critical success factors that have had a significant impact on the business strength of Ford Motor Company are manufacturing capability, profitability, market share, and product line. The critical success factors are given a rating of severe competitive disadvantage, mild competitive disadvantage, equal or neutral, mild competitive advantage, or great competitive advantage to determine the overall rating of low, medium, or high for Ford's business strength in the auto industry.

Manufacturing Capacity Ford's car and truck production capacity for the North American market has increased to an annual level more than 1 million units higher than in 1985. Most of the increase came from expansion and modernization of existing plants; some came from sources other than the North American facilities.
Rating: Great competitive advantage.

Market Share Ford's U.S. car market share rose by 1.5 percentage points from 1987 to 21.8 percent in 1988—the highest Ford share in ten years. Ford truck sales reached an all-time high in the U.S. truck industry market, and Ford's truck share remained strong at 29 percent.
Rating: Great competitive advantage.

Product Line In the past decade, the Ford Taurus was the most successful car of the decade. The best-selling autos in the United States have been the Ford Escort and Taurus. Ford continued to lead the truck market with the F-series pickup. Ford also leads in 9 of the 16 market segments in which it competes.
Rating: Great competitive advantage.

Profitability A combination of lower sales volume and higher product development and marketing costs (i.e., incentives averaging slightly over $1000 per vehicle) caused Ford to lose $37 million in its North American operations in the September 1989 quarter, the first time this has happened since 1982. But Ford does have the highest capacity utilization rate (95 percent) and the lowest cost per unit among domestic makers and is the company best equipped to weather a mild slowdown.
Rating: Mild competitive advantage.

- *Overall rating of Ford's business strength in the U.S. automotive industry is high.*

In summary, the U.S. automotive industry attractiveness is in the medium-low range whereas Ford Motor Company business strength is high. Thus, Exhibit 3 shows where Ford would fall on the matrix.

Exhibit 3 *Industry Attractiveness–Business Strength Matrix*

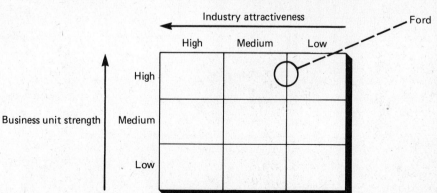

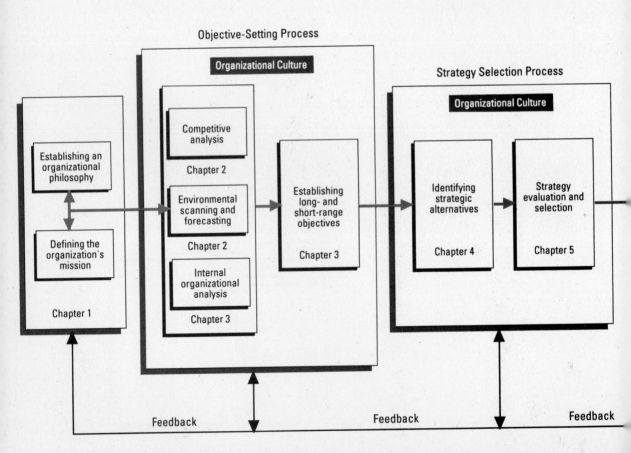

STRATEGIC MANAGEMENT PROCESS

Strategy Formulation

Objective-Setting Process

Organizational Culture

Strategy Selection Process

Organizational Culture

Establishing an organizational philosophy

Defining the organization's mission

Chapter 1

Competitive analysis

Chapter 2

Environmental scanning and forecasting

Chapter 2

Internal organizational analysis

Chapter 3

Establishing long- and short-range objectives

Chapter 3

Identifying strategic alternatives

Chapter 4

Strategy evaluation and selection

Chapter 5

Feedback

Feedback

Feedback

PART FOUR
STRATEGY IMPLEMENTATION

Strategy Implementation →

Organizational Culture

Strategy, structure, and organizational leadership	Developing budgets, functional strategies, and motivational systems	Strategic control systems
Chapter 6	Chapter 7	Chapter 8

Feedback   Feedback

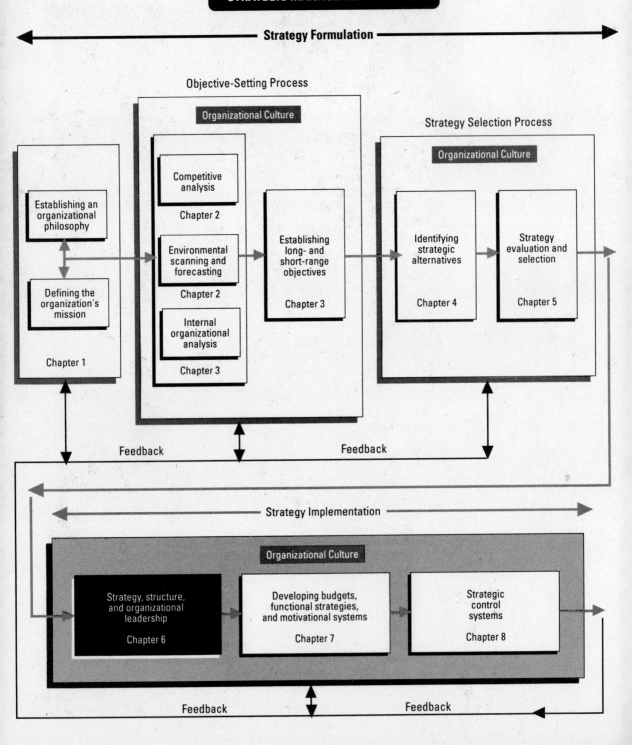

STRATEGIC MANAGEMENT PROCESS

Strategy Formulation

Objective-Setting Process

Organizational Culture

Establishing an organizational philosophy

Defining the organization's mission

Chapter 1

Competitive analysis

Chapter 2

Environmental scanning and forecasting

Chapter 2

Internal organizational analysis

Chapter 3

Establishing long- and short-range objectives

Chapter 3

Strategy Selection Process

Organizational Culture

Identifying strategic alternatives

Chapter 4

Strategy evaluation and selection

Chapter 5

Feedback

Feedback

Strategy Implementation

Organizational Culture

Strategy, structure, and organizational leadership

Chapter 6

Developing budgets, functional strategies, and motivational systems

Chapter 7

Strategic control systems

Chapter 8

Feedback

Feedback

CHAPTER 6
Strategy, Structure, and Organizational Leadership

LEARNING OBJECTIVES

After studying this chapter, you should be able to

1. Define organization.
2. Describe the organizing process.
3. Discuss the functional, product, customer, and geographic methods of departmentation.
4. Discuss the contingency approach to organizing.
5. Outline three questions that need to be answered before an effective structure can be designed.
6. Outline several reasons why a business might be restructured.
7. Define organizational leadership.
8. Describe the function of a board of directors.
9. Present the responsibilities of a board of directors.
10. Define due care for a member of a board of directors.

Strategies are carried out through organizations. An *organization* is a group of people working together in a coordinated effort to attain a set of objectives that could not be achieved by individuals working separately. *Organizing* is the grouping of activities necessary to attain a set of objectives and the assignment of each grouping to a person who has the authority necessary to manage the people performing the activities. Thus, organizing basically is the division of labor accompanied by the delegation of authority. The framework that defines the boundaries of the organization and within which the organization operates is the organizational structure.

In addition to developing a structure appropriate for implementing strategy, organizations must have effective leadership if they are to be successful in achieving their objectives. Leadership is a critical element in strategy implementation. Both organizational structure and leadership are explored in this chapter in relation to their impact on the strategy implementation process.

STRATEGY AND STRUCTURE

A major part of an organization's strategy for attaining its objectives concerns how the organization is structured. The structure of an organization is reflected in how groups compete for resources, where responsibilities for profits and other performance measures lie, how information is transmitted, and how decisions are made. In addition to clarifying and defining strategy through the delegation of authority and responsibility, the structure of the organization can either facilitate or inhibit strategy implementation.

In a ground-breaking study of organizational strategy, Alfred D. Chandler described a pattern in the evolution of organizational structures.[1] The pattern was based on studies of du Pont, General Motors, Sears, Roebuck & Co., and Standard Oil Company, with corroborating evidence from many other firms. The pattern Chandler described was that of changing strategy, followed by administrative problems, leading to decline in performance, revised structure, and a subsequent return to economic health. In summary, Chandler concluded that structure follows strategy. In other words, changes in strategy ultimately led to or resulted in changes in the organization's structure. Chandler's work related particularly to growth and to the structural adjustments that were made to maintain efficient performance during market expansion, product line diversification, and vertical integration.

Although subsequent research has supported the existence of a relationship between strategy and structure, it is clear that strategy is not the only variable that has a bearing on structure.[2] It can safely be concluded that the process of matching structure to strategy is complex and should be undertaken with a thorough understanding of the historical development of the current structure, the requirements of the organization's environment and technology, and the political relationships that might be affected. The process of departmentation, which is the primary means used to structure an organization, is briefly discussed in the next section.

DEPARTMENTATION

While thousands of different organizational structures exist, almost all are built on the concept of departmentation. *Departmentation* is the grouping of activities into related work units. The work units may be related on the basis of work functions, product, customer, geography, or time.

Functional

Functional departmentation occurs when organizational units are defined by the nature of the work they perform. Although different terms may be used, most organizations have three basic functions: production, sales, and finance. Production refers to the actual creation of something of value, either goods or services or both. The distribution of goods or services created is usually referred to as sales or marketing. Finally, any organization, manufacturing or service, must provide the financial structure necessary for carrying out its activities.

Each of these basic functions may be broken down as necessary. For instance, the production department may be split into maintenance, quality control, engineering, manufacturing, and so on. The marketing department may be grouped into advertising, sales, and market research. (Figure 6.1 shows a typical functional departmentation.)

Figure 6.1 Functional Departmentation

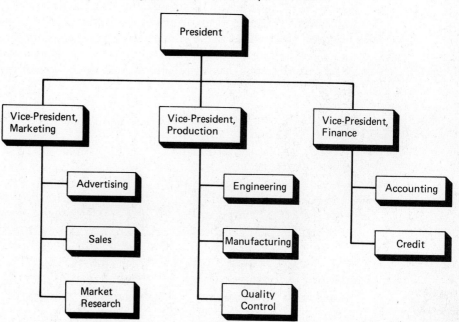

The primary advantage of functional departmentation is that it allows for specialization within functions. It also provides for efficient use of equipment and resources. However, functional departmentation can be accompanied by some negative effects. Members of a functional group may develop more loyalty to the functional group's objectives than to the organization's objectives. If the group's objectives and the organization's objectives are not mutually supportive, this can lead to problems. Conflict may also develop between different departments striving for different objectives.

Product or Service

Under *departmentation by product or service,* all the activities needed to produce and market a product or service are grouped together. This system allows employees to identify with a particular product and thus develop esprit de corps. It also facilitates managing each product as a distinct profit center. Product departmentation provides opportunities for training executive personnel by letting them experience a broad range of functional activities. Problems can arise if departments become overly competitive to the detriment of the overall organization. A second potential problem is that facilities and equipment may have to be duplicated. Product departmentation adapts best to large multiproduct organizations. Figure 6.2 illustrates product departmentation at the Allied Corporation.

Geographic

Geographic departmentation is the grouping of activities by geographic area. It is most likely to occur in organizations that maintain physically dispersed and autonomous operations or offices. Departmentation by territories permits the use of local workers and/or salespeople. This can create customer goodwill and an awareness of local feelings and desires. It can also provide a high level of service. Of course, having too many geographic locations can be very costly.

Figure 6.2 Product Departmentation

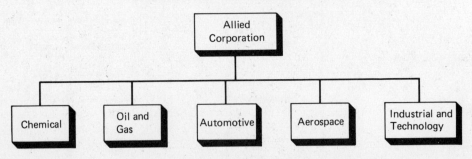

Figure 6.3 Customer Departmentation

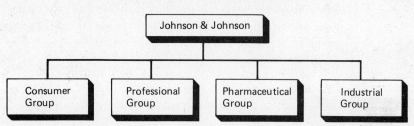

Customer

Another type, *customer departmentation,* is based on division by customers. A common example is an organization that has one department to handle retail customers and one to handle wholesale or industrial customers. (Figure 6.3 shows departmentation by customer for Johnson & Johnson.) This type of departmentation has the same advantages and disadvantages as product departmentation. For example, if the Professional Group and the Pharmaceutical Group in Figure 6.3 became too competitive with each other for corporate resources, the organization's overall performance could be damaged.

Other Types

Several other types of departmentation are possible. Departmentation by simple numbers is practiced when the most important ingredient to success is the number of workers. Organizing for a local United Way drive might be an example. Departmentation by process or equipment is another possibility. A final type of departmentation is by time or shift. Organizations that work around the clock may use this type of departmentation.

Departmentation is practiced not only for division of labor but also to improve control and communications. Typically, as an organization grows, it adds levels of departmentation. A small organization may have no departmentation at first. As it grows, it may departmentalize first by function, then by product, then by geography. Many different department mixes are possible for a given organization. The appendix at the end of this chapter summarizes the potential strengths and weaknesses of organizational structure types.

CONTINGENCY APPROACH TO ORGANIZING

No organizational structure is applicable to all situations. Recognition by management practitioners and scholars that there is no universal best way to organize has led to the evolution of a contingency or situational approach to organizing. The *contingency approach to organizing* recognizes that the most appropriate organizational structure depends primarily on the organization's objectives and strategy but also is influenced by the size and growth stage of the organization, the environmental conditions it faces, and the technology it employs.

Organizational Size and Growth Stage

Size and growth stage is a key variable in determining an organization's structure. The most appropriate structure for a small computer company, for instance, would be considerably different from the most appropriate structure for the IBM Corporation. Thus, as an organization grows (in terms of both employees and product line) it requires different organizational structures.

Several attempts have been made to develop a model for describing the various stages of organizational growth.[3] The basic idea behind these models is that organizations grow along a continuum from simple to complex. Furthermore, the models describe positions along the continuum and postulate that as an organization reaches a particular point on the continuum a different organizational structure should be implemented.

Many of the growth-stage models developed from the work of Alfred Chandler. Although Chandler did not specifically develop a growth-stage model, his work was one of the first to demonstrate the relationship between structure and growth or size of the organization.[4]

Later, J. Thomas Cannon proposed five stages of organizational growth:[5]

1. *Entrepreneurial Stage* Decisions are made mostly by the top person. The organizational structure is rather informal, with minimal coordination requirements. Communications are also on an informal basis.
2. *Functional Development Stage* Decisions are made more and more through other managers and less and less by the top manager. The organizational structure is based on specialization by functions, and problems of coordination among functions arise. Communications become more important and more difficult. The problems associated with this stage move an organization into the third stage.
3. *Decentralization Stage* Management copes with the problems of a growing functional business by decentralizing. Organizational structures are developed on a division or product basis. The idea is to develop minibusinesses within the organization that can be managed under the conditions described earlier in the entrepreneurial stage. However, problems arise. Flexibility in shifting resources from one area to another in order to exploit new opportunities is reduced. Expenses are often increased from duplication of effort. Finally, top management may feel that they have lost control of the minibusinesses in the decentralization stage. These problems often cause an organization to move into one of the final two stages.
4. *Staff Proliferation Stage* This stage involves adding staff at the corporate level to assist top management in planning and control of the minibusinesses. Today, virtually all large organizations have corporate staffs. The greatest

problems with adding staff are the inherent conflict that develops between line and staff and the time delays associated with staff review of proposals.

5. *Recentralization Stage* Sometimes, organizations resolve the problems of the decentralization and staff proliferation stages by recentralization. Recentralization is very similar to the functional development stage, with many of the same problems. Computerization of information and sophisticated control systems enable the management of organizations to move to this stage.

Obviously, not all organizations pass through these stages in sequence. They move through the stages in different and often unpredictable ways. However, it does appear that as organizations move from small, single-product organizations to large, multiproduct organizations, organizational structures change with this growth in size. It also appears that increasing organizational size fosters more rules, procedures, and job descriptions, which are all devices that formalize behavior.

Organizational Environment

A classic study relating organizational structure to environment examined 20 industrial organizations and identified two distinct organizational structure types.[6] One, labeled *mechanistic systems,* had a rigid delineation of functional duties, precise job descriptions, fixed authority and responsibility, and a well-developed organizational hierarchy. The other, labeled *organic systems,* had less formal job descriptions, greater emphasis on adaptability, more participation, and less fixed authority. The study found that successful organizations in stable and established industries tended to have mechanistic structures. Successful organizations in dynamic and changing industries tended to have organic structures. Another study that examined the relationship between organizational structure and environment concluded that, in order to be successful, organizations operating in a dynamic environment needed a relatively flexible structure, those in a stable environment needed a more rigid structure, and those in an intermediate environment needed a structure somewhere between the two extremes.[7]

Many other studies have been conducted on the relationship between environment and organizational structure.[8] In general, most have concluded that the most effective structure for a particular organization depends to some extent on the conditions of its environment.

Technology and Structure

One of the classic studies examining the relationship between organizational structure and the technology used by an organization analyzed 100 organizations in Great Britain.[9] This study classified organizations along a scale of technical complexity based on their method of production. The study also identified the following three methods of production: (1) unit or batch production (e.g., custom-made products), (2) large-scale or mass production (e.g., an assembly line operation), and (3) continuous-flow or process production (e.g., a chemical or paper plant). The unit production method is at the lower end of the technical complexity scale whereas the continuous-flow method is at the upper end.

Each organization was classified into one of the three categories, and a number of organizational variables was investigated. This study yielded several findings relating to organizational structures:

- The number of levels of management increased as technical complexity increased.[10]
- Using the previously discussed definition of organic and mechanistic systems, organic systems predominated in organizations using unit or continuous-flow production methods, whereas mechanistic systems predominated in organizations using a large-scale production method.[11]
- No significant relationship was found between technical complexity and organizational size.[12]
- The ratio of managers and supervisors to total personnel increased with technical complexity.[13]

Another study analyzed the relationship between technology and structure in 43 organizations, classified along a continuum from technical diffuseness to technical specificity. Technically diffuse organizations were described as having a wider product line, producing products that vary from year to year, and producing more made-to-order products. Organizations described as having technical specificity produced products that had much less variation and change. Similar to the findings of earlier studies, this study found significant relationships between technology and organizational structure.[14]

Many additional studies have investigated the relationship between technology and structure.[15] Although much research has been concerned with whether size or technology is the more important variable, most studies have concluded that technology plays a key role in determining an organization's structure.

ASSESSING AN ORGANIZATION'S STRUCTURE

There are several points at which the management of an organization should assess the appropriateness of its structure.[16] One obvious point is when the organization is having severe performance problems in achieving its objectives. Leadership changes, such as with retirements, resignations, or terminations, almost always lead to changes in organizational structure. Finally, changes in organizational strategy should lead to an assessment of the appropriateness of the structure.

Many other symptoms also point to an ineffective organizational structure.

According to Peter Drucker, the multiplication of management levels is the most common and most serious symptom.[17] Too many management levels make coordination and communication difficult, if not impossible. Another symptom of organizational ineffectiveness is too many meetings attended by too many people. Some organizations, unfortunately, seem to be structured in such a fashion that meetings are the norm, not the exception. In effective organizational structures, the need for meetings should be minimized. Another common symptom of an ineffective structure is when too much attention is directed toward following proper procedures or resolving interdepartmental conflicts. Effective organizational structures help resolve interdepartmental conflicts quickly. Other problems that often result from an inappropriate organizational structure include lack of opportunities for general management development, too much concentration on operational issues, lack of coordination among business units within the organization, neglect of special markets, excessive decision making at the top, and overworked key personnel.[18] In the final analysis, the effectiveness of an organization's structure is reflected in how well the organization achieves its objectives. An effective structure should facilitate the accomplishment of organizational objectives.

GUIDELINES IN DESIGNING EFFECTIVE ORGANIZATIONAL STRUCTURES

Because no organizational structure is applicable to all situations, there are no absolute guidelines for choosing the one best structure. For example, one of the oldest, largest, and most successful organizations is the Roman Catholic church. Its organizational structure, which has changed little over the years, is extremely simple. Basically, the parish priest reports to a bishop, and the bishop reports to a cardinal who, in turn, reports to the pope. On the other hand, large business organizations regularly change structures and often have many layers of management between the president and operative employees. This section offers some general guidelines for designing organizational structures.

Simple Structures

Peter Drucker has proposed that the simplest organizational structure that will do the job is the best one.[19] He postulated that the following three questions need to be answered before an effective structure can be designed:[20]

1. In what area is excellence required in order to achieve the organization's objectives?
2. In what areas would lack of performance endanger the results, if not the survival, of the organization?
3. What values are truly important to the company? Product quality? Product safety? Customer service?

The answers to these questions identify the functions and activities that are essential for achieving organizational objectives. These activities should serve as the basis for developing an organizational structure. Other activities should be ranked according to the contribution they make in achieving organizational objectives. This contribution determines the ranking and placement of activities. Key activities should never be subordinate to non-key activities. Revenue-producing activities should never be subordinate to non-revenue-producing activities. Structuring the organization on the basis of the contribution made in achieving organizational objectives greatly enhances the likelihood that these same objectives will be achieved.

Simple Structure, Lean Staff

As an organization grows and succeeds, it tends to evolve into a more and more complex structure. Just how this takes place varies; frequently, a major cause is an increase in staff positions, especially at high levels. Many managers seem to feel a need for more staff and a more complex structure as the organization grows; they seem inclined to equate staff size with success.

In their study, Thomas Peters and Robert Waterman found that many of the best-performing companies had managed to maintain a simple structure with a small staff.[21] A simple structure with a lean staff better allows an organization to adjust to a fast-changing environment and is also conducive to innovation. A simple structure and a lean staff are naturally intertwined in that one breeds the other: A simple structure requires fewer staff, and a lean staff results in a simple structure.

Peters and Waterman outline four characteristics or practices that enable organizations to maintain a simple structure and a lean staff:[22]

1. Extraordinary divisional integrity. Each division has its own functional areas, including product development, finance, and personnel.
2. Continual formation of new divisions and rewards for this practice.
3. A set of guidelines that determine when a new product or product line will become an independent division.
4. The moving of people and even products among divisions on a regular basis without causing disruption.

Peters and Waterman postulate that the successful organizations of the future will be variations of the simple, divisionalized line and staff structure and that they will have the above characteristics.

REASONS FOR RESTRUCTURING AN ORGANIZATION

Unfortunately, the terms *restructuring* or *reorganizing* are used primarily in connection with organizational changes made during troubled times. Some of the restructuring changes made include layoffs in personnel to deal with profitability or cash flow problems, sales of assets to reduce levels of debt, divestments of business units or idle assets, and major capital borrowings to increase returns an equity.

However, businesses can be restructured during good times as well. Changes in structure may be needed to deal with increases in a company's size, diversity of products, or customer base; acquisitions to broaden product lines; or joint ventures to enter larger and broader fields of business.

One recent study found that most of the Fortune 500 companies are or recently were involved in some form of restructuring, for the following reasons:[23]

- To improve profitability
- To improve productivity
- To meet competition
- To refocus strategically
- To improve balance sheet ratios
- To enhance growth rates

Many forces interact to influence organizational structure, but an organization's structure cannot be changed every time one of these forces changes. If it did, the organization would be in a continuous state of reorganization. Unfortunately, some organizations do seem to be in such a state, which generally only results in confusion and chaos. Changes in organizational structure cannot offset a bad strategy, poor product offerings, or having the wrong people in key positions.

MANAGEMENT ACTIONS REQUIRED IN RESTRUCTURING AN ORGANIZATION

After it has been determined that a particular organizational structure is inappropriate, certain steps need to be taken to move to a more appropriate structure. First, top management must decide what it is trying to achieve with the new structure. Some of the objectives of a reorganization may be to increase productivity, increase sales, improve service, control costs, eliminate overlaps in responsibilities, maximize utilization of critical staff skills, establish clearly defined functional units, or decentralize the decision-making process.[24]

Next, top management must decide on what structure is to be used. Organizational structures of all types and varieties exist. Each has its own potential strengths and vulnerabilities. The appendix at the end of this chapter summarizes the various organizational styles and outlines the potential strengths and weaknesses of each in terms of their competitive response, market response, and internal functioning.

Finally, top management should establish a timetable for implementing the changes. This timetable should then be communicated to all levels of management.

For best results, the active participation of all management levels should be encouraged throughout the restructuring process. Participation creates a feeling of "ownership" and leads to greater acceptance of the new structure when it is implemented. Top management should inform all levels of management why it feels reorganization is necessary and should encourage open discussion of these reasons. Management should also attempt to explain how reorganization will benefit not only the organization but also the individuals involved in the changes. Example 6.1 shows how Ralston Purina uses many of the principles described in this chapter in structuring its business.

ORGANIZATIONAL LEADERSHIP

A critical ingredient in strategy implementation is the skills and abilities of the organization's leaders. A leader is an individual who is able to influence the attitudes and opinions of others. Unfortunately, too many senior managers are merely able to influence employee actions and decisions. Leadership is not a synonym for management; it is a higher order of capability.[25]

Organizational leadership—the ability to influence the attitudes and opinions of others in order to achieve a coordinated effort from a diverse group of employees—is a difficult task. However, one of the key methods available to management is creating an overall sense of direction and purpose through effective strategic planning.

How is this accomplished? First, most employees have some idea about the performance of the organization and have some degree of understanding of the strengths, weaknesses, opportunities for, and threats to their organization. In other words, they have a general idea about what their organization should be doing. Next, each employee also has a concept of what the organization is presently doing. Finally, employees are influenced by the organizational structure and leadership and develop a concept of what they should be doing to improve organizational performance and for their own self-interest.[26] Figure 6.4 graphically shows how employees develop these three perceptions. Obviously, the challenge of leadership in an organization is to develop systems that bring these three perceptions in line or as close as possible. In addition, in order for any organization to be successful, its leadership must have a clear vision of the organization's mission and objectives, must be effective in communicating this vision, must have the will to change difficult things in the business, and must demand uncompromising integrity.[27] Example 6.2 describes the leadership style of Ken Olsen, who has been called America's most successful entrepreneur.

Another area of interest in organizational leadership is the complementary relationship between manager selection and organizational strategy. Many contend that without a linkage between manager selection and strategy, an organization risks either sacrificing a well-planned strategy to a manager who is ill suited to implement it or hiring a key manager without a clear rationale

Ralston Purina's Management Structure

Ralston Purina Company was founded in 1894. Today it is

- The world's largest producer of dry dog and dry and soft-moist cat foods, which are marketed under the Purina brand name
- The largest wholesaler baker of fresh bakery products in the United States, with such popular brands as Wonder breads and Hostess sweet baked goods
- The world's largest manufacturer of dry cell battery products, including the Eveready and Energizer brand products
- A producer of breakfast cereals, such as Chex products, and cookies, crackers, and snack foods
- A major producer of isolated soy proteins and, outside the United States, of feeds for livestock and poultry

In the 1988 annual report, William P. Stiritz, chief executive officer of Ralston Purina, stated the following about the company's organization structure:

> We still believe a decentralized organization structure is the most rational way to manage the corporation. Our operating units are sized to stand alone and each has the scale required to compete in its respective market. All of our operating units are strong cash providers: high achievers do not subsidize under-performers.
>
> We maintain a corporate staff which is limited in size and scope. Most of the staff functions that support the operations are organized as independent service businesses and, where possible, subjected to outside competition. Managers are rewarded for the quality and value of services provided, not for the size of their departments. The intent is to constrain bureaucratic behavior and keep overhead costs low.
>
> We try to keep the operating environment simple and straightforward. We keep management layers to a minimum—there are no group officers or staff and no management committees of consequence. As a result, the lines of communication throughout the company are short. Moreover, we do not impose a standardized regimen of management systems and processes upon the operating companies. In this way we try to avoid the type of organizational structure that focuses excessively on control in favor of one that encourages creative thinking and innovation.

Source: 1988 Annual Report.

for that particular choice.[28] The assumption here is that the style of managers can and does influence their effectiveness in carrying out particular strategies. On the other hand, matching managerial style to an organization's unique situation is a most difficult and challenging task. It is apparent, however, that certain organizational cultures and strategies are better suited for certain styles of leadership. Thus, when an organization is experiencing difficulties or is operating in a considerably different environment, it is not unusual for that

Figure 6.4 Sources of the Individual Perceptions of Organizational Strategies

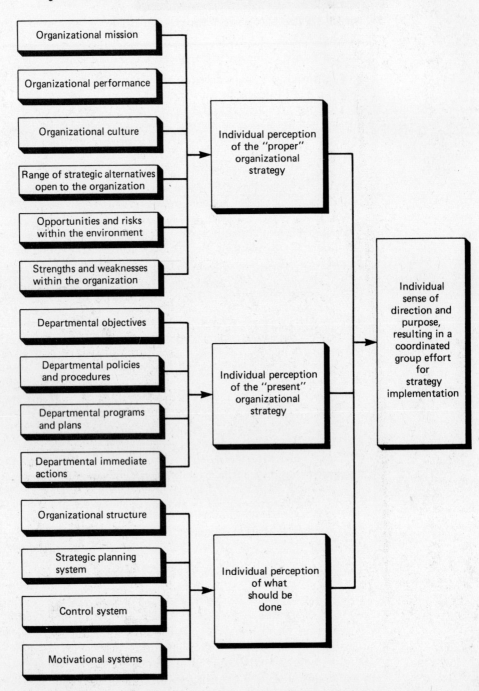

Source: Adapted from LaRue Tone Hosmer, "The Importance of Strategic Leadership," *Journal of Business Strategy* 3 (Fall 1982):56.

STRATEGY IN ACTION Example 6.2

Ken Olsen: America's Most Successful Entrepreneur

Ken Olsen was called America's most successful entrepreneur by *Fortune* magazine. He started Digital Equipment Corporation (DEC) from nothing, turned it into a $7.6-billion business in 29 years, and is IBM's most serious challenger in 20 years.

Olsen's technical interest began at the age of 14, when he and his brother built a radio station. In 1944, he joined the Navy, where he received his first formal training in engineering. In 1947 he entered MIT and left in 1952 with a master's degree in electrical engineering.

Olsen had his first exposure to IBM in 1951, when he was working on the nation's first air defense system as a research assistant. He was shocked at the regimentation and insularity of the culture Thomas Watson had created. He was later heard saying about IBM, "I can beat these guys at their own game."

The church has played an integral part of Olsen's life, and coincidentally it is where he first received management experience—as a Sunday school superintendent. Many of the church's puritan values have been vital to Olsen's management style. He believes in the philosophies of the colonial-age primers: humility, gentleness, peace, neatness, temperance, and long suffering. These values, not microchips, are Olsen's favorite topics of conversation.

Olsen's management style is quirky, contradictory, and demanding. He encourages executives to voice their differences and seek product flaw advice from factory workers. He is an autocrat, yet he rarely issues direct orders. He declares that "a good manager never has to make any decisions at all." In order to make the necessary business decisions, he utilizes committees. Olsen is a firm believer that this method forces the correct decision to arise. Another one of Olsen's techniques is "pulse management": He probes into a particular area of the company and tries to solve a problem. In 1985, he was using this technique and became irritated with the number of different plugs needed to connect DEC cable products together. He worked on the problem and learned everything necessary about the plugs. This probing led to the current standardized plug.

organization to change its top management in anticipation that a new management team will better enable the organization to meet the situation.

BOARDS OF DIRECTORS

Boards of directors are an integral part of an organization's leadership and have recently received increased attention in regard to their role in strategy implementation. A *board of directors* is a group of people elected by the stockholders of an organization and serves primarily to see that the organization is well managed for all of the organization's stakeholders.[29] The board is the body to whom management is accountable for its actions. Example 6.3 illustrates the importance of the role played by the board of RJR Nabisco.

STRATEGY IN ACTION Example 6.3

RJR Nabisco's Board of Directors

RJR Nabisco's president and chief executive, F. Ross Johnson, surprised Wall Street during the latter part of 1988 by announcing he was considering the biggest leveraged buy-out in history. Many felt that RJR's board would passively go along with Johnson. The board, however, surprised everyone by setting up a special five-member committee to review proposals for buy-outs. The committee made it clear that any sale or breakup would be done on the committee's terms. Not only did the committee give no breaks to the group headed by Johnson, it solicited offers from other groups.

The board of RJR saw their task not as just getting the best immediate price for RJR but as ensuring that shareholders didn't get cut out of possible future gains for the company. They also defined their fiduciary duty as looking out for shareholders, employees, and communities in which RJR operates. Ultimately, the board rejected Johnson's bid and sold out to Kohlberg Kravis Roberts & Co. for about $23.7 billion, which was considerably higher than Johnson's original bid price.

In serving the needs and interests of an organization's stakeholders, the primary responsibilities of the board include the following:

- Evaluating and approving the philosophy, mission, policies, objectives, and strategies
- Overseeing the capitalization, resource allocation, and other financial matters
- Approving or disapproving diversifications, mergers, acquisitions, and divestments
- Establishing the chief executive officer's compensation
- Appraising management's performance
- Ensuring that the organization is developing management talent
- Providing for succession to the chief executive officer's position

Composition of the Board

Most large publicly owned organizations have both inside and outside directors. Inside directors are employees of the organization and include the chief executive and chief operating officers. Outside directors come from a wide variety of sources. Commercial bankers, investment bankers, attorneys, and chief executives of other companies are frequently used sources. In the past, the boards of most organizations were composed mostly of white males. However, in recent years women and minorities, as well as representatives of public-interest groups, have begun to appear on corporate boards.

The number of people on the board varies from organization to organization. It is not unusual for large organizations to have 15 to 20 members on the board.

Structure of the Board

It is a fairly common practice in large organizations to have the chairman of the board also serving as the chief executive officer and concentrating on strategic planning and external relations. The chief operating officer (or president) is then concerned with day-to-day operations and reports to the chairman. Critics of this approach agree that it gives the chairman too much authority and undercuts the independence of the board. They feel that the chairman of the board should have authority over the board functions but should not run the company.

Boards of directors normally have one or more standing or permanent committees. Board committees have different functions but basically serve as the eyes and ears of the full board in particular areas of organizational activities. They keep the full board informed through reports or minutes of committee meetings. Some of the typical committees of the board include the following: executive, audit, compensation, nominating, finance, social responsibility, and planning.

Executive Committee The executive committee is normally granted the power to act with the authority of the full board between board meetings. Typically, the executive committee is involved directly with the chief executive. A chief executive may use this committee as a sounding board on general management problems or issues that affect the organization as a whole.

Audit Committee The audit committee has taken on added significance in recent years due to the pressure for greater exposure of company financial information, increased exposure of directors to legal liability, and legal actions in which public accounting firms have been charged with deficiencies in audits.[30] The most common responsibilities of audit committees are selecting or recommending auditors to the board and/or stockholders, determining the scope of the audit, reviewing the audit results, and reviewing internal accounting procedures. Normally the audit committee only consists of outside directors.

Compensation Committee Compensation committees make recommendations to the board on the compensation (including salary, bonuses, fringe benefits, and stock options) for certain employees of the organization.[31] Normally, these employees include employee directors and officers of the organization.

Nominating Committee The primary responsibility of the nominating committee is to recommend candidates for board membership to the full board.[32]

Finance Committee The finance committee is concerned with the financial decisions of the organization. Its primary responsibilities include reviewing and making recommendations on the financial policies of the organization, monitoring the organization's financial condition and its requirements for funds, making recommendations on financing to be undertaken, reviewing and making recommendations on capital expenditure programs, and evaluating financial planning. As can be seen, the finance committee's role differs from the audit committee's role, which is to provide an independent check on financial reporting and controls. Thus, unlike the audit committee, the membership of the finance committee normally includes employee directors such as the chief executive officer and the chief financial officer.

Social Responsibility Committee   A relatively new committee for most boards, the social responsibility committee is primarily concerned with the effect of the organization on the community, its employees, consumers, the public, and the organization's natural environment.

Planning Committee   The planning committee is primarily concerned with the strategic planning process of the organization.[33] Its functions include reviewing mission statements, objectives, and strategies; monitoring performance against objectives; assessing the organization's strategic planning process; and advising the chief executive officer on strategic issues.

Legal Responsibilities of the Board

Most states have laws requiring the board of directors to "manage" the business of the organization. Generally courts do not require that directors do this on a day-to-day basis. Rather, the board is primarily required to establish broad policies, approve major transactions, and provide general supervision of the management of the organization.

In handling these responsibilities, directors are charged with the duty of due care. *Due care* requires that a director act with the same degree of care, diligence, and skill that a prudent person would exercise under similar circumstances in like positions. Due care is a flexible standard that may have a wide latitude.

The law also recognizes that business decisions require the exercise of judgment and involve risks. Under what is frequently called the *business judgment rule*, theoretically short of fraud, self-dealing, or gross abuse of discretion, a court normally will not interject its own ideas about what should or should not have been done. However, a 1985 decision of the Delaware Supreme Court (*Smith* v. *Van Gorkom*) held that the "business judgment rule" did not protect the directors of the Trans Union Corporation from personal liability in setting too low a price for the sale of the company. The court ruled that the directors were personally liable to the stockholders for the difference between the fair price that might have been received if the directors had acted properly and the lower actual sales price.[34] Interestingly, no charges were made that the directors acted fraudulently or profited personally at the expense of the stockholders. Thus, in minimizing problems of due care and business judgment, a director would be wise to attend board and committee meetings regularly, read all material furnished by management, ask questions at meetings, study all SEC filings, review annual and quarterly reports to stockholders, discuss in full all major actions before the board, make independent inquiries regarding the organization, and register objections when appropriate.[35]

SUMMARY OF LEARNING OBJECTIVES

1. Define an organization.
   An organization is a group of people working together in a coordinated effort to attain a set of objectives that could not be achieved by individuals working separately.
2. Describe the organizing process.
   Organizing is the grouping of activities necessary to attain a set of objectives and the assignment of each grouping to a person who has the authority necessary to manage the people performing the activities.
3. Discuss the functional, product, customer, and geographic methods of departmentation.
   Functional departmentation occurs when organizational units are defined by the nature of the work they perform. Under product departmentation, all the activities needed to produce and market a product or service are grouped together. Geographic departmentation is the grouping of activities by geographic area. Customer departmentation is based on division by customers.
4. Discuss the contingency approach to organizing.
   The contingency approach to organizing recognizes that the most appropriate organizational structure depends primarily on the organization's objectives but also is influenced by the size and growth stage of the organization, the environmental conditions it faces, and the technology it employs.
5. Outline three questions that need to be answered before an effective structure can be designed.
   The questions are as follows:

   - *In what area is excellence required in order to achieve the organization's objectives?*
   - *In what areas would lack of performance endanger the results, if not the survival, of the organization?*
   - *What values are truly important to the company? Product quality? Product safety? Customer service?*

6. Outline several reasons why a business might be restructured.
   A business might be restructured to improve profitability, to improve productivity, to meet competition, to refocus strategically, to improve balance sheet ratios, and to enhance growth rates.

7. Define organizational leadership.

   Organizational leadership is the ability to influence the attitudes and opinions of others in order to achieve a coordinated effort from a diverse group of employees.

8. Describe the function of a board of directors.

   A board of directors is a group of people elected by the stockholders of an organization and serves primarily to see that the organization is well managed for all of the organization's stakeholders.

9. Present the responsibilities of a board of directors.

   The primary responsibilities of the board include the following:

   - *Evaluating and approving the philosophy, mission, policies, objectives, and strategy of the organization*
   - *Overseeing the capitalization, resource allocation, and other financial matters*
   - *Approving or disapproving diversifications, mergers, acquisitions, and divestments*
   - *Establishing the chief executive officer's compensation*
   - *Appraising management's performance*
   - *Ensuring that the organization is developing management talent*
   - *Providing for succession to the chief executive officer's position*

10. Define due care for a member of a board of directors.

    Due care requires that a director act with the degree of care, diligence, and skill a prudent person would exercise under similar circumstances in like positions.

REVIEW QUESTIONS

1. Define organization.
2. Explain the organizing process.
3. Discuss the relationship between strategy and structure.
4. Explain functional, product, geographic, and customer departmentation.
5. Explain the contingency approach to organizing.
6. Name some symptoms that may indicate an inappropriate organizational structure.
7. Discuss several reasons why an organization might be restructured.
8. What general steps need to be taken in restructuring an organization?
9. What is organizational leadership?
10. Outline the primary responsibilities of a board of directors.
11. Describe the responsibilities of the following committees of a board of directors:
    a. Executive
    b. Audit
    c. Compensation
    d. Nominating
    e. Finance
    f. Social responsibility
    g. Planning

12. What is due care?
13. What is the business judgment rule?

DISCUSSION QUESTIONS

1. Describe some of the ways in which an organization's structure can either positively or negatively influence the implementation of strategy.
2. Draw an organizational chart for your college or university. What type of structure does your college or university currently use? Do you think it is effective? How could it be restructured?
3. Choose an organization that has recently been reorganized. Be prepared to discuss why you think the reorganization was necessary.
4. "Most of the organizations that I am familiar with are constantly reorganizing." Do you agree or disagree? Why?

REFERENCES AND ADDITIONAL READING

1. A. D. Chandler, *Strategy and Structure* (Cambridge, Mass.: MIT Press, 1962).
2. Some relevant research includes J. Child, "Organization Structure, Environment, and Performance: The Role of Strategic Choice," *Sociology* 6 (1972):1–22; and R. Rumelt, *Strategy, Structure, and Economic Performance* (Boston: Harvard Business School, Division of Research, 1974).
3. See, for instance, Malcolm S. Salter, "Stages of Corporate Development," *Journal of Business Policy* 1, no. 1 (Spring 1970):23–27; Alan Filley and Robert House, *Managerial Process and Organizational Behavior* (Glenview, Ill.: Scott, Foresman, 1969), pp. 443–455; and Donald H. Thain, "Stages of Corporate Development," *Business Quarterly*, Winter 1969, pp. 32–45.
4. Alfred D. Chandler, Jr., *Strategy and Structure* (Cambridge, Mass.: MIT Press, 1962), p. 14.
5. J. Thomas Cannon, *Business Strategy and Policy* (New York: Harcourt Brace Jovanovich, 1968), pp. 525–528.
6. Tom Burns and G. M. Stalker, *The Management of Innovation* (London: Tavistock Institute, 1962).
7. Paul Lawrence and Jay Lorsch, "Differentiation and Integration in Complex Organizations," *Administrative Science Quarterly* 12 (June 1967):1–47; and Paul Lawrence and Jay Lorsch, *Organization and Environment* (Homewood, Ill.: Irwin, 1969).
8. See, for instance, Jeffrey Pfeffer and Gerald Salancik, *The External Control of Organizations* (New York: Harper & Row, 1978); and Michael Crozier and Jean-Claude Thoenig, "The Regulation of Complex Organized Systems," *Administrative Science Quarterly* 21 (1976):547–570.
9. Joan Woodward, *Management and Technology* (London: H.M.S.O., 1958).
10. Ibid., p. 16.
11. Joan Woodward, *Industrial Organization: Theory and Practice* (London: Oxford University Press, 1965), p. 64.
12. Woodward, *Management and Technology*, p. 20.
13. Ibid., pp. 16–17.

14. Edward Harvey, "Technology and the Structure of Organizations," *American Sociological Review* 33, no. 2 (April 1968):247–259.
15. See, for instance, Denise M. Rousseau and Robert A. Cooke, "Technology and Structure," *Journal of Management* 10 (Fall/Winter 1984):345–361; Pradip N. Khandwalla, "Mass-Output Orientation of Operations Technology and Organization Structure," *Administrative Science Quarterly* 19 (1974):74–97; and Peter M. Blau, Cecilia Falbe, William McKinley, and Phelps K. Tracy, "Technology and Organization in Manufacturing," *Administrative Science Quarterly* 21 (1976):20–40.
16. See, for instance, John R. Kimberly, "The Anatomy of Organizational Design," *Journal of Management* 10 (Spring 1984):123–125.
17. Peter Drucker, *Management: Tasks, Responsibilities and Practices* (New York: Harper & Row, 1974), p. 546.
18. Arnoldo C. Hax and Nicholas S. Majluk, "Organization Design: A Case Study on Matching Strategy and Structure," *Journal of Business Strategy* 4 (Fall 1983):75.
19. Drucker, *Management*, pp. 601–602.
20. Ibid., pp. 530–531.
21. Thomas J. Peters and Robert H. Waterman, Jr., *In Search of Excellence* (New York: Harper & Row, 1982), pp. 306–318.
22. Ibid., p. 310.
23. Much of the discussion in this section is drawn from Michael L. Tennican, "Reinvigorating Corporate Profitability," *Journal of Business Strategy*, Winter 1987, pp. 4–10.
24. Jack M. Kaplan and Eileen E. Kaplan, "Organizational Restructuring," *Management Review* 73 (January 1984):15–16.
25. LaRue Tone Hosmer, "The Importance of Strategic Leadership," *Journal of Business Strategy* 3 (Fall 1982):55.
26. Ibid., p. 57.
27. David C. Shanks, "The Role of Leadership in Strategy Development," *Journal of Business Strategy*, January/February 1989, p. 36.
28. Milton Leontiades, "Choosing the Right Manager to Fit the Strategy," *Journal of Business Strategy* 3 (Fall 1984):69.
29. For an in-depth discussion of boards of directors, see Jeremy Bacon and James K. Brown, *Corporate Directorship Practices: Role, Selection and Legal Status of the Board* (New York: The Conference Board, 1975).
30. See Jeremy Bacon, *Corporate Directorship Practices: The Audit Committee* (New York: The Conference Board, 1979), Report No. 766.
31. See Jeremy Bacon, *Corporate Directorship Practices: The Compensation Committee* (New York: The Conference Board, 1982), Report No. 829.
32. See Jeremy Bacon, *Corporate Directorship Practices: The Nominating Committee and the Director Selection Process* (New York: The Conference Board, 1981), Report No. 812.
33. See James K. Brown, *Corporate Directorship Practices: The Planning Committee* (New York: The Conference Board, 1981), Report No. 810.
34. Bacon and Brown, *Corporate Directorship Practices: Role, Selection and Legal Status of the Board*, p. 77.
35. Richard M. Leisner, "Boardroom Jitters," *Barron's*, April 22, 1985, p. 34.

Chapter 6: Strategy, Structure, and Organizational Leadership

Ford Motor Company has a relatively simple structure, yet it is strategically mapped out to reflect the changing nature and focus of Ford's business. Ford has three basic strategic business units—the Automotive Group, Diversified Products Operations (DPO), and Financial Services. Each of these strategic businesses also has several different business units. Exhibit 1 shows Ford's organizational structure.

AUTOMOTIVE STRATEGIC BUSINESS UNIT

The Automotive Group is divided into two divisions, the North American Automotive Group (NAAO) and the International Automotive Operations (IAO). The NAAO has more than 50 assembly and manufacturing facilities in the United States. Currently, this group is experiencing the greatest amount of difficulty in boosting its sales, with 1988 marking the first time that Ford did not outearn its larger rival, General Motors. Although Ford is the only domestic auto manufacturer gaining market share, its share of the U.S. passenger car market was only 22.3 percent during the first ten months of 1989. General Motors' share of the market is down a full percentage point to 35.1 percent, but still GM is controlling the market. The NAAO is also experiencing difficulties with its line of automobiles. Despite advertising that "Quality Is Job One," Ford has had to submit to periodic recalls on various models.

International Automotive Operations has operations in 22 countries, grouped into three main regions—Europe, Latin America, and Asia Pacific. Ford also has international business relationships with auto manufacturers in nine countries. Although IAO has been in position in prior years to balance the lagging sales in the U.S. automobile market, analysts predict that industry-wide auto sales are expected to slip in Europe after the five greatest record years in auto history. Also, Ford and its rival counterparts are going to find out that not only are the Japanese tough competitors in the U.S. car market, they will be major contenders with the introduction of the Nissan in northern England, and Toyota and Honda have plans for plant facilities in Europe to be operational in the mid-1990s. This trio is expected to capture 13.5 percent of current industry sales, thus claiming a significant portion of Ford IAO's current share.

DIVERSIFIED PRODUCTS OPERATIONS STRATEGIC BUSINESS UNIT

The Diversified Products Operation encompasses all of Ford's support businesses. As Ford's intercompany supply organization, it plays an important role in saving supplier costs.

Exhibit 1 *Organizational Chart, Ford Motor Company*

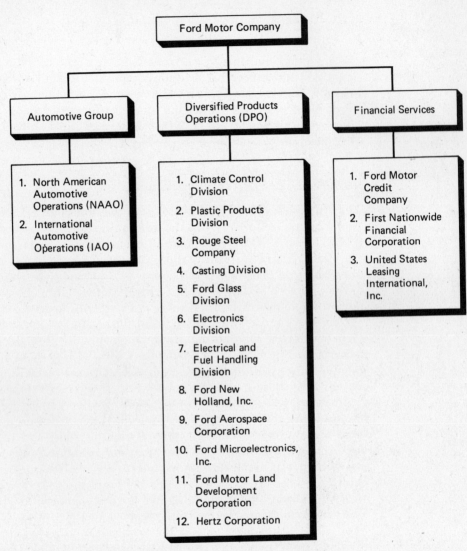

FINANCIAL SERVICES STRATEGIC BUSINESS UNIT

Ford Financial Services has one primary division, Ford Credit and Insurance Services. This group oversees the operations of Ford Motor Credit and the financing operations of Ford's overseas automotive affiliates. First Nationwide Financial Corporation and U.S. Leasing International, Inc., comprise the world's second largest finance company that lends money to dealers, retail automotive customers, and agricultural equipment customers in addition to offering insurance products.

FORD'S LEADERSHIP

Henry Ford

In 1914, with a team of investors, Henry Ford started what we know today as the Ford Motor Company. In his years as CEO he took on several different leadership styles. He became a hero in the eyes of the laborers when he raised the wage rate to five dollars an hour for an eight-hour day. On the other hand, he practiced an autocratic leadership style in ensuring that all employees were heavily supervised while working during that eight-hour period. Although Henry Ford was an authoritarian, he was not viewed that way until the employees began to entertain the idea of starting a labor union. They were terrified to raise the issue of labor union talks for fear of losing their jobs. Henry Ford was noted in his remaining years as being autocratic and unresponsive to his employees' needs.

Henry Ford II

When Henry Ford II took the reins as CEO of Ford Motor Company upon the retirement of his grandfather, he was faced with a large, inefficient, nearly bankrupt organization. The finance department was literally nonfunctional owing to Henry Ford Sr.'s dislike for the IRS and accountants. The company was losing nearly $10 million a month. Unlike his grandfather, Henry II saw the importance of the finance function. To him, it was an integral part of a company's success. He immediately took action to clean up the finance department, as well as the rest of the company. He hired a group of young, talented former Air Force officers whose specialty was correcting seemingly uncorrectable problems. Among this group was Robert McNamara, who later left Ford and served as secretary of defense under Presidents Kennedy and Johnson. With the help of the "Whiz Kids" Henry Ford II turned the Ford Motor Company around, and it was once again a profitable organization. However, with change there comes a certain amount of resistance. Henry Ford II had made several adjustments in the financial operations process without consulting a large percentage of his senior management staff or operations staff to see how smoothly the changes could be implemented. Thus, his management style was somewhat like his grandfather's.

Henry Ford II retired in October 1979, handing over the responsibilities of CEO to Philip Caldwell.

Philip Caldwell

Philip Caldwell was much more democratic in his leadership style than his predecessors. He felt that, in making a decision, it was very important to consider the input of those who were closest to the problem. Although this was different from the style of previous CEOs, he still made all primary decisions on the basis of his own analysis. Caldwell was also different in that he often became involved in special problems personally. One such area of special involvement was the design of the Topaz/Mercury. Because he felt strongly about the new aerodynamic design, he deviated from his typical style and approved the design without input from his management team. Another difference in Caldwell's leadership style was his involvement with the employees, particularly the union workers. Under Caldwell, the company initiated two programs that boosted employee morale. His concern for the well-being of his employees led to UAW local 898 at Rawsonville electing him an honorary member of the union, a first for both top management and the union.

Donald Petersen

Donald Petersen became president in 1980 and CEO in 1985. He is the Ford leader credited with guiding the company to record profits and the most successful cultural revolution in automotive industry history. In 1987, under Petersen, Ford Motor Company took on a new structure that reflected the changing nature of Ford's business. He guided Ford into producing the highest-quality products on a world scale. His style of leadership has been described as democratic, primarily because he used the resources of his management team to make decisions about the changes and their implementation.

Harold Poling

Harold Poling, the current CEO, has been with the company in many capacities and has worked under many of the past CEOs. The primary challenge facing him is increasing Ford's international market and strengthening its position as a quality car manufacturer against foreign car makers. Thus far, Poling has used the same type of management style as Petersen. Poling plans to make further strides in efficiency and quality and to continue to push the new products already on the drawing board. His management style has been described as democratic. He is very conscious of the talent housed in his management staff and feels that their input is essential.

Future Leadership Issues

Although the leaders and management styles of Ford Motor Company have changed over the years, there has been one underlying concern for the stockholders. Until 1979, Ford Motor Company's management team had always been headed up by a member of the Ford family. During the 1980s, this tradition changed quite a bit. However, it is important to note that two younger members of the Ford family presently serve on the company's board of directors and also work as managers in the company. Exhibit 2 summarizes the members on the board of directors. Edsel B. Ford II serves as general sales manager, Lincoln-Mercury Division, while William Clay Ford, Jr., serves as chairman and managing director—Ford Motor Company (Switzerland) S.A.

The Ford family has a combined voting power that constitutes 40 percent of the company stock, and in recent years, the two younger members of the Ford family have made known their desire for an increased say in the operations and decisions of the company. Soon after Petersen's retirement, each of them was given board committee assignments.

Exhibit 2 Ford's Board of Directors

Donald E. Petersen
Chairman of the Board   Committees: Finance; Executive; Organization Review and Nominating (chairman)

William Clay Ford
Vice-chairman of the Board   Committees: Finance (chairman); Executive (chairman); Organization Review and Nominating

Harold A. Poling
Vice-chairman of the Board   Committees: Finance; Executive

Philip E. Benton, Jr.
Executive Vice-president   Committees: Finance; Executive

John A. Betti
Executive Vice-president   Committees: Finance; Executive

Philip Caldwell
Retired Chairman of the Board and Chief Executive Officer, Ford Motor Company; Presently Senior Managing Director, Shearson Lehman Hutton Inc.   Committees: Audit; Organization Review and Nominating

Colby H. Chandler
Chairman of the Board and Chief Executive Officer, Eastman Kodak Company   Committees: Audit (chairman); Organization Review and Nominating

Michael D. Dingman
Chairman of the Board, The Henley Group, Inc.   Committees: Compensation and Option; Organization Review and Nominating

Edsel B. Ford II
General Sales Manager, Lincoln-Mercury Division

William Clay Ford, Jr.
Chairman and Managing Director, Ford Motor Company (Switzerland) S.A.

Allan D. Gilmour
Executive Vice-president   Committees: Finance; Executive

Roberto C. Goizueta
Chairman of the Board, The Coca-Cola Company   Committees: Compensation and Option; Organization Review and Nominating

Marian S. Heiskell
Director, The New York Times Company   Committees: Audit; Organization Review and Nominating

Irvine O. Hockaday, Jr.
President and Chief Executive Officer, Hallmark Cards, Inc.   Committees: Audit; Organization Review and Nominating

Continued

Exhibit 2 (*Continued*)

Drew Lewis
Chairman and Chief Executive Officer, Union Pacific Corporation   Committees: Compensation and Option; Organization Review and Nominating

Ellen R. Marram
President, Nabisco Biscuit Company   Committees: Audit; Organization Review and Nominating

Kenneth H. Olsen
President and Chief Executive Officer, Digital Equipment Corporation   Committees: Compensation and Option; Organization Review and Nominating

Carl E. Reichardt
Chairman of the Board and Chief Executive Officer, Wells Fargo & Company   Committees: Audit; Organization Review and Nominating

Louis R. Ross
Executive Vice-president   Committees: Finance; Executive

Stanley A. Seneker
Executive Vice-president   Committees: Finance; Executive

Clifton R. Wharton, Jr.
Chairman and Chief Executive Officer, Teachers Insurance and Annuity Association—College Retirement Equities Fund   Committees: Compensation and Option (chairman); Organization Review and Nominating

APPENDIX TO CHAPTER 6: Strengths and Weaknesses of Organizational Structure Types

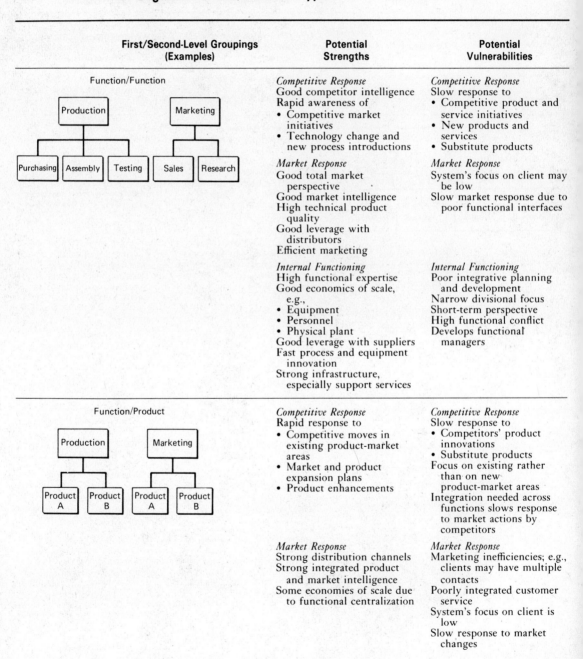

First/Second-Level Groupings (Examples)	Potential Strengths	Potential Vulnerabilities
Function/Function	*Competitive Response* Good competitor intelligence Rapid awareness of • Competitive market initiatives • Technology change and new process introductions	*Competitive Response* Slow response to • Competitive product and service initiatives • New products and services • Substitute products
	Market Response Good total market perspective Good market intelligence High technical product quality Good leverage with distributors Efficient marketing	*Market Response* System's focus on client may be low Slow market response due to poor functional interfaces
	Internal Functioning High functional expertise Good economics of scale, e.g., • Equipment • Personnel • Physical plant Good leverage with suppliers Fast process and equipment innovation Strong infrastructure, especially support services	*Internal Functioning* Poor integrative planning and development Narrow divisional focus Short-term perspective High functional conflict Develops functional managers
Function/Product	*Competitive Response* Rapid response to • Competitive moves in existing product-market areas • Market and product expansion plans • Product enhancements	*Competitive Response* Slow response to • Competitors' product innovations • Substitute products Focus on existing rather than on new product-market areas Integration needed across functions slows response to market actions by competitors
	Market Response Strong distribution channels Strong integrated product and market intelligence Some economies of scale due to functional centralization	*Market Response* Marketing inefficiencies; e.g., clients may have multiple contacts Poorly integrated customer service System's focus on client is low Slow response to market changes

(Continued)

181

First/Second-Level Groupings (Examples)	Potential Strengths	Potential Vulnerabilities
	Internal Functioning Strong supply channels Functional and product expertise Some economies of scale due to functional centralization	*Internal Functioning* Poor integrative planning and resource allocation across functions Product synergies not considered Economies of scale not fully realized
Function/Customer 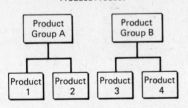	*Competitive Response* Rapid resource allocation to existing functional and market areas Rapid response to • Existing market diversity • Competitors' moves in existing market areas High competitive intelligence *Market Response* Total market awareness Good market intelligence High leverage with distributors Full line sales	*Competitive Response* Slow response to • New products • New technologies Competitors' product initiatives Innovation/growth restricted to existing market areas *Market Response* Marketing inefficiencies, e.g., • Product knowledge lessened • Possible product overlap System's focus on customer needs is low Possible variances in product quality
	Internal Functioning High technical expertise High leverage with suppliers High economies of scale: • Capacity • Facilities	*Internal Functioning* Poor integrative product planning and development Economies in scale not fully realized, e.g., duplication of staff
Product/Product Product Group A — Product Group B Product 1 Product 2 Product 3 Product 4	*Competitive Response* Good product planning and management Rapid resource allocation to existing product areas Rapid response to • Competitive initiatives in existing product areas • Product and service enhancement *Market Response* Strong distribution channels Tailored customer support systems Sales force has high product knowledge	*Competitive Response* Lack of total market perspective Diffused authority for critical functions Divisional rather than corporate focus, leading to inability to perceive competitor in its totality Low competitive intelligence *Market Response* Distributors may face multiple contacts Possible marketing inefficiencies; e.g., clients may have multiple contacts Poorly integrated customer service Poor market intelligence Poor technical product quality System's focus on client is low

First/Second-Level Groupings (Examples)	Potential Strengths	Potential Vulnerabilities
	Internal Functioning Develops general managers High product focus and morale Possible product technology synergies	*Internal Functioning* Possible product synergies not realized Functional inefficiencies Low economies of scale: • Capacity • Staff Low technical expertise Poor internal support systems Corporate attention dissipated
Product/Function Product A → Production, Marketing Product B → Production, Marketing	*Competitive Response* Good product planning and management Rapid resource allocation to existing product areas Product enhancement potential is high	*Competitive Response* Lack of total market perspective Divisional rather than corporate focus, leading to inability to perceive competitor in its totality Focus on existing rather than new product areas Possible product synergies not considered Low competitive intelligence
	Market Response High technical product quality Tailored customer support systems Sales force has high product knowledge Strong product intelligence	*Market Response* Possible marketing inefficiencies; e.g., clients may have multiple contacts Poorly integrated customer service Poorly integrated market intelligence Distribution and supply positions weakened by lack of total corporate approach
	Internal Functioning Develops general managers High product focus and morale Possible product technology synergies within departments High technical product expertise High functional expertise	*Internal Functioning* Functional inefficiencies Inefficient capacity and staff utilization Corporate attention dissipated Conflicting goals (divisional vs. corporate)
Product/Customer Product A → Government, Business Product B → Government, Business	*Competitive Response* Good product planning and management Rapid resource allocation to existing product-market areas Rapid response to • Existing market diversity • Competitive initiatives in existing product-market areas • Customer needs	*Competitive Response* Lack of total product-market perspective Divisional rather than corporate focus, leading to inability to perceive competitor in its totality Focus on existing rather than new products Diffused authority for critical functions Possible product synergies not considered

Continued

First/Second-Level Groupings (Examples)	Potential Strengths	Potential Vulnerabilities
	Market Response Good market intelligence and focus Sales force has high product knowledge Tailored customer support systems	*Market Response* Possible marketing inefficiencies: • Sales force may compete for overlapping markets • Clients may have multiple contacts Poorly integrated customer service System's focus on client is low Poorly integrated market intelligence Weakened by lack of corporate-wide approach
	Internal Functioning Develops general managers High product-market focus and morale	*Internal Functioning* Poor internal support systems Functional inefficiencies Inefficient capacity and staff utilization Low technical product quality Low functional expertise Corporate attention dissipated
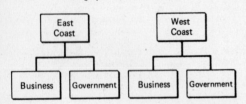 Geographic Area/Customer	*Competitive Response* Rapid response to • Existing market diversity • Customer needs • Existing market expansion plans High market preemption potential	*Competitive Response* Lack of total market perspective May not have authority over all critical functions Divisional rather than corporate focus, leading to inability to perceive competitor in its totality Innovation restricted to existing markets
	Market Response Strong marketing and sales Good customer service Facilitates client planning and coordination High market intelligence Particularly suitable for key account strategies	*Market Response* Overresponse to client whims Marketing inefficiencies; e.g., clients may have multiple contacts Low product intelligence Sales force faced with broader product line and consequently lower product knowledge Weakened distribution channel position
	Internal Functioning Develops general managers High market integration internally	*Internal Functioning* Corporate attention dissipated Market overlap may cause internal competition Low functional skills Poor internal support systems and integration Inefficient capacity and staff utilization

First/Second-Level Groupings (Examples)	Potential Strengths	Potential Vulnerabilities

Customer/Function

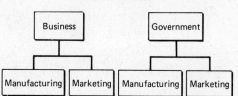

Competitive Response
Rapid response to
• Existing market diversity
• Customer needs
• Market expansion plans
• Competitors' market initiatives

Competitive Response
Lack of total market perspective
Divisional rather than corporate focus, leading to inability to perceive competitor in its totality
Slow response to
• Competitors' product innovations
• Product expansion plans
Low competitive intelligence

Market Response
Strong marketing and full-line sales
High leverage with distribution channels
High product quality
High market intelligence

Market Response
Marketing inefficiencies:
• Product knowledge lessened
• Product priority conflict
• Possible market product overlap
Low product intelligence

Internal Functioning
High function expertise
Good internal support systems
High leverage with suppliers

Internal Functioning
Product priority conflict (if multiproduct)
Low economies of scale (across divisions)
Poor integration between functions

Customer/Product

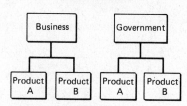

Competitive Response
Rapid response to
• Customer needs
• Market and product expansion plans
• Competitive moves in existing product-market areas
• Product enhancements
Rapid resource allocation to product-market areas

Competitive Response
Lack of total market perspective
Divisional rather than corporate perspective, leading to inability to perceive competitor in its totality
Low competitive intelligence
Slow response to competitors' product innovations

Market Response
Strong marketing and sales; e.g., sales force has high product knowledge
Good market intelligence and expertise
Good customer service

Market Response
Marketing inefficiencies: e.g., client may have multiple contacts
System's focus on client is low
Possibly overresponsive to client whims

Internal Functioning
Develops general managers
High product and market focus and morale

Internal Functioning
Low functional expertise
Poor internal support systems
Low capacity and staff utilization
Product innovation/enhancement overlaps
Possible product synergies may be overlooked

Source: Adapted from Ian C. MacMillan and Patricia E. Jones, "Designing Organizations to Compete," *Journal of Business Strategy* 4 (Spring 1984):22–26.

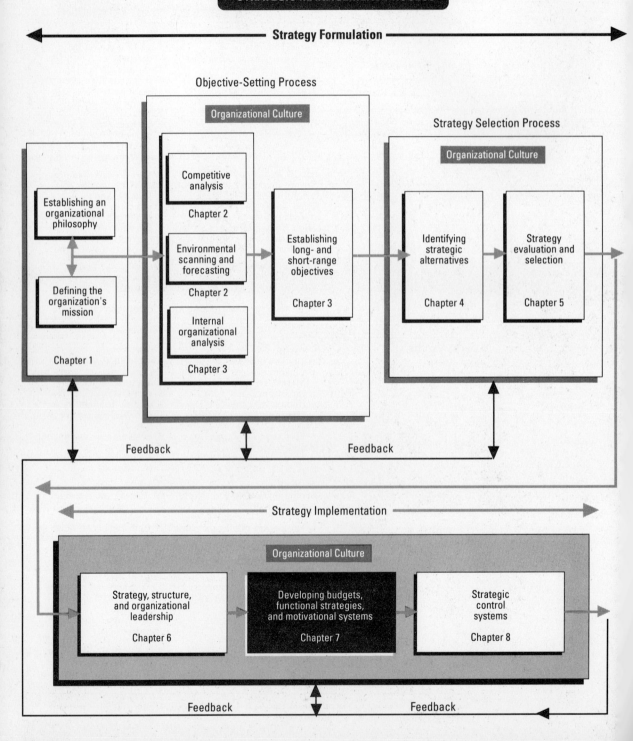

STRATEGIC MANAGEMENT PROCESS

Strategy Formulation

Objective-Setting Process

Organizational Culture

Competitive analysis

Chapter 2

Environmental scanning and forecasting

Chapter 2

Internal organizational analysis

Chapter 3

Establishing long- and short-range objectives

Chapter 3

Establishing an organizational philosophy

Defining the organization's mission

Chapter 1

Strategy Selection Process

Organizational Culture

Identifying strategic alternatives

Chapter 4

Strategy evaluation and selection

Chapter 5

Feedback   Feedback

Strategy Implementation

Organizational Culture

Strategy, structure, and organizational leadership

Chapter 6

Developing budgets, functional strategies, and motivational systems

Chapter 7

Strategic control systems

Chapter 8

Feedback   Feedback

LEARNING OBJECTIVES

After studying this chapter, you should be able to

1. Explain the role of budgets in achieving organizational objectives.

2. Describe flexible budgets.

3. Outline the conditions that must exist to ensure that the budgeting process helps in strategy implementation.

4. Define functional strategies.

5. Explain the role of marketing strategy.

6. Discuss the activities involved in financial management.

7. Categorize the activities involved in production/operations management.

8. Describe the three basic categories of research and development.

9. Define organizational rewards.

After objectives are established, corporate-level and business unit strategies are selected, and an organizational structure is chosen, several activities must take place to ensure that the strategy is successful. First, the financial resources of the business must be allocated to make certain that each organizational unit is adequately supported. This is accomplished through the budgeting process. Next, strategies must be developed for each of the functional (marketing, finance, production, and so on) areas of the business. These functional strategies must complement each other and support the corporate-level or business unit strategy. Finally, employees must be encouraged to direct their efforts toward the accomplishment of organizational objectives. The motivational systems used by a business should provide this encouragement. The purpose of this chapter is to discuss each of these activities—budgeting, functional strategies, and motivational systems—in more depth and describe their importance in the successful implementation of strategy.

DEPLOYMENT OF RESOURCES THROUGH BUDGETING

Budgeting is a process by which management specifies the resources it will employ to achieve the organization's objectives. It also provides the means of measuring the successful accomplishment of the stated objectives within a specific time period, normally one year.[1] The following types of budgets can be developed: sales budget, production budget, capital budget, direct materials budget, direct labor budget, overhead budget, selling and administrative expense budget, cash flow budget, budgeted income statement, and a budgeted balance sheet. Each of these budgets can be prepared for the organization as a whole or for various components of an organization (e.g., business units or functional areas). Figure 7.1 describes some of the more common types of budgets.

Although budgets may be expressed in other terms, the dollar is the most common denomination. Budgets that may be expressed in units other than

Figure 7.1 Types and Purposes of Budgets

Type of Budget	Brief Description or Purpose
Revenue and expense budget	Provides details for revenue and expense plans
Cash flow budget	Forecasts cash receipts and disbursements
Capital budget	Outlines specific expenditures for plant, equipment, machinery, inventories, and other capital items
Production, material, or time budget	Expresses physical requirements of production or material or the time requirements for the budget period
Balance sheet budgets	Forecasts the status of assets, liabilities, and net worth at the end of the budget period

dollars include equipment budgets, which can be expressed in numbers of machines, or material budgets, which can be expressed in pounds, pieces, and gallons. Budgets not expressed in dollars are normally translated into dollars for incorporation into an overall budget.

Flexible Budgets

Flexible budgets vary with the volume of sales or some other measure of output. Flexible budgets are generally limited in application to expense budgets. Under a flexible budget, material, labor, advertising, and other expenses are allowed to vary with the volume of output. Flexible budgets are more useful for evaluating what expenses should have been under a certain set of circumstances.

Zero-based Budgeting

The key difference between traditional budgeting and zero-based budgeting (ZBB) is that ZBB does not build from the previous year's budget. Traditional budgeting systems produce a set of numbers based on the previous year's budget. Those numbers do not necessarily justify the need for the activity or function or identify its effectiveness or priority.

ZBB requires managers to analyze each existing or newly proposed budget item as if no money had ever been allocated for the item. Each function or activity under a manager's control is identified, evaluated, and ranked in order of its importance. Then each year every function and activity in the budget is matched against all other claimants for an organization's resources. ZBB should enable an organization to react to changing environmental conditions and to reallocate resources effectively to business units where the greatest return can be achieved.

Participative and Nonparticipative Budgets

Budgets can also be classified as being participative or nonparticipative. Under a *nonparticipative budgeting process*, top management sets the budget, issues it to lower-level managers, and then holds these lower-level managers accountable for performance in accordance with the budget. Under a *participative budgeting process*, lower-level managers submit budgets for their organizational units, which top management combines into an overall organizational budget. Some degree of participation in the budgeting process seems to exist in most organizations today.[2]

Dangers in the Budgeting Process

Budgets are not without their dangers. One of the greatest potential dangers is inflexibility. Inflexibility poses a special threat to organizations operating in an industry characterized by rapid change and/or severe competition. It can also lead to the subordination of organizational objectives to the budget. In this case, staying within the budget becomes more important than meeting objectives.

Budgets can hide inefficiencies. The fact that an expenditure was made in the past often becomes justification for continuing the expenditure, when in fact the situation may have changed considerably.

Budgets can also become inflationary and inaccurate. This often happens in a participative budgeting system when lower-level managers pad their budgets because they know they will be cut by upper levels of management. Since the lower-level manager is never certain of how severely the budget will be cut, the result is often an inaccurate and unrealistic budget. Some of the methods employed in the budgeting game, as it is often called, are budgeting a low sales figure or a high expense figure by exaggerating the problems facing the business unit or functional area. In addition, money can be saved on the budget in the short run by not investing in research, ordering new equipment, or conducting training programs. Of course, cutting these budget items can have negative effects in the long run. Figure 7.2 identifies some of the symptoms and possible causes of a weak budgeting process. Identifying and rectifying these symptoms goes a long way toward eliminating many of the dangers described in this section.

Strategy and the Budgeting Process

Unfortunately, many managers view the budgeting process as merely being a financial exercise rather than being part of the strategy implementation process. In order for the budgeting process to be useful in strategy implementation the following conditions must exist:

1. Senior management must have a strong commitment to the budgeting process.
2. Budgets must be based on the objectives of the business. For example, across-the-board budget cuts communicate that all business units or functional areas of the business are of equal importance. If budgets are based on organizational objectives, it is natural that some business units or functional areas will be cut more than others.
3. Regular reviews of the operating results in comparison to the budget must be conducted.
4. All levels of management must be required to explain budget variances.[3]

DEVELOPING FUNCTIONAL STRATEGIES

Functional strategies describe the means or methods to be used by each functional area of the organization in carrying out the corporate-level or business unit strategy. Functional strategies differ from corporate or business unit strategies in several respects. First, functional strategies usually cover a much shorter time span than do corporate strategies. Second, functional strategies are much more specific and action-oriented than are corporate strategies. The corporate strategy is designed to give general direction; the functional strategy is designed to give more specific direction. Finally, functional strategy development requires much more active participation by lower levels of management. In fact, input by lower management levels at the development stage is essential in the successful implementation of functional strategies.

Functional strategies can be developed for any unit within an organization. However, the functional areas of organizations normally include most, if not all, of the following:

- Marketing
- Finance
- Production/operations
- Human resources/personnel
- Research and development

Marketing Strategies

Marketing consists of those activities intended to move products or services from the producer to the consumer or market. The basic role of marketing in an organization is to have the right products or services in the right quantity at the right place at the right time.[4] When this role is performed effectively,

Figure 7.2 *Identifying a Weak Budgeting Process*

Symptom	Possible Cause
If, after the budgeting process is complete, the organization experiences the following symptoms:	Problems can possibly be traced to the following budgeting deficiencies:
• Programs and projects are having difficulty in getting established	• Short-range objectives are not synchronized with long-range objectives
• Shortly after the beginning of the year, much to the surprise of management, a hiring freeze or expenditure curtailment is imposed	• Key economic, business, or internal assumptions either are not considered or are faulty
• The organization experiences unexpected additional cash requirements	• A realistic cash flow analysis with varying assumptions was not prepared
• Key financial returns such as return on assets/return on investment are disappointing	• The organization did not consider steady or improved productivity and increased fixed cost more than required; or real growth expectations did not materialize

Source: Adapted from Cosmo S. Trapani, "Six Critical Areas in the Budgeting Process," *Management Accounting* 64 (November 1982):55.

profits are earned and customers are served efficiently. *Marketing strategy* is concerned with matching existing or potential products or services with the needs of customers, informing customers that the products or services exist, having the products or services at the right time and place to facilitate exchange, and assigning a price to the products or services. Example 7.1 shows the marketing strategy developed by Wal-Mart.

The marketing strategy selected by an organization is dependent on whether the organization is attempting to reach new or existing customers and whether its products or services are new or already exist. A classification

---

STRATEGY IN ACTION Example 7.1

Wal-Mart's Marketing Strategy

Wal-Mart is a Delaware corporation with its principal offices located in Betonville, Arkansas. It currently operates 1117 discount department stores, 84 Sam's Wholesale Clubs, 112 deep-discount drug stores, 3 full-time craft stores, and 2 hypermarkets. The company sells merchandise through these various discount stores.

In 1945, Sam M. Walton opened his first variety store in Newport, Arkansas. In 1946, James L. Walton opened a similar store in Vesalles, Missouri. The two brothers accumulated 15 additional stores before opening the first store that was called Wal-Mart in 1962.

Wal-Mart became a publicly held corporation in 1970. The company stock began trading on the New York Stock Exchange in mid-1972.

The company focused on selling products exclusively in small towns and medium-sized cities. This niche proved to be quite profitable for the Arkansas-based firm.

In 1983, the company opened its first three Sam's Wholesale Clubs and its first deep-discount drug store. In 1988, it opened its first two hypermart stores.

The company currently operates Wal-Mart stores in Alabama, Arkansas, Colorado, Florida, Georgia, Illinois, Indiana, Iowa, Kansas, Kentucky, Louisiana, Minnesota, Mississippi, Missouri, Nebraska, New Mexico, North Carolina, Oklahoma, South Carolina, Tennessee, Texas, Virginia, West Virginia, and Wisconsin. Most Wal-Mart stores have an average size of approximately 61,500 square feet. However, store sizes range between 30,000 and 100,000 square feet.

Wal-Mart has been effective in selling goods at low prices. The company determines its competitors' prices and then makes sure its prices match them. Wal-Mart feels its company has excellent programs designed to sell quality products at low prices. Under the "Everyday Low Price" program, name brand products are sold at low prices every day. The purpose behind this policy is to have consumers associate the Wal-Mart store with name brand products at a low price. The "Items Merchandising" policy emphasizes displaying name brand products in a manner that attracts consumers' attention. The "Store-Within-a-Store" policy emphasizes the many types of products sold at Wal-Mart. These policies have effectively positioned Wal-Mart as an industry leader of discount stores.

system for marketing strategies based on the type of customer and type of product or service is illustrated in Figure 7.3.

With a *marketing penetration strategy*, the organization attempts to gain greater control in a market in which it already has a product or service. Management must carefully consider several factors in using a market penetration strategy. These include

- The reaction of competitors
- The capacity of the market to increase usage or consumption and/or the availability of new customers
- The costs involved in gaining customers from competition, stimulating more usage or consumption, or attracting new customers

A *market development strategy* consists of introducing the organization's existing products or services to customers other than the ones it currently serves. Considerations in using a market development strategy include

- The reaction of competitors
- An understanding of the number, needs, and purchasing patterns of the new customers
- Determination of the organization's adaptability to new markets

An organization using a *product development strategy* creates a new product or service for existing customers. Considerations in a product development strategy include

- The competitive response
- The impact of the new product or service on existing products or services
- The ability of the organization to deliver the product or service

With a *diversification marketing strategy*, an organization offers a new product or service to new customers. Considerations in using this strategy include

- Developing a considerable knowledge of the new customer's needs

Figure 7.3 Marketing Strategies by Customer and Products or Services.

Products or Services	Customer	
	Existing	**New**
Existing	Market penetration	Market development
New	Product development	Diversification

Source: Adapted from H. Igor Ansoff, *Corporate Strategy* (New York: McGraw-Hill, 1965), p. 109.

- Making certain that the new product or service meets those needs
- Knowing that the organization has the human talent to serve the new customers

After the basic marketing strategy is determined, more specific strategies are required. These activities are often called the *marketing mix.* They include

- Determining the exact type of product or service that is to be offered (product strategy)
- Deciding how the product or service is to be communicated to customers (promotion strategy)
- Selecting the method for distributing the product or service to the customer (channel strategy)
- Establishing a price for the product or service (price strategy)

Determination of the appropriate marketing mix is crucial in the success of any organization. Figure 7.4 outlines several questions that when answered give direction in determining the appropriate marketing mix for a particular organization.

Product positioning, which is often used as an aid in developing a marketing strategy, uses marketing research techniques to determine where proposed

Figure 7.4 *Questions in Determining the Appropriateness of a Marketing Mix*

Consistency

1. Do the individual elements of the mix fit together to form a logical relationship, or are they fragmented?
2. Does the mix fit the organization, the market, and the environment into which it will be introduced?

Sensitivity

1. Are customers more sensitive to certain marketing mix variables than others?
2. Are customers more likely to respond favorably to a decrease in price or an increase in advertising?

Cost

1. What are the costs of performing the various marketing mix activities?
2. Do the costs exceed the benefits in terms of customer response?
3. Can the organization afford the marketing mix expenditures?

Timing

1. Is the marketing mix properly timed?
2. Is promotion scheduled to coincide with product or service availability?

Source: Adapted from Roger A. Kerin and Robert A. Peterson, *Strategic Marketing Problems* (Boston: Allyn & Bacon, 1978), p. 7.

---

and/or present brands or products are located in the market. This tool enables managers to decide whether they want to leave their present product and marketing mix alone or whether they want to reposition the product. It allows an organization to develop marketing strategies oriented toward target customers. Developing strategies of this type is frequently called *target marketing*. For example, an organization may develop a market segmentation strategy in which its products are aimed at a homogeneous submarket of a larger market. Another organization might develop a combining strategy that involves combining relatively homogeneous submarkets into a larger target market.

Financial Strategies

Financial management is primarily concerned with two functions. The first function, acquiring funds to meet the organization's current and future needs, is normally the responsibility of the treasurer. The second function is recording, monitoring, and controlling the financial results of an organization's operations and is normally the responsibility of the controller.

The activities of financial management can be grouped into five categories:

1. Determining the magnitude and characteristics of funds necessary to conduct business operations
2. Allocating resources in the most efficient manner
3. Serving as an interface with creditors and stockholders concerning the financial condition of the organization
4. Recordkeeping
5. Providing financial data to top management in determining the feasibility of various strategic alternatives.

Figure 7.5 outlines just some of the questions that need to be answered in developing a financial strategy.[5]

Two important considerations in financial management that influence all functional areas of an organization are capital budgeting and cash flows. Both are important to the implementation of strategies at all levels of the organization.

Capital Budgeting   *Capital assets* are assets that are used in the physical process of producing an organization's goods or services and are normally used for a number of years. Since the amount of money involved is so large, generally organizations carefully plan and evaluate expenditures for capital assets. Furthermore, an organization's current capital allocations directly affect its future strategic options. Inefficient capital allocation can slow an organization's growth, strain its financing capacity, and severely limit its strategic options.[6]

The process of determining how much to spend on capital assets and which assets to acquire is called capital budgeting. Capital budgets are developed on the basis of sales forecasts and the anticipated plant and equipment needed to meet those expected sales. Methods for evaluating various investment options

Figure 7.5 Potential Questions That Need Answering in Developing a Financial Strategy

Determining Magnitude and Characteristics of Necessary Funds

1. What are cash flow requirements?
2. How are credit and collections to be handled?
3. Are long-term bonds, stock issues, or short-term bank borrowing to be used?
4. How is inventory control to be handled?

Allocating Resources

1. Are the long-term benefits from the proposed project commensurate with the long-run costs?
2. What types of budgets are to be developed?

Serving as an Interface with Creditors and Stockholders

1. What methods are to be used in paying dividends?
2. What credit terms are going to be requested from suppliers?

Recordkeeping

1. Are profit-center accountability systems to be established?
2. Are financial statements to be prepared for each organizational unit?
3. What reports are to be prepared for various levels of management, and when?

Providing Financial Data on Various Strategic Alternatives

1. What is the value of the company that is under consideration for acquisition?
2. What are the financial implications of the proposed liquidation of a certain part of the organization?

are based on the marginal cash flow that results from each option. After the marginal cash flows have been estimated, several techniques can be used to evaluate the investment options. The primary techniques used are the present value, internal rate of return, payback period, and accounting rate of return.

Cash Flow Analysis Cash is essential to the survival, growth, and profitability of any organization. The cash flow process is basically an asset transformation process. An organization must start with a certain amount of cash. It then purchases goods and services or invests in capital assets. The purchased goods and services and capital are then used to produce a product or service, which results in an inventory. Sale of the inventory results in an accounts receivable. The collection process then turns accounts receivable into cash. And, if the cash flow process works properly, the cycle repeats itself continuously.

Of course, the cash flow process is complicated by several factors. Credit from suppliers, outside financing, and retained earnings add to the resources in the cycle. On the other hand, debt reduction, dividends, and operating losses reduce the resources in the cycle. Furthermore, the periodic acquisition of large capital assets complicates the cycle. Actually, the cash flow cycle is often somewhat erratic and subject to disruptions.

The determination of the sources of cash flowing into an organization and the uses of that cash by the organization is called a sources and uses of funds analysis or funds flow analysis. This analysis is particularly useful in determining how well an organization is achieving its financial resource objectives.

Production/Operations Strategies

Production/operations management, which evolved from the field of production or manufacturing management, is concerned with selecting, designing, and updating the systems that produce the organization's products or services and with operating those systems. Production or operating systems, which consist of the activities and processes necessary to transform inputs into products or services, exist in all organizations whether they are private, public, profit, nonprofit, service, or manufacturing. Generally, the operating system of an organization takes up the largest part of its financial assets, personnel, and expenses. It is being increasingly recognized that no amount of marketing, advertising, or financial manipulation can make an organization healthy if its products/services, facilities, technologies, and people are not of competitive quality.[7] Example 7.2 illustrates Polaroid's manufacturing strategy.

The activities of production/operations management can be categorized into two main areas: (1) system design and (2) operations planning and control. *System design* starts with product or service design, which largely determines the production capabilities needed. Process selection, site location, layout of facilities, equipment selection, and design of work methods are all part of the design phase of operations management. Obviously, it is impossible to design efficient production systems and facilities without knowledge of the corporate objectives and strategies.

The *operations planning and control* phase involves planning production levels in light of demand forecasts, scheduling work through the operating system, and allocating employees throughout the system. This phase includes production control, inventory control, quality control, cost control and improvement, and facility maintenance. The operations planning and control activities must be closely coordinated with the design activities. For example, the design objectives of the operating system would most likely dictate the most appropriate control system. Similarly, the design objective would also affect the number and types of personnel needed. Figure 7.6 outlines some of the major considerations in developing a production/operations strategy.

It is important to note here that many of the activities in marketing, finance, and production/operations have considerable overlap. For example, product design is an operations activity that directly relates to marketing. Process design and equipment acquisition are operations activities that cannot be undertaken independently of finance. Thus, close coordination and cooperation are required in the development of functional strategies for all of these areas.

Human Resource/Personnel Strategies

Human resource/personnel management includes those organizational activities that are concerned with determining the human resources (both quantity

STRATEGY IN ACTION Example 7.2

Polaroid's Manufacturing Strategy

There is much more to Polaroid's business than instant photography, particularly chemically based photography. Polaroid Corporation is in the instant-imaging business. It designs, manufactures, and markets worldwide a variety of imaging systems—technologies and products based on the interaction of light and matter. Its research and development work in imaging also provides avenues of exploration into related fields such as microelectronics and high-density information storage, retrieval, and transfer. Polaroid is involved in such fields as magnetic media, graphic arts, fiber optics, medical diagnostics, photovoltaics, holography, plastic LCD technology, electronic image processing, electrostatic echo ranging, and commercial optics.

Polaroid has described its manufacturing strategy as follows:

> In recent years, quality control in our manufacturing units has taken on new meaning. We have adopted a variety of statistical quality control systems. Production lines are equipped with test devices for process control, and those devices are in turn linked by computer. We are able to determine whether parts or products are within specifications and trace individually coded units to determine problem areas. This ongoing, process-oriented approach to quality control is far more efficient than traditional sampling techniques. Quality control consciousness and a QC presence are constantly on the production floor. With data continuously collected and analyzed, product quality is enhanced.
>
> The revolution taking place in Polaroid's manufacturing is more than a technological one. It is here that some of the most innovative work redesign has already occurred and will continue to take place. The trend is moving away from strict linear organizations of processes and assemblies toward work teams—sociotechnical groups—where individuals take greater responsibility for quality of production and the approach to supervision is more facilitative.

Source: Career Opportunities at Polaroid, company publication.

and quality) that the organization needs to achieve its objectives: recruiting, hiring, training, developing, and counseling employees; developing compensation systems; developing disciplinary systems; acting as a liaison with unions and government organizations; and handling other matters such as employee safety and corporate communications. The strategic alternatives of any organization are feasible from a human resource perspective if (1) the organization, business unit, or function has or can obtain the talent necessary to carry it out; and (2) the costs of acquiring, retaining, developing, and motivating the needed talent are economically feasible.[8]

In adapting a strategic perspective to human resource management, an organization should

1. Use its strategies (corporate-level, business unit, and functional) to identify what human resources are needed and how they should be allocated

2. Develop and implement personnel practices that select, reward, and develop employees who best contribute to the accomplishment of organizational objectives
3. Use its resources to compete for or retain employees who are needed to reach its objectives
4. Develop mechanisms that match employees' competencies to the organization's present and future needs as determined by the nature of the product or service and the market.[9]

Figure 7.7 poses several questions that must be addressed in developing a human resource strategy, and Example 7.3 shows the human resource strategy developed at Mary Kay Cosmetics.

Research and Development Strategies

Products or services become obsolete—not only from a technical but also from an economic standpoint—more rapidly today than ever before. The same applies to methods of production. For example, one of the primary reasons for

Figure 7.6 *Considerations in Developing a Production/Operations Strategy*

Stage of System	Considerations
Birth of the system	What are the objectives and strategies of the organization? What product or service will be offered?
Product design and process selection	What is the form and appearance of the product? Technologically, how should the product be made?
Design of the system	What capacity do you need? Where should the facility be located? What physical arrangement is best to use? How do you maintain desired quality? How do you determine demand for the product or service? What job is each worker to perform? How will the job be performed, measured; how will the workers be compensated?
Start-up of the system	How do you get the system into operation? How long will it take to reach the desired rate of output?
The system in steady state	How do you maintain the system? How can you improve the system? How do you revise the system in light of changes in corporate strategy?
Termination of the system	How does a system die? What can be done to salvage resources?

Source: Richard B. Chase and Nicholas J. Aquilano, *Production and Operations Management,* 3rd ed. (Homewood, Ill.: Irwin. 1981), p. 13.

Figure 7.7 Considerations in Developing a Human Resource Strategy

1. Does the organization have methods for quantifying and expressing its human resource needs?
2. To what extent can human resources be transferred between business units or functions to meet the strategic plan?
3. To what extent can human resources be developed in business units or functional areas to implement the strategic plan?
4. Are there mechanisms for shifting resources between business units or functional areas, for example from a declining unit to a growing unit?
5. Are reward systems designed to encourage employees to contribute to accomplishing the strategic plan?
6. Are training and development programs oriented toward developing skills needed to implement the strategic plan?
7. Are performance evaluation and appraisal systems consistent with the objectives of the organization?
8. Are human resource policies and procedures consistent with the finance and marketing strategies?
9. Are human resource services such as employment, compensation, and training coordinated and directed toward the accomplishment of organizational objectives?

Source: Adapted from Lloyd Baird, Ilan Meshoulam, and Ghislaine DeGive, "Meshing Human Resources Planning with Strategic Business Planning: A Model Approach," *Personnel* 60 (September–October 1983):22–29.

the economic difficulties faced by the steel industry in the United States is the technical obsolescence of its production facilities. An effective way for an organization to safeguard against either product or production process obsolescence is through research and development (R&D) efforts.

The R&D efforts of organizations can be divided into three basic categories:

1. *Basic Research.* Basic research enlarges technical knowledge without having a specific application of the knowledge. Colleges, universities, and several federal government agencies are active in performing basic research. Furthermore, an interesting trend is developing in which private enterprise organizations are funding basic research at colleges and universities in anticipation that useful commercial applications can be developed from the basic research findings.
2. *Applied Research.* Applied research enlarges technical knowledge in such a manner that a useful commercial application will result from the research.
3. *Development Research.* Development research uses available knowledge in the introduction of new or improved products or services or production techniques.

Most private enterprise organizations devote a significant portion of their R&D budgets to applied and development research.

An important consideration in R&D strategy is the outlook or orientation that an organization is going to assume in its R&D efforts. Basically, four orientations exist: innovative, protective, catch-up, or combination.

STRATEGY IN ACTION Example 7.3

Mary Kay's Pink Cadillacs

Mary Kay Cosmetics, Inc., target of jokes about its pink Cadillacs, is doing nicely, thank you, 3½ years after founders Mary Kay Ash and her son Richard R. Rogers took the company private in a $469 million deal.

Sales have increased 63.1 percent since 1985, the last year the company was publicly traded, reaching $406 million in 1988—all through the efforts of 185,000 sales "consultants," most of them women and some of them rich women. Consultants earn money by selling cosmetics at home presentations and recruiting other consultants.

Since Ash founded the company in 1963, 33 consultants have each been paid more than $1 million in commissions. In February alone, 10 "national directors" earned more than $20,000 each, with the top director getting $40,303.53.

Mary Kay has an estimated 2 percent of the cosmetic market, but claims as much as 9 percent of the skincare products segment and about 3.5 percent of the so-called glamour segment, primarily makeup.

Every year the company stages four sessions in which thousands of Mary Kay consultants descend on Dallas for a production number extravaganza. Top sellers are awarded minks, crowned and throned on stage at the Dallas Convention Center, and treated to a reception at Ash's pink mansion.

But it is the cars that have become the company signature. Top achievers are given pink Cadillacs to drive for the rest of their lives, getting a new one every two years as long as they maintain their high performance. Lesser efforts are rewarded by smaller cars—Buicks and Pontiacs. There are about a thousand Mary Kay pink Cadillacs on the road, plus 1000 Buicks and 3000 Pontiacs.

Behind the company's flamboyance is a detailed program telling consultants everything from how to set up business and do their accounting to how they should dress. It provides a detailed code of ethics and outlines how to win prizes.

Source: Adapted from *Atlanta Journal and Constitution*, July 5, 1989, p. E-5.

An *innovative R&D strategy* is primarily concerned with developing new products or services or production techniques. Most of the firms in the pharmaceutical and biomedical fields use the innovative approach.

A *protective R&D strategy* is concerned with improving present products and/or production techniques. The emphasis is primarily on maintaining the firm's present position.

Closely related to the protective R&D strategy is the *catch-up R&D strategy*. A firm that uses this strategy basically researches competitive products or services and incorporates their best features into its own products or services. This type of R&D strategy has been used by many foreign organizations and governments in developing products designed to compete with U.S. firms. On the other hand, U.S. firms have also used this strategy to catch up with foreign firms (e.g., the industrial application of robotics).

A final approach to an R&D strategy is a *combination* of any of the above three approaches. For example, IBM often uses a protective strategy for its existing products, but also uses an innovative strategy in developing new products.

The choice of what R&D strategy orientation is to be used by a particular organization depends on its size, its degree of technological leadership, its environment, and its competitors. Figure 7.8 outlines several questions that need to be considered in developing an R&D strategy.

STRATEGY AND MOTIVATIONAL SYSTEMS

Encouraging employees to work hard toward the achievement of organizational objectives is one of the most significant challenges for any management team. There is little doubt that highly motivated employees can significantly increase the likelihood that organizational objectives will be achieved. In fact, one study on the relationship between middle management and strategy implementation found that middle managers can redirect, delay, or even sabotage the implementation of a strategy that they believe compromises their self-interest.[10]

In most cases, the organizational reward system is one of the most effective motivational tools available to organizations. The design and use of the organizational reward system reflects management's attitude about performance and significantly influences the entire organizational climate. Few things in an organization evoke as much emotion as the organizational reward system.

Organizational rewards include all types of rewards, both intrinsic and extrinsic, that are received as a result of employment by the organization. Intrinsic rewards are internal to an individual and are generally derived from involvement in certain activities or tasks. The feelings of satisfaction and accomplishment that are derived from doing a job well are examples of intrinsic rewards. On the other hand, extrinsic rewards are tangible rewards that are directly controlled and distributed by the organization. An employee's pay and hospitalization insurance are examples of extrinsic rewards.

Incentive pay plans attempt to tie pay to performance and are used by many organizations to motivate employees to work toward organizational objectives. Unfortunately, most incentive programs are designed only for top management. Lower levels of management and operative employees do not normally participate. In order for pay to be an effective motivator in strategy implementation, it should be tied to performance and used at all levels in the organization.

Two major problems seem to exist in the design of most management incentive pay programs:

1. The plans are not coupled to the industry's performance. Thus, managers may receive a high reward for achieving a 15 percent growth rate while the industry is growing at a rate of 25 percent.

Figure 7.8 Checklist of Questions on Developing an R&D Strategy

1. Which technical know-how is available or has to be developed for the new product?
2. What kinds of research resources are required for the development of the new product, and are the resources available?
3. What research personnel are required or available?
4. What is the estimated applied research time?
5. What is the expected development time?
6. What is the earliest possible introduction time of the new product, and what is the latest one?
7. What additional labor and research resources are required for speeding up the research time?
8. What are the consequences (e.g., financial) of an earlier or better completion of the research phase compared with the optimal introduction time of the new product?
9. What synergy effects are likely to occur, taking into account other research projects?
10. Which technologies required for the development of this product are relevant for the research policy of the company in the long run?
11. What technological developments have been realized by competition in this area?
12. Are the technologies that are required to develop the product completely new to the organization?
13. What is the innovation value of the new product, and how long will this innovation value exist?
14. Will the new product require continuous defensive research to keep the product features up-to-date; what resources will probably be required for this?
15. What are the estimated design costs and production costs of a prototype or pilot plant?
16. Which additional research resources will make it possible to design a product essentially different from competitive products?
17. What is the probability of technical success?
18. How and with what additional resources could this probability of technical success be influenced?

Source: Adapted from T. Bemelmans, "Strategic Planning for Research and Development," *Long Range Planning* 12 (April 1979):41.

2. The plans are one-dimensional. For example, if compensation is based solely on return on assets, managers may be tempted to eliminate assets or investments critical to long-term growth.[11]

Thus, incentive programs must be properly designed or they can actually work against successful strategy implementation.[12]

Some organizations, in an attempt to relate individual rewards to organization performance, have designed stock option programs in which all employees can participate. This indirectly ties individual rewards to organizational performance.

Many other organizational factors influence the motivation level of employees. In the final analysis, the management team is the key element in determining the level of motivation in an organization. Peter Drucker has suggested several personal characteristics of managers that can significantly lower the level of motivation among employees:

- Lack of integrity of character
- Tendency to focus on people's weaknesses rather than on their strengths
- Interest in who is right rather than what is right
- Disposition to value intelligence more than integrity[13]

Motivated employees are something that some organizations have, and many others wish they had. In the final analysis, motivated employees play a significant role in the successful implementation of organizational strategy.

SUMMARY OF LEARNING OBJECTIVES

1. Explain the role of budgets in achieving organizational objectives.
   Budgeting is a process by which management specifies the resources it will employ to obtain the organization's objectives. It also provides the means of measuring the successful accomplishment of the stated objectives within a specified time period, normally one year.
2. Describe flexible budgets.
   Flexible budgets vary with the volume of sales or some other measure of output.
3. Outline the conditions that must exist to ensure that the budgeting process helps in strategy implementation.
   The conditions are as follows:
   - *Senior management must have a strong commitment to the budgeting process.*
   - *Budgets must be based on the objectives of the business.*
   - *Regular reviews of the operating results in comparison to the budget must be conducted.*
   - *All levels of management must be required to explain budget variances.*
4. Define functional strategies.
   Functional strategies describe the means or methods to be used by each functional area of the organization in carrying out the corporate-level or business unit strategy.
5. Explain the role of marketing strategy.
   Marketing strategy is concerned with matching existing or potential products or services with the needs of customers, informing customers that the products or services exist, having the products or services at the right time and place to facilitate exchange, and assigning a price to the products or services.
6. Discuss the activities involved in financial management.
   The activities of financial management can be grouped into five categories:
   - *Determining the magnitude and characteristics of funds necessary to conduct business operations*

- *Allocating resources in the most efficient manner*
- *Serving as an interface with creditors and stockholders concerning the financial condition of the organization*
- *Recordkeeping*
- *Providing financial data to top management in determining the feasibility of various strategic alternatives.*

7. Categorize the activities involved in production/operations management.
The activities of production/operations management can be categorized into two main areas: system design and operations planning and control.

8. Describe the three basic categories of research and development.
The R&D efforts of organizations can be divided into these basic categories:
- *Basic research: Basic research enlarges technical knowledge without having a specific application of the knowledge.*
- *Applied research: Applied research enlarges technical knowledge in such a manner that a useful commercial application will result from the research.*
- *Development research: Development research uses available knowledge in the introduction of new or improved products or services or production techniques.*

9. Define organizational rewards.
Organizational rewards include all types of rewards, both intrinsic and extrinsic, that are received as a result of employment by the organization. Examples of organizational rewards include pay, fringe benefits, and praise and recognition.

REVIEW QUESTIONS

1. What is a budget?
2. Describe the following budgeting systems:
   a. Flexible budgets
   b. Zero-based budgeting
3. What are some guidelines in identifying a weak budgeting process?
4. What is the purpose of functional strategies?
5. Describe the following marketing strategies:
   a. Market penetration strategy
   b. Market development strategy
   c. Product development strategy
   d. Diversification marketing strategy
6. What are the primary activities of financial management?
7. What is capital budgeting?
8. Describe the cash flow process.
9. What are the main activities in production/operations management?
10. Outline several questions that need to be answered in developing a production/operations strategy.
11. Outline several questions that need to be answered in developing a human resource strategy.
12. Describe the three basic categories of research and development.

13. Outline some of the organizational rewards that can influence the level of motivation in an organization.
14. Describe some of the personal characteristics of managers that can influence the level of motivation in an organization.

DISCUSSION QUESTIONS

1. Do you think that the functional strategies in marketing, finance, and production are generally in conflict? Why or why not?
2. If you were the chief executive of a medium-size company, how would you ensure that all the functional strategies interrelate and help the company achieve its overall objectives?
3. What system would you use to motivate functional-area managers not only in achieving their objectives but also in working cooperatively with other functional-area managers?

REFERENCES AND ADDITIONAL READING

1. Cosmo S. Trapani, "Six Critical Areas in the Budgeting Process," *Management Accounting* 64 (November 1982):52.
2. Carolyn Conn, "Budgets: Planning and Control Devices?" *Managerial Planning* 29, no. 4 (January–February 1981):37.
3. Srinivasan Umapatny, "How Successful Firms Budget," *Management Accounting,* February 1987, pp. 25–27.
4. See Milton Leontiades, "The Importance of Integrating Marketing Planning with Corporate Planning," *Journal of Business Research* 11 (December 1983):457–473.
5. For a more in-depth look at problems in developing financial strategies, see Steward C. Meyers, "Finance Theory and Financial Strategy," *Interfaces* 14 (January–February 1984):26–137.
6. Joseph V. Rizzi, "Capital Budgeting: Linking Financial Analysis to Corporate Strategy," *Journal of Business Strategy* 4 (Spring 1984):81.
7. Wickham Skinner, "Getting Physical: New Strategic Leverage from Operations," *Journal of Business* 3 (Spring 1983):75.
8. Lee Dyer, "Bringing Human Resources into the Strategy Formulation Process," *Human Resources Management* 22 (Fall 1983):261.
9. Lloyd Baird, Ilan Meshoulam, and Ghislaine DeGive, "Meshing Human Resources Planning with Strategic Business Planning: A Model Approach," *Personnel* 60 (September–October 1983):17.
10. William D. Guth and Ian C. MacMillan, "Strategy Implementation Versus Middle Management Self-interest," *Strategic Management Journal,* July–August 1986, p. 313.
11. Ray Stata and Modesto A. Maidique, "Bonus System for Balanced Strategy," *Harvard Business Review* 58 (November–December 1980):157.
12. For a more in-depth discussion see Mark R. Hurwich, "Strategic Compensation Designs That Link Pay to Performance," *Journal of Business Strategy,* Fall 1987, pp. 79–83.
13. Peter F. Drucker, *Management: Tasks, Responsibilities, Practices* (New York: Harper & Row, 1974), p. 462.

Chapter 7: Developing Budgets, Functional Strategies, and Motivational Systems

During the past eight years, Ford has emphasized three main functional strategies. These strategies have been aimed at Ford's customers, its facilities and equipment, and its employees. In addition to Ford's commitment to its consumers and employees, the company has also continued to use a strategy directed toward fulfilling its social responsibilities.

MARKETING STRATEGY

The marketing strategy aimed at Ford's customers has been designed to create an image in the customer's mind that Ford is synonymous with quality. Ford has created an image of high-quality, fuel-efficient, and appealing products. Philip Benton, president of the Ford Automotive Group, has described Ford's marketing strategy as follows:

> What our customers define as quality is what we must deliver. We have relearned in recent years that the successful automakers consistently provide customers with that they need and want, at a price they feel offers good value, in a product that meets their expectations of safety and quality. Our challenge is to go beyond that—to exceed customer expectations and, indeed, to generate customer enthusiasm. (1988 annual report, p. 6)

In 1989, sales of new cars and trucks in the U.S. market were estimated at 14.8 million units, and Ford's share was 22 percent. There will be an expected loss of market share by American manufacturers totaling more than 6 percentage points by 1994 to Japanese competitors. Ford Motor Company is expected to lose approximately 1 point. In light of this information, Ford has placed more emphasis on customer satisfaction. To obtain feedback from its customers for product improvement, Ford has designed a questionnaire (see Exhibit 1).

Ford's marketing strategy is supported by its "Partners in Excellence" program. Under this program, Ford employees, dealers, and suppliers worldwide play increasingly important roles in assuring the levels of quality and customer satisfaction Ford seeks. At the manufacturing and assembly level, joint United Auto Workers (UAW)–Ford "Best-in-Class" education and training programs continue to strengthen quality efforts. Ford also works closely with suppliers on quality objectives. All suppliers to North America Automotive Operations (NAAO) must have earned Ford's Q1 Preferred Quality Award by January 1, 1990, to qualify for new business. Over 2100 supplier locations have earned the award.

To help ensure quality customer service, Ford has joined with a number of dealers and community colleges across the country to develop a two-year work/study program called Ford ASSET (Automotive Student Service Educa-

Exhibit 1 Questionnaire for Ford Customers

Automarket Research 10-Day Survey

SELLING DEALER:

Please make any corrections in your name and address here.

PHONE ( )

SALESPERSON:

PLEASE MARK AS FOLLOWS: ⊖ This questionnaire should be completed by the principal driver of the vehicle indicated. Please answer only based on your experience with the dealership where you bought your vehicle. Do not report experience with any other dealership. Thank you.

ABOUT THE SALE AND DELIVERY OF NEW VEHICLE

1. How satisfied were you with your treatment by the dealership sales personnel?
- a. Helpfulness, courtesy of dealership sales personnel
- b. Product knowledge of salesperson
- c. Explanation of your vehicle's operating features
- d. Explanation of the warranty coverage and maintenance requirements
- e. Overall satisfaction with sales treatment

2. At the time of delivery, how satisfied were you with your dealership's preparation of your vehicle in the following areas?
- a. Exterior appearance and cleanliness
- b. Interior appearance and cleanliness
- c. Operation of accessories (e.g., horn, wipers, radio, air conditioner, heater, defroster, etc.)
- d. Overall satisfaction with new vehicle preparation

ABOUT THE DEALERSHIP SALES STAFF

3. Prior to purchase, did the salesperson offer you a test drive? Yes / No

4. Prior to or at the time you took delivery, did someone from the dealership:
- a. Give you the opportunity to purchase an extended service contract?
- b. Introduce you to someone in the Service Department?
- c. Explain to you what to do if you need service?
- d. Explain to you the Quality Commitment?

5. At the time you took delivery, how much fuel was provided? Full / ¾ Full / ½ Full / ¼ Full / Less Than ½ Full

6. a. Since taking delivery, have you been contacted by anyone from the dealership where you bought the vehicle? Yes / No
b. Since taking delivery, how was the contact made? Telephone / Letter / Personal Contact
c. Were you contacted by your salesperson? Yes / No If no, go to Question 8.

ABOUT THE SERVICE DEPARTMENT

7. a. Since taking delivery, have you taken your new vehicle for any kind of service including warranty repair work? If yes, where have you taken this vehicle for service to:
Go to Question 8.1
- b. How satisfied were you with the service received at Beaudry Ford?

(Rating scale: Completely Satisfied / Very Satisfied / Fairly Well Satisfied / Somewhat Dissatisfied / Very Dissatisfied)

PFQ704   000475

ABOUT YOUR DEALERSHIP OVERALL

8. To sum it all up, overall how satisfied have you been with the dealership where you bought your vehicle (taking into account the new vehicle preparation and service you may have received)?

(Rating scale: Completely Satisfied / Very Satisfied / Fairly Well Satisfied / Somewhat Dissatisfied / Very Dissatisfied)

9. All things considered, how likely would you be to:
- a. Recommend the salesperson to someone else?
- b. Recommend the dealership to someone else?
- c. Recommend a Ford Motor Company product to someone else?

(Rating scale: Definitely Would / Probably Would / Likely Would / Probably Would Not / Definitely Would Not)

ABOUT YOUR NEW VEHICLE

10. If you have returned your vehicle for service, what was the reason? Check those that apply.
- Paint/exterior moldings
- Interior
- Transmission
- Brakes/steering
- Engine
- Electrical system
- Wheels/tires
- Other (please describe)

11. Although you've had your vehicle for only a brief period, tell us how satisfied you are with it in the following areas.
- a. Exterior quality of workmanship (fit and finish)
- b. Interior quality of workmanship (fit and finish)
- c. Engine power and pickup
- d. Smoothness of the transmission
- e. Riding comfort
- f. Ease of handling
- g. Fuel economy
- h. Quietness
- i. Operation of the accessories (e.g., radio, air conditioner, heater, defroster, etc.)
- j. Overall satisfaction with this vehicle

(Rating scale: Completely Satisfied / Very Satisfied / Fairly Well Satisfied / Somewhat Dissatisfied / Very Dissatisfied)

GENERAL

12. What make vehicle did you previously drive?
- Ford Motor Company
- General Motors
- Chrysler Corporation
- European import
- Japanese import
- Other

13. Have you previously purchased any other vehicle(s) from the dealership where you bought this vehicle (either new or used)? Yes / No

Please answer the following for purposes of classifying your response.

ABOUT YOU

14. Are you: Male / Female

15. Are you: Married / Single

16. Please your age bracket: Under 20 / 20–24 / 25–29 / 30–34 / 35–39 / 40–44 / 45–49 / 50–54 / 55–59 / 60–64 / 65 or over

17. Your education:
- Some high school
- High school graduate, no college
- Some college
- College graduate
- Postgraduate degree

18. Which of the following approximates your total annual household income?
- $15,000 or less
- $15,001–$25,000
- $25,001–$35,000
- $35,001–$45,000
- $45,001–$55,000
- $55,001–$65,000
- $65,001–$80,000
- $80,001–$100,000
- $100,001–$125,000
- $125,001–$150,000
- Over $150,000

Additional comments: (What can your dealership do to improve customer treatment?)

Please return the completed questionnaire directly to Automarket Research in the postage-paid envelope provided or mail to: Automarket Research, P.O. Box 8021, Royal Oak, MI 48068-9917

5555   2222   3573552

tional Training). ASSET helps provide Ford and Lincoln-Mercury dealerships with well-qualified entry-level service technicians.

MANUFACTURING STRATEGY

Complementing Ford's marketing strategy has been its investment in new facilities and equipment. Technological development and modernization of facilities has been a major strategic thrust at Ford. Since 1984, the company has spent over $18 billion in capital expenditures for equipment and special tools. Through the use of automation, Ford has been able to cut its labor costs and improve the overall quality of its plants.

Ford has also implemented the concept of project management into many of its plants. In the Escort facilities at the Wayne assembly plant, Ford has placed its new stamping and body facility strategically adjacent to its assembly facility. This location offers efficiencies in overall operations through the use of the just-in-time concepts and improved quality through greater automation. Project management entails the use of teamwork and communication to get the job completed on time and within budget.

HUMAN RESOURCE STRATEGY

Ford has focused on gaining commitment from its employees through a human resource strategy that has both monetary and educational components. Through its profit sharing program, the company introduced a bonus system based on annual profits. The program encourages employees to work harder to ensure maximum profits for the company. This illustrates one motivational system used by Ford in achieving its objectives.

Ford offers an extensive employee benefit package. It includes several options for medical coverage for families and single adults, dental insurance plans, and in some instances eye care. To ensure that quality people are running its business, Ford has developed a continuing-education program for its employees. When an employee completes job-related college-level or high school equivalency (GED) courses, Ford reimburses him or her for tuition and textbooks.

In 1988, there were more than 140,000 enrollments by both salaried and UAW-represented hourly employees in educational and personal-development activities. And since 1985, more than 2,000 top managers from around the world have attended Ford's Executive Development Center in Detroit.

Ford spends millions of dollars to maintain several personal-development seminars. The philosophy behind these seminars is that if the employees are motivated and content with themselves as individuals, they will carry out the strategy of the company effectively.

SOCIAL RESPONSIBILITY STRATEGY

Ford has also developed a strategy to meet its social responsibilities. One example is its commitment to minority dealers and suppliers. Another is the financial support of education and community programs.

In 1988, the number of minority-owned Ford and Lincoln-Mercury dealerships rose by 30 percent to 308, highest among the Big Three automakers. Business with minority suppliers also grew substantially, from $341 million in 1987 to $481 million in 1988.

Ford contributed more than $28 million for educational and community support in 1988—the majority to United Way campaigns and social, educational, and cultural programs. Grants for education (primarily college level) and funds to match employees' gifts to schools and universities reached $9.6 million, up from $7.6 million in 1987.

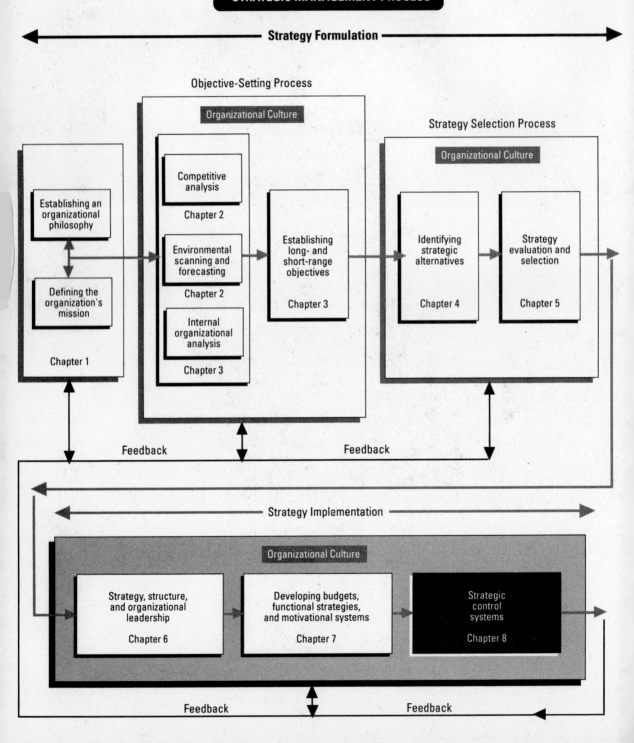

STRATEGIC MANAGEMENT PROCESS

Strategy Formulation

Objective-Setting Process

Organizational Culture

Establishing an organizational philosophy

Defining the organization's mission

Chapter 1

Competitive analysis

Chapter 2

Environmental scanning and forecasting

Chapter 2

Internal organizational analysis

Chapter 3

Establishing long- and short-range objectives

Chapter 3

Strategy Selection Process

Organizational Culture

Identifying strategic alternatives

Chapter 4

Strategy evaluation and selection

Chapter 5

Feedback   Feedback

Strategy Implementation

Organizational Culture

Strategy, structure, and organizational leadership

Chapter 6

Developing budgets, functional strategies, and motivational systems

Chapter 7

Strategic control systems

Chapter 8

Feedback   Feedback

CHAPTER 8
The Strategic Control Process

LEARNING OBJECTIVES

After studying this chapter, you should be able to

1. Explain the relationship between strategy formulation and the strategic control processes.

2. Describe the three basic elements in the strategic control process.

3. Outline typical areas in which organizations establish quantitative criteria for evaluation.

4. Discuss several sources that provide quantifiable data on organizational performance measures.

5. Explain the auditing process.

6. Describe the characteristics of an effective strategic control system.

7. Explain the role of MIS in the strategic control process.

8. Describe a strategy review.

The basic premise of strategic management is that the chosen strategy will achieve the organization's objectives. However, the possibility of this not occurring gives rise to the need for the strategic control process. In the *control process* top management determines how well or whether the chosen strategy is achieving the organization's objectives.

The strategic control process should alert management to a problem or potential problem before it becomes critical. Control is accomplished by comparing actual performance to objectives and then taking action to correct any deviations from the objectives. The need for control is essential. However, the nature and degree of strategic control is a complex and sensitive issue. The implementation of control systems often only leads to more controls which, in turn, lead to more controls. In order to avoid this trap, managers must remember that control is only one phase in the strategic management process and is not an end in itself. Control systems must be designed to provide information that facilitates the accomplishment of organizational objectives. Too much information can be as bad as or worse than not enough information.

STRATEGY FORMULATION AND THE STRATEGIC CONTROL PROCESS

The strategic control and strategy formulation processes are closely interrelated. Figure 8.1 illustrates the relationship. The desired results (long- and short-range objectives) of an organization are established during the strategy formulation process. Control systems measure outputs from functional areas of the organization. Evaluation of performance occurs when the output of the control system is compared to the long- and short-range objectives. Finally, feedback occurs when the results of this comparison are used to make adjustments in the objectives of the organization, changes in strategy, changes in the organizational structure, or changes in the management team.

THREE ELEMENTS OF THE STRATEGIC CONTROL PROCESS

The strategic control process has three basic elements: (1) objectives of the business, (2) evaluation of performance, and (3) feedback (or corrective action). All three elements are essential in maintaining effective strategic control.

Objectives of the Business

The objectives of the business should be the starting point in evaluating an organization's success. As will be recalled, establishing organizational objectives was described in detail in Chapter 3. Ideally, objectives should be quantifiable and measurable.

Quantitative criteria should be established for all key objectives of the organization. Key objectives are those that are essential for the survival and success of the organization. Most organizations establish quantitative criteria for evaluation on factors such as

- Dividend payments
- Earnings per share
- Employee turnover, absenteeism, tardiness, and grievances
- Growth in sales
- Market share
- Net profit
- Profit-sales ratios
- Return on investment
- Stock price

Example 8.1 illustrates du Pont's system of financial controls. As can be seen, du Pont uses quantitative criteria.

However, the use of quantitative criteria for evaluation can cause problems. First, most quantitative criteria are only geared to the short-term profit objectives of the organization. Pressure is exerted by stockholders and the financial community for steady increases in earnings per share on a quarterly basis.

Figure 8.1 *Relationship Between Strategic Planning and the Strategic Control Process*

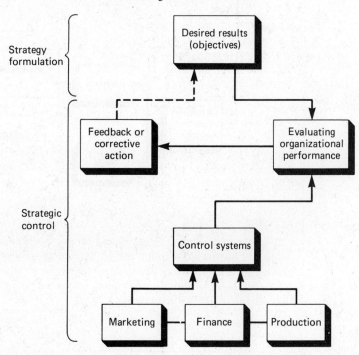

Du Pont's System of Financial Control

Du Pont's system of financial control (shown diagrammatically in the figure below) has received wide recognition.

The figure is divided into two main groupings. The upper group represents investment turnover, which is derived by combining current assets and fixed investments in the form of property, plant, and equipment, and then dividing total investment into sales.

The lower group begins with an analysis of the income statement. Sales minus cost of sales gives earnings, and earnings divided by sales gives earnings as a percent of sales. Return on investment is calculated by multiplying turnover by earnings as a percent of sales.

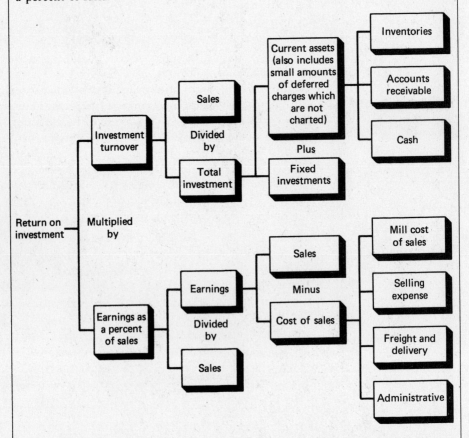

Return on investment is calculated for each operating division, department, or product. This has been called the *profit center approach* to looking at performance. Management compares division, department, or product performance not only to determine how to allocate additional resources but also to determine incentive bonuses for individual managers.

Source: Adapted from Lawrence J. Gitman, *Principles of Managerial Finance*, 5th ed. (New York: Harper & Row, 1980), pp. 111–113.

Concern about immediate profit maximization makes it rather difficult to implement a strategy that cannot be immediately measured and has returns that are long-term in nature. A second problem with the use of quantitative criteria is that the set of criteria used at one particular point during the implementation of a strategy more than likely will change over time. For example, during the development phase of a new product, the most important criteria would probably relate to production efficiency and research and development. Later, criteria related to marketing and financial considerations would become more important. Finally, different accounting methods provide different results on many of the quantitative criteria. If quantitative measures are to be used in control, the accounting procedures used in the calculations must be consistently applied.

Evaluating Organizational Performance

Unfortunately, performance evaluation is often viewed as being synonymous with the control process when in fact it is only part of the total control process. The overriding purpose of performance evaluation is to identify problem areas in an organization. Evaluating performance requires comparing actual performance to planned performance, that is, comparing the output from the control systems to the objectives of the business. After this comparison has been made, corrective action can be taken, if necessary.

In evaluating performance, it is useful for a business not only to evaluate its performance against its objectives but to compare itself against its competitors. The following sources provide quantifiable data on organizational performance measures.

1. *Computerized Data Bases.* Computerized data bases provide financial information about companies and markets from a variety of sources. Two of the major firms in the computerized data base field are Standard and Poor's (S&P) Corporation and Value Line. These firms provide disks containing the information. Standard and Poor's uses the name Compustat for its data base. Compustat offers basic annual and historical data files on over 5000 organizations. Some of the information provided by Compustat includes income statement data, balance sheet data, and information on stock prices. In addition, Compustat adjusts the data to achieve comparability between time periods and companies. The information provided by Value Line is similar to Compustat.

2. *Dun's Review.* Each year (normally during November) Dun and Bradstreet publishes in *Dun's Review* key business ratios for the retail, wholesale, and manufacturing industries. Ratios in this listing include

   a. Current assets to current liabilities
   b. Net profits on net sales (percent)
   c. Net profits on tangible net worth (percent)
   d. Net profits on net working capital (percent)
   e. Net sales to tangible net worth

f. Net sales to net working capital
g. Collection period (days)
h. Net sales to inventory
i. Fixed assets to tangible net worth (percent)
j. Current debt to tangible net worth (percent)
k. Total debt to tangible net worth (percent)
l. Inventory to net working capital (percent)
m. Current debt to inventory (percent)

Furthermore, each year in December *Dun's Review* provides a qualitative evaluation of what it feels are the five best-managed companies for the year.

3. *Forbes.* Each year in January, *Forbes* publishes its measures of performance for over 1000 organizations. *Forbes* measures these organizations on their profitability (in terms of return on stockholders' equity and total capital), growth (in terms of both earnings per share and sales), debt-equity ratios, net profit margins, and stock market performance. *Forbes* uses these measures to rank the organizations in terms of their profitability, growth, and stock market performance.

4. *Fortune.* Each year in May, *Fortune* provides financial and other information on the 500 largest U.S. industrial corporations. The information provided includes sales, assets, net income, stockholders' equity, number of employees, net income as a percent of stockholders' equity, earnings per share, and total return to investors. In June, the same information is provided for the second 500 largest industrials.

Feedback or Corrective Action

Output from the strategic control process influences all other phases of the strategic management process. For example, if the profits for a particular SBU, division, or product are significantly below projections, then a complete reexamination of the unit's objectives and strategy is in order. However, the poor performance may only be due to the personal ineptness or negligence of certain managers, and in this case these managers must change or be replaced.

Furthermore, output from the control phase of strategy implementation provides information essential to the objective-setting process. As will be recalled from Chapter 2, answering the question "Where are we now?" is the first step in the objective-setting process. Properly designed control systems provide valuable information for answering this question.

Thus, the entire strategic management process is a feedback system that must be constantly adjusted based on information from the control system and from the organization's environment. Figure 8.2 illustrates this feedback system. The dashed lines indicate that information from the control process influences and should be used in all other phases of the strategic management process. Viewing the process as a feedback system only enhances the system's effectiveness. Otherwise, when performance deviations occur, piecemeal and often only stopgap measures are taken such as firing managers or reorganizing. These actions may very well be necessary, but they should be undertaken only after a review of the entire strategic management process.

Figure 8.2 *Strategic Management Process as a Feedback System*

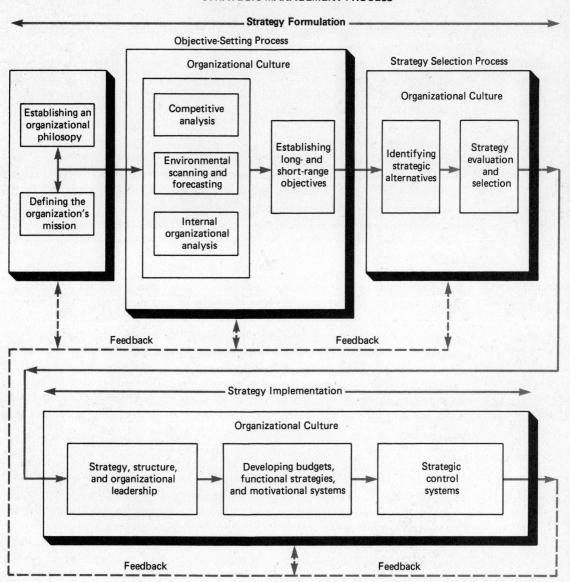

STRATEGIC MANAGEMENT PROCESS

METHODS USED IN STRATEGIC CONTROL SYSTEMS

Many methods are used in strategic control systems. Some senior managers feel that the only way to get an adequate picture of what is happening in the company is through personal observation. Thus, they make visits to various facilities. Other frequently used methods of control are described in the following sections.

Budgets

Budgets are probably the most widely used control methods. Preparation of the budget determines how the resources of the organization are to be allocated among its various units. On the other hand, the administration of the budget is a method of control.

After the budget is prepared, the controller's department in large organizations keep records on expenditures and periodically prepares reports showing the budgets, actual expenditures, and differences (or variances, as they are frequently called). For smaller organizations, this function is often handled by the owner-manager, the office manager, or an independent service organization such as a bank or accounting firm. After the report is prepared, generally it is sent to the people responsible for the particular area or function covered by the budget. It is at this point that variances must be analyzed and corrective action taken, if necessary. Furthermore, in effective budgeting control systems, each manager meets with his or her subordinates to review variances and determine corrective actions. This process is repeated from the bottom to the top of the organization. At higher levels of management, written reports are often required that outline the reasons for variances and the corrective actions that are being taken.

Of course, it is entirely possible that the budget, which is actually only a forecast of expected results and requirements, may need revising. Normally, for larger organizations a budget review committee (generally composed of the top executives of the organization) meets regularly to review and revise the budget. In the final analysis, preparation, administration, and corrective action taken on budget variances are key elements in successful strategy implementation.

Audits

Another frequently used method of control is an audit. *Auditing* has been defined by the American Accounting Association (AAA) to be "a systematic process of objectively obtaining and evaluating evidence regarding assertions about economic actions and events to ascertain the degree of correspondence between those assertions and established criteria and communicating the results to interested users."[1]

Basically, the audit process focuses on the financial assertions made by a business and on how well those assertions represent events that have occurred.

People who perform the audit function can be divided into three basic groups: independent, government, and internal auditors.

Independent Auditors

Independent auditors or certified public accountants (CPAs) are professionals who provide their services to organizations for a fee. Their primary function is to examine the financial statements of a client. However, independent auditors also perform other work such as bookkeeping and accounting services, tax accounting, management consulting, and the preparation of financial statements for clients.

In order to offer their services to the public, CPAs must meet a series of standards of education and experience and must pass a uniform national examination. The license to practice as a CPA is granted by individual states. Audits of financial statements by CPAs determine whether the statements have been prepared according to an objective set of rules, called generally accepted accounting principles (GAAP), and whether the statements fairly represent the activities of the organization. In making this determination, CPAs use a set of standards called generally accepted auditing standards (GAAS).

Government Auditors

Two government agencies—the General Accounting Office (GAO) and the Internal Revenue Service (IRS)—are primarily responsible for performing government audits of organizations. Government audits are conducted to determine the organization's compliance with federal laws, statutes, policies, procedures, and rules. Auditors from the GAO perform audits of other government agencies and companies with government contracts. The Internal Revenue Service, on the other hand, is primarily concerned with compliance with the federal tax laws (Internal Revenue Code) and, of course, can audit any private enterprise organization.

Internal Auditors

Internal auditors are organizational employees whose primary responsibility is to determine whether organizational policies and procedures are being carried out correctly and to safeguard organizational assets. Internal auditors are also frequently called upon to assess not only the efficiency of various organizational subunits but also the efficiency of control systems within the organization. Top management and an organization's board of directors are the most frequent users of the information gained by internal auditors.

Management Audits

Management audits systematically examine, analyze, and evaluate the overall performance of an organization's management team. Management audits can be performed by outside consultants (the consulting division of independent certified public accounting firms often performs management audits) or by an organization's own internal audit staff. Management audits have been performed in organizations with such diverse interests as the Roman Catholic church and Procter & Gamble.[2]

DESIGNING EFFECTIVE STRATEGIC CONTROL SYSTEMS

In today's environment, floods of data and information can be generated to the point that the entire control system becomes meaningless. In order to be effective, control systems must meet several basic requirements:

1. *Control Systems Should Be Economical.* In designing a control system for a particular area or function in an organization, management should always ask, What is the minimum information needed to have control over this area or function? Too much information can be just as bad as too little.

2. *Control Systems Should Be Meaningful.* Controls must be related to the key objectives of the organization. At lower levels of management, control systems should give managers useful information about the activities they control and influence. A careful analysis should be made not only of what is needed but also of what is not needed.

3. *Control Systems Should Provide Timely Information.* Frequent and rapid feedback does not necessarily mean better control. The key question is whether the information is provided in time to be of use to the management team. In certain cases, information is needed almost daily. For example, when an organization is test marketing a new product, rapid feedback on the results is essential. However, in a long-range research and development project, frequent feedback on progress may actually be counterproductive. Thus, control systems should be designed to correspond to the time span of the activity or function being measured.

4. *Control Systems Should Provide Qualitative Information on Trends.* For example, knowing whether a particular product's market share is going up or down or remaining stable is probably at least as important as knowing the actual percentage of market share. Knowing whether a new product is on schedule in terms of its market introduction is as important as knowing whether it is within budget. Qualitative information such as this can signal problem areas much more quickly than a mere presentation of quantitative data and thus can facilitate quicker action to solve the problem.

5. *Control Systems Should Facilitate Action.* Information from the control system must be directed to those people in the organization who can take action based on it. Providing a control report to a manager "for informational purposes only" usually means that the report will be ignored by the manager and may, in fact, lead the manager to ignore other useful reports. Not everyone in an organization has to receive all the reports.

6. *Control Systems Should Be Simple.* Generally, it is safe to say that if someone needs to know the mechanics and methodology of the control system before it can be used, then more than likely the system needs to be redesigned. Complex control systems often only confuse people and accomplish little. The key to an effective control system is its usefulness, not its complexity.

Example 8.2 illustrates McKesson Drug Company's strategic control system for handling order entry information.

McKesson Drug Company's Strategic Information System

A striking change has occurred in wholesale drug distribution over the past decade. The number of wholesale drug distributors has decreased by over 50 percent. A second major change has been the decreasing share of direct distribution by manufacturers. Today, over 60 percent of the pharmaceuticals ordered by pharmacies are provided by wholesale drug distributors. McKesson Drug Company is one of the largest of these distributors.

In order to better serve its customers—retail pharmacies—McKesson developed one of the most widely cited examples of successful strategic control systems. The system is called Economost. It was instituted to reduce costs and to tie retail pharmacy customers closer to McKesson. One motivation for developing the system was that McKesson's principal customers, the independent pharmacies, were failing. Economost was aimed at giving these independents many of the advantages enjoyed by the chains, enabling them to compete better and thus preserving the market served by McKesson.

Using Economost, a customer may order from McKesson by passing through his or her store and simply keying McKesson's seven-digit identifier into a hand-held electronic order entry device. The customer then transmits the order via McKesson's 800 WATTS line to McKesson's national data center. The same or the following day, McKesson delivers the items ordered. The requested items come delivered in cartons that match the aisle arrangement and major departments of the drug store; no sorting is required, and the shelves can be restocked with a single pass. Price stickers are provided, and the customer has the option of specifying numerous retail options.

McKesson also provides retail pharmacists with valuable management control information, much of which would be too expensive for an independent to provide for itself. A monthly "Management Purchase Report" is available to all Economost customers; it shows what items have been ordered and the prices at which they have been sold, and indicates profit margins for items, departments, and the pharmacy as a whole.

Source: Adapted from Eric K. Clemons and Michael Row, "A Strategic Information System: McKesson Drug Company's Economost," *Planning Review*, September–October 1988, pp. 14–19.

ROLE OF MANAGEMENT INFORMATION SYSTEMS IN THE STRATEGIC CONTROL PROCESS

A management information system (MIS) is a formal system designed to provide information in order to facilitate strategy formulation and strategic control. The basic idea behind an MIS, regardless of its sophistication, is to provide managers with information in a systematic and integrated manner rather than a sporadic and piecemeal manner.

Careful design and implementation of an MIS is essential. Obviously, the value of an MIS is enhanced when its design and implementation are aligned with the organization's strategy. Furthermore, the value of an MIS is considerably enhanced if the following guidelines are followed:

- The MIS must be designed and implemented to meet the needs of those managers who are making strategic decisions.
- The MIS must be designed and implemented through close cooperation between MIS personnel and managers who make strategic decisions.
- Output from the MIS must be presented in a form that is most appropriate for strategic decision making. Information overload must be avoided.
- A good starting point in MIS design is an examination of the information systems that currently exist in the businesses.
- A good MIS must be flexible in order to accommodate the changing environment of the business.

Businesses that do align their MIS with their strategy will undoubtedly gain a competitive advantage. The likelihood that a strategy will be successful is enhanced when the necessary MIS is available to provide information on how well the strategy is working.[3]

CONDUCTING A STRATEGY REVIEW

A *strategy review* is an examination of an organization's strategy to determine if the existing strategy has produced the desired results. An organization normally undertakes a strategy review under the following conditions:

- An existing strategy has failed to produce the desired results.
- A fundamental change has occurred in the organization's environment.
- A new management team would like to set its own course of action.[4]

Figure 8.3 diagrams the strategic review process. The possible conclusions reached in Figure 8.3 call for changes that must be made by senior management. In the final analysis, a strategy review should provide the basis for making changes that will ensure that future organizational objectives are successfully achieved.

For most organizations, senior management gives a general strategy review in the annual report. Example 8.3 gives such a review for Apple Computer.

SUMMARY OF LEARNING OBJECTIVES

1. Explain the relationship between strategy formulation and the strategic control process.

   The long- and short-range objectives of a business are established in the strategy formulation process. The strategic control process provides information on how well the strategy is being accomplished.

Figure 8.3 *Strategy Review*

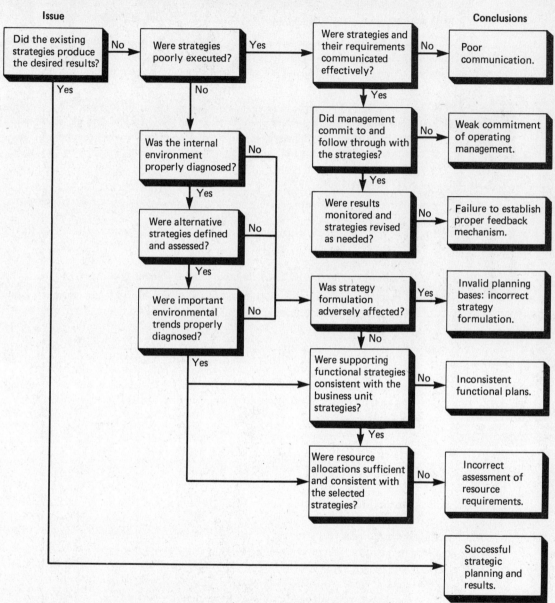

Source: Adapted from Jeffrey A. Schmidt, "The Strategic Review," *Planning Review,* July/August 1988, p. 15.

2. Describe the three basic elements in the strategic control process.
   The three elements in the strategic control process are (1) objectives of the business, (2) evaluation of performance, and (3) feedback (or corrective action).

STRATEGY IN ACTION Example 8.3

Strategy Review at Apple Computer

One source for a general strategy review given by a company's management is its annual report. John Sculley, chairman, president, and chief executive officer of Apple Computer, provides the following strategy review for Apple:

> Products that change the world also change the companies that create them.
>
> In 1988, what changed Apple's world was the Macintosh™ II. Its global acceptance positioned Apple as a mainstream business computer company, and continued to strengthen our leadership position in education. And the rich user environment of the Macintosh II reaffirmed what differentiates Apple from every other computer maker—our values:
>
> > We place the individual—not the organization—at the center of the computing universe.
> > We believe that an organization can only be as productive as its individual members, so improving the computer user's experience is at the center of everything we do.
> > We build tools specifically designed to increase personal productivity.
>
> It all started with the Apple™ II, the first computer to put real power in the hands of nontechnical users. But today, the most complete expression of that goal is the Macintosh II, a computer that embodies Apple's vision of the future.
>
> It is our platform for the 1990s. Its 32-bit Motorola microprocessor, easily augmented million-character memory, and wide-open architecture make it our most powerful personal computer. But its Multifinder system software and revolutionary application languages such as HyperCard™ use that power to make it our most *personal* personal computer.

Source: 1988 annual report.

3. Outline typical areas in which organizations establish quantitative criteria for evaluation.
   These areas include dividend payments; earnings per share; employee turnover, absenteeism, tardiness, and grievances; growth in sales; market share; net profit; profit-sales ratios; return on investment; and stock price.
4. Discuss several sources that provide quantifiable data on organizational performance measures.
   Several sources are computerized data bases such as Standard and Poor's Corporation and Value Line, Dun's Review, Forbes, and Fortune.
5. Explain the auditing process.
   Auditing focuses on the financial assertions made by a business and on how well those assertions represent events that have occurred.
6. Describe the characteristics of an effective strategic control system.
   Effective control systems should be economical, be meaningful, provide timely information, provide qualitative information on trends, facilitate action, and be simple.

The Macintosh II is the platform for a new generation of Apple tool sets for everything from information management and programming to interactive learning and computer-aided design. And while it has changed the way the world perceives Apple, it has also brought about fundamental changes in Apple's world.

Because of its higher performance and greater sophistication, the Macintosh II has enabled us to enter new markets in business, education, and government.

Those markets required new channels of distribution—high-end dealers, systems integrators, original equipment manufacturers (OEMs), and value added resellers (VARs).

Those new channels required new kinds of Apple sales and support—team selling with direct Apple involvement for larger customers, and heightened emphasis on customer satisfaction.

Those larger customers, in turn, required new levels of sophistication in networking and communications, as well as solutions.

And this required a new generation of software, peripherals, and networking and communications products. All of which, ultimately, required us to reshape Apple into a new kind of company—with a new organization that will be more responsive to customers, can accommodate continuing growth, and yet will preserve the basic values that are the foundation of our success.

So even though the Apple II remains an important part of our business and even though the other members of the Macintosh family are global best-sellers, to understand the pivotal role of the Macintosh II in 1988 is to have a clear vision of Apple's future.

7. Explain the role of MIS in the strategic control process.
   An MIS is a formal system designed to provide information in order to facilitate strategy formulation and strategic control.
8. Describe a strategy review.
   A strategy review is an examination of an organization's strategy to determine if the existing strategy has produced the desired results.

REVIEW QUESTIONS

1. Describe the relationship between strategy formulation and strategic control.
2. What are the three basic elements in the strategic control process?
3. Outline some typical areas in which organizations establish quantitative criteria for evaluation.

4. List several sources that provide quantifiable data on organizational performance measures.
5. Describe the following:
   a. Audit
   b. Independent auditors
   c. Government auditors
   d. Internal auditors
6. Outline the characteristics of an effective control system.
7. What is the purpose of an MIS?
8. What is a strategy review?

DISCUSSION QUESTIONS

1. "Controls only necessitate the need for more controls." Discuss your views on this statement.
2. What are some of the major problems associated with using budgets as control devices?
3. Do you think that all organizations should have a team of internal auditors that reports directly to the board of directors? What are some of the possible negative consequences of having a group such as this?
4. When a strategy has not been successful, the most effective way to take corrective action is to change the management team. Do you agree? Why or why not?

REFERENCES AND ADDITIONAL READING

1. AAA Committee on Basic Auditing Concepts, 1971.
2. William T. Thornhill, *Complete Handbook of Operational and Management Auditing* (Englewood Cliffs, N.J.: Prentice-Hall, 1981), p. 73.
3. Dhruba Sen, "Using It to Support Business Strategy," *Accountancy*, July 1987, pp. 137–140.
4. Jeffrey A. Schmidt, "The Strategic Review," *Planning Review*, July/August 1988, p. 14.

Strategy in Action Case Study: Ford Motor Company

Chapter 8: Strategic Control Process

The issue that must be addressed in strategy review is, Did the existing strategies produce the desired results? The answer to this question for Ford Motor Company is that Ford's strategies during the 1980s have proven to be very successful.

During the early 1980s, Ford faced a number of critical challenges: soaring interest rates, a severe worldwide recession, and intense foreign competition. The time was at hand to reshape one of the world's largest enterprises. And in a short time, Ford accomplished what many said was impossible.

Ford people revitalized the company, strengthened its businesses, and set on a new course for the future. Ford invested billions of dollars in new tooling, new technology, and a whole new generation of vehicles.

Ford has emerged as a pacesetter in automotive transportation and other critical technologies. Consider some of the company's major achievements since 1980:

- Ford has reached the level of producing the highest-quality cars and trucks of any domestic manufacturer.
- Ford is a pioneer in the employee involvement and participative management movements.
- Ford has brought about 30 new vehicle lines to market.
- Ford's technology has leaped a generation. It is a global leader in automotive electronics, robotics, ergonomics, and aerodynamics.
- Ford has been lauded for a new generation of distinctively designed, meticulously engineered "driver's" cars and trucks.

OVERVIEW OF RESULTS OF FORD'S STRATEGY

Donald E. Petersen, chairman of the board and chief executive officer, and Harold A. Poling, vice-chairman of the board and chief operating officer, give the following review of the results of Ford's strategy in the company's annual report:

A review of Ford's three major business elements—the Automotive Group, Diversified Products Operations and the Financial Services Group—shows strength and growth.

In the Automotive Group, Ford's U.S. car-market share rose by 1.5 percentage points from 1987 to 21.7 percent in 1988—the highest Ford share in 10 years. Ford truck sales reached an all-time high in the largest U.S. truck-industry market ever recorded and our truck share remained strong at 29 percent. Our U.S. profits were down slightly from 1987, primarily because of less favorable product mix and higher product and marketing costs.

In Canada, Ford's combined car and truck sales set a record. Car-market share was up 1.6 percentage points, the largest gain in the industry.

In Europe, Ford remained the fourth largest seller of cars in that highly competitive market, with an 11.5 percent share. Car sales were almost even with 1987's record, and truck sales set a record. Our truck share, at 11.1 percent, remained the third highest in Europe.

In Latin America, Ford had truck sales leadership in Argentina and Venezuela. In the Asia-Pacific region, Ford retained car sales leadership in Australia and in New Zealand. And in the booming Taiwan market, Ford Lio Ho led in car sales for the first time.

Our exports of North American–made cars and trucks rose sharply to about 41,000 units, an 83 percent increase over 1987. The Middle East continued to be the strongest growth area.

Diversified Products Operations' 10 automotive and non-automotive businesses registered a record $13.3 billion in sales, up $1.4 billion from 1987. All of the ongoing non-automotive components were profitable for the first time since 1977.

In December 1988, we sold to a Brazilian company three Philco Brazil operations that make consumer electronics products. The sale did not include other Philco-managed operations that produce automotive audio equipment and climate control components for the Brazilian market.

Reflecting the growing significance of automotive electronics, we began construction of two new components plants last fall.

Ford Aerospace Corporation, in acquiring BDM International, Inc., increased its capabilities to provide professional and technical services in national defense and security, communications, energy, logistics, space and manufacturing technology.

During the year, our Financial Services Group continued to expand by means of both internal growth and acquisitions. Through our First Nationwide Financial Corporation subsidiary, we have become America's second largest savings and loan operation, with assets of approximately $35 billion.

Although Financial Services Group earnings were down from 1987—caused primarily by lower net interest margins and higher credit losses—Ford Motor Credit Company, First Nationwide Financial Corporation, United States Leasing International, Inc., and Ford's international credit affiliates continued to contribute importantly to the company's total earnings.

FORD'S FUTURE STRATEGY—STRENGTHENING COMPETITIVENESS

Petersen and Poling went on to describe Ford's future strategy as follows:

The automotive business remains our core element. To ensure that we maintain our competitive capabilities worldwide, we are supplementing our own strong internal resources through a number of associations with other automakers and component suppliers. These mutually beneficial cooperative ventures give us access to markets and customers we might not otherwise reach.

Our longest-standing relationship has been with Mazda Motor Corporation, in which we hold a 25 percent interest. We will mark the 10th anniversary of our equity association with Mazda in 1989. We also have important relationships with Volkswagen in South America and with Kia Motors Corporation in South Korea. We also are working on various projects with Nissan Motor Company, Ltd.

In addition, Ford has joined six other American companies in forming a consortium to explore business opportunities in the USSR, including the possible sale and assembly of Ford vehicles.

Even as our associations with others grow, we continue our historic internal commitment to ensure that the company's long-range scientific and technological needs are met. Ford's research covers a wide spectrum of activities involving power-train, electronic and manufacturing systems, materials and design analysis, and the physical and chemical sciences. Out of such research has come a recent technological breakthrough—a catalyst that would reduce the need for platinum as a catalytic agent for helping to control exhaust emissions.

By far our most ambitious advanced project is Alpha. It involves research and development into areas that include—but also go beyond—technology. Alpha's mission is to promote improvements in all elements of our business. People from various areas of the company and suppliers work together to find innovative ways to improve products and processes, resulting in quality and productivity improvements. These new developments are incorporated into the business as soon as possible. An example is the automated underbody decking system used to produce the 1989 Ford Thunderbird and Mercury Cougar at our Lorain (Ohio) Assembly Plant. The system aligns the underbody components, such as the powertrain, suspension and exhaust, and accurately attaches them to the vehicle body.

CONTINUED COMMITMENT TO ACHIEVING ESTABLISHED OBJECTIVES

Ford summarizes its commitment to achieving its objectives as follows:

Only the strongest performers will survive in the highly competitive years ahead, and Ford fully intends to be one of them. To do so, we know we must be the very best in every field in which we compete. We have identified several key priorities to guide us in this effort. Our objectives are to

- Provide high-quality products and services that meet our customers' needs and exceed their expectations at a cost that represents superior value.
- Continue our efforts to instill a people-oriented culture throughout the company. The only way to attain the level of excellence we seek is through teamwork, respect and communication.
- Identify, implement and refine the most cost-efficient operating and business processes while carrying out the most ambitious worldwide investment actions we have ever undertaken.
- Continue to strengthen our partnerships with our dealers and suppliers. We are each partners in assuring the levels of customer satisfaction needed for our individual and collective successes.

We believe that if we continue to focus on these priorities, if we concentrate on our core values, and if we keep applying ourselves diligently to the basics of running the business, we will maintain our momentum—and Ford will continue to perform strongly in the years ahead. (1989 annual report)

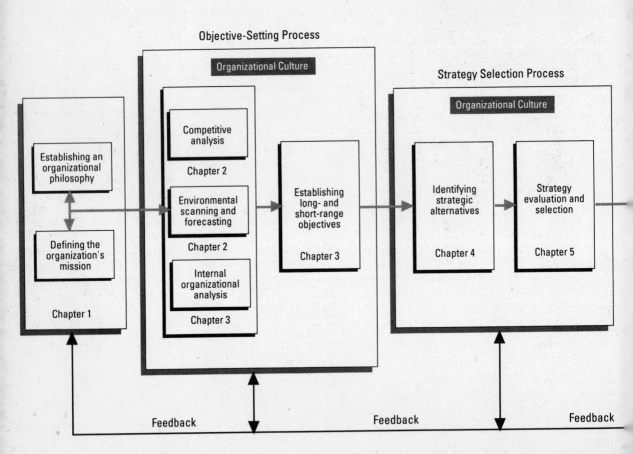

STRATEGIC MANAGEMENT PROCESS

Strategy Formulation

Objective-Setting Process

Organizational Culture

Strategy Selection Process

Organizational Culture

Establishing an organizational philosophy

Defining the organization's mission

Chapter 1

Competitive analysis

Chapter 2

Environmental scanning and forecasting

Chapter 2

Internal organizational analysis

Chapter 3

Establishing long- and short-range objectives

Chapter 3

Identifying strategic alternatives

Chapter 4

Strategy evaluation and selection

Chapter 5

Feedback   Feedback   Feedback

PART FIVE
APPLICATION OF STRATEGIC MANAGEMENT

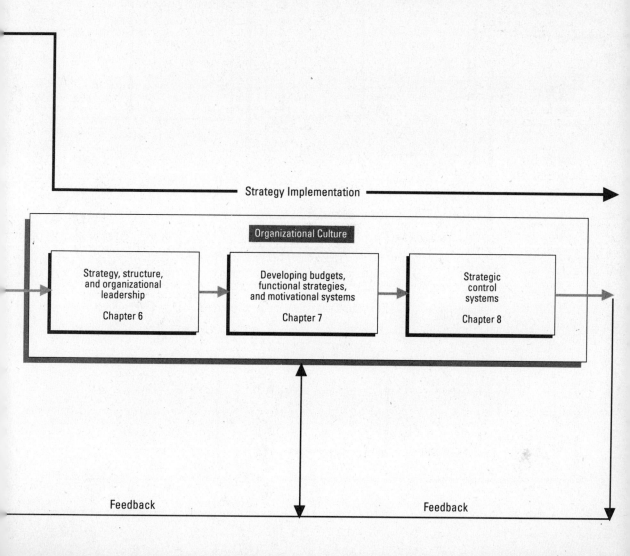

Strategy Implementation

Organizational Culture

Strategy, structure, and organizational leadership

Chapter 6

Developing budgets, functional strategies, and motivational systems

Chapter 7

Strategic control systems

Chapter 8

Feedback

Feedback

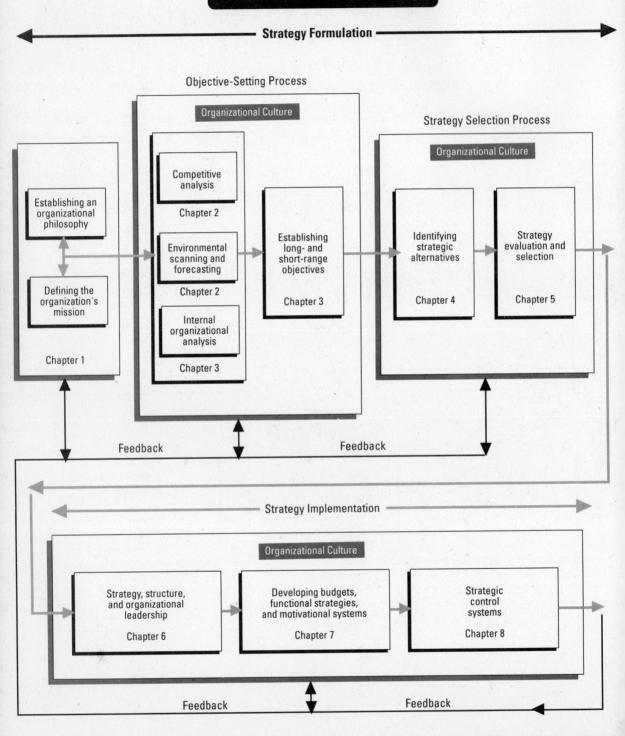

STRATEGIC MANAGEMENT PROCESS

Strategy Formulation

Objective-Setting Process

Organizational Culture

Strategy Selection Process

Organizational Culture

Establishing an
organizational
philosophy

Defining the
organization's
mission

Chapter 1

Competitive
analysis

Chapter 2

Environmental
scanning and
forecasting

Chapter 2

Internal
organizational
analysis

Chapter 3

Establishing
long- and
short-range
objectives

Chapter 3

Identifying
strategic
alternatives

Chapter 4

Strategy
evaluation and
selection

Chapter 5

Feedback   Feedback

Strategy Implementation

Organizational Culture

Strategy, structure,
and organizational
leadership

Chapter 6

Developing budgets,
functional strategies,
and motivational systems

Chapter 7

Strategic
control
systems

Chapter 8

Feedback   Feedback

CHAPTER 9
Global Strategy:
Formulation and Implementation

LEARNING OBJECTIVES

After studying this chapter, you should be able to

1. Outline the basic reasons for international business involvement.

2. Define global industry and global strategy.

3. Define multinational corporation (MNC).

4. Present the unique environmental forces in global strategy formulation.

5. Outline the generic global strategy options available to a business.

6. Explain comparative advantage.

7. Discuss competitive advantage in international business.

8. Define the value-added chain.

9. Define exporting, importing, and licensing.

10. Outline guidelines for successfully formulating and implementing global strategies.

An important factor in the strategic management process of any business is the increasing internationalization of business activity. The internationalization of American companies has been dramatic, with companies such as IBM, Eastman Kodak, Exxon, BankAmerica, and American Express having large and growing international business activities. The same kind of experience can be observed among non-American companies such as Volkswagen, Nestlé, British Petroleum, Phillips, Toyota, and Olivetti. Therefore, the purpose of this chapter is to examine the unique aspects of the strategy formulation and implementation processes in international business activities.

REASONS FOR INTERNATIONAL BUSINESS INVOLVEMENT

Generally, the decision to extend an organization's operations to other countries has two objectives: profit and stability. In terms of profit, international operations give organizations the chance to meet the increasing demand for goods and services in foreign countries. In addition, new sources of demand (in other countries) for an organization's output may have a stabilizing effect on the organization's production process. Example 9.1 describes the reasons that the Campbell Soup Company moved into international business activities.

Organizations deciding to move into international business usually do so for one of four basic reasons:

1. *Exploit a Technological Lead.* When an organization creates a new product, it at first enjoys a distinct competitive advantage. As the product becomes less unique and this advantage erodes, the organization often attempts to build new markets elsewhere. In addition, as costs begin to play a more critical part in the production of the product, the organization often sets up production and/or marketing facilities nearer to the markets it is serving.
2. *Exploit a Strong Trade Name.* A successful product often induces organizations to set up operations on an international basis. Foreign brands often are considered better—as a result of snob appeal or on the basis of superior quality. This is especially evident in the foreign car market.
3. *Exploit Advantages of Scale.* Larger organizations can more easily assemble the funds, physical assets, and human resources needed to produce and distribute goods on a larger scale than can smaller organizations.
4. *Exploit a Low-Cost Resource.* When costs of production are a critical concern, an organization may set up international operations in areas where the resource and/or labor costs are relatively lower than they are domestically.

DEFINING GLOBAL INDUSTRY, GLOBAL STRATEGIES, AND MULTINATIONAL CORPORATIONS

A *global industry* is one in which the strategic positions of competitors in major geographic or national markets are fundamentally affected by their overall

Campbell Soup Company Moves into Europe

Campbell Soup Company is betting that the marketplace of the future is outside the United States. For the past several years, the company that made its initial fortune putting condensed soup on U.S. grocery shelves has pushed hard to establish market niches overseas. Campbell has bought about a dozen small and medium-size food companies that make fancy cookies, frozen foods, and "shelf-stable" products, such as pasta and other packaged and canned goods. Many of the acquisitions (see below) have been in Europe, where the planned removal of trade restraints in 1992 offers a shot at 320 million consumers.

Campbell's global push began in the early 1980s, when R. Gordon McGovern, Campbell's president and chief executive officer, persuaded Campbell directors that the company had to act fast to counter moves by rival U.S. food companies, such as Heinz and CPC, which had been aggressively courting foreign consumers for decades. "We were extremely vulnerable," McGovern recalls.

The company initially decided to expand quickly through acquisitions, rather than spend years building support for Campbell-brand products. It also moved rapidly to acquire or establish affiliations with other companies to improve distribution.

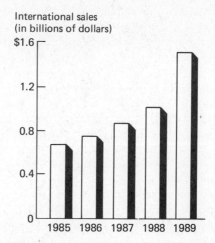

International sales
(in billions of dollars)

Key Brands Abroad

Name/Product Line	Country
Biscuits Delacre	Belgium
Biscuits and cookies	
Continental Foods	Belgium
Condiments, soups, and sweets	

Continued

Example 9.1 (*Continued*)

Name/Product Line	Country
Eugen Lacroix	West Germany
Premium soups and sauces	
Freshbake Foods	United Kingdom
Frozen meals and vegetables	
Groko	Netherlands
Frozen vegetables	
Lamy-Lutti	France
Chocolates, candy, and gum	
Lazzaroni & Co.	Italy
Biscuits and seasonal cakes	
Theodor Kattus	West Germany
Pasta, condiments, and sauces	

Source: Adapted from Vindu P. Goel, "Campbell Seeks to Boost Global Presence," *Wall Street Journal*, September 26, 1989, p. A10.

---

global positions.[1] For example, IBM's strategic position in competing for computer sales in France and Germany is significantly improved by the technology and marketing skills developed elsewhere in the company combined with a coordinated worldwide manufacturing system.[2] *Global strategies* are the alternatives chosen by a particular organization in order to compete in global industries on a worldwide, coordinated basis.

A *multinational corporation* (MNC) has the following characteristics:

1. It maintains a production, assembly, sales, or service presence in two or more countries.
2. A considerable portion of its sales, profits, and assets come from its international activities. For example, it has been suggested that when operations in other countries account for 35 percent of of sales and profits, an organization is considered multinational. It has also been suggested that an organization becomes multinational when 20 percent of its assets are in other countries.
3. It considers opportunities throughout the world, even though it may not do business in every region and country of the world.
4. It has a worldwide perspective and orientation in managerial decision making. In other words, the organization makes managerial decisions regarding the use of its resources—funds, technology, and business know-how—on a global basis.[3]

Example 9.2 describes the 20 largest U.S. multinational corporations.

Twenty Largest U.S. Multinational Corporations

The 20 largest U.S. multinational corporations are summarized below. As can be seen, many of the companies have substantial revenues and profits from outside the United States.

Rank	Company	Foreign Revenue (millions)	Total Revenue (millions)	Foreign Revenue as % of Total	Foreign Operating Profit (millions)	Total Operating Profit (millions)	Foreign Operating Profit as % of Total	Foreign Assets (millions)	Total Assets (millions)	Foreign Assets as % of Total
1	Exxon	$50,337	$ 69,888[b]	72.0	$3,910[a]	$5,219[a]	74.9	$30,740	$ 69,484	44.2
2	Mobil	27,388[b]	46,025[b]	59.5	1,858[a]	1,407[a]	132.1	17,581	37,233	47.2
4	IBM	25,888	51,250	50.5	3,184[a]	4,789[a]	66.5	27,604	57,814	47.7
5	Ford Motor	19,926	62,716	31.8	825[a]	3,285[a]	25.1	18,842	37,933	49.7
6	General Motors	19,837	102,814	19.3	-186[a]	2,945[a]	D-P	16,120	72,403	22.3
7	Texaco	15,494	31,613	49.0	1,170	1,187	98.6	10,279	34,940	29.4
7	Citicorp	10,940	23,496	46.6	522[a]	1,058[a]	49.3	86,117[c]	184,013[c]	46.8
9	E. I. du Pont de Nemours	9,955[d]	26,907	37.0	644[a]	1,791[c]	36.0	8,035	26,733	30.1
9	Dow Chemical	5,948	11,113	53.5	684	1,285	53.2	6,049	12,242	49.4
10	Chevron	5,605	24,352	23.0	808[f]	1,055[f]	76.6	7,862	34,583	22.7
11	BankAmerica	4,659	12,483	37.3	439[a]	-518[a]	P-D	37,263	104,189	35.8
12	Philip Morris	4,573	20,681	22.1	346	3,624	9.5	3,209	17,642	18.2
13	Procter & Gamble	4,490	15,439	29.1	143[a]	709[a]	20.2	3,461	13,055	26.5
14	RJR Nabisco	4,488	15,978	28.1	491	2,617	18.8	3,856	17,019	22.7
15	Chase Manhattan	4,356	9,460	46.0	119[a]	585[a]	20.3	40,940	94,770	43.2
16	ITT[g]	4,180	17,437	24.0	484	1,128	42.9	4,677	35,805	13.1
17	Eastman Kodak	4,152	11,550	35.9	389	724	53.7	4,016	12,902	31.1
18	Coca-Cola	4,019	8,669	46.4	858	1,372	62.5	2,065	8,373	24.7
19	Xerox[g]	3,996[b]	13,046[b]	30.6	158	473	33.4	4,758	19,299	24.7
20	Amoco	3,931[b]	18,478[b]	21.3	263[a]	747[a]	35.2	6,070	23,706	25.6

[a]Net income.
[b]Includes other income.
[c]Average assets.
[d]Includes excise taxes.
[e]Operating income after taxes.
[f]Net income before corporate expenses.
[g]Includes proportionate interest in unconsolidated subsidiaries and affiliates.
Note: D-P: Deficit over profit; P-D: Profit over deficit.

Source: Adapted from "The 100 Largest U.S. Multinationals," *Forbes,* July 27, 1987, p. 152.

An MNC does not necessarily have to develop a global strategy. It can allow its foreign operations to be autonomous on a country-by-country basis. However, most MNCs do develop global strategies in competing in world markets.

UNIQUE ENVIRONMENTAL FORCES IN GLOBAL STRATEGY FORMULATION

When a business decides to extend its operations into foreign markets, some unique environmental forces must be dealt with in the strategy formulation process.

Cultural Differences

In order to understand the differences between U.S. and international management, it is necessary to understand differences in culture. Obviously, U.S. managers and French managers do not see the world in the same way because they come from different cultures. *Culture* can be defined as something that is shared by all or almost all members of some social group, something that the older members of the group try to pass on to the younger members, and something (as in the case of morals, laws, and customs) that shapes behavior or structures one's perception of the world."[4] In other words, people living in different countries develop different values and different ways of relating to each other. For example, North Americans tend to stand far apart while talking; Middle Easterners stand close. In some cultures bribery is condoned in certain business situations; North Americans consider bribery a crime. Scheduled meeting times and punctuality is expected by North Americans; but in the Middle East and China the people have more relaxed views of time.[5]

Numerous cultural differences influence the social, economic, technical, and political environment of a country. Success in the international business environment requires that these differences be recognized in managing international business activities.

Payment for International Transactions

International trade requires exchanging currency from one country into that of another. *Foreign exchange rates* (the rate of exchange for one currency to another currency, e.g., French francs to American dollars) present certain problems as the rates fluctuate in value. In fact, a change in foreign exchange rates can wipe out profits earned on an international transaction.

The problem of foreign exchange rates arises because of the time lag between the time of a sale and the delivery of and payment for the product or service. Because two different countries are involved and the changes in supply and demand for the two currencies vary, the importer can pay a different amount than originally expected. Figure 9.1 shows the effects of exchange rate changes on importers and exporters.

Tariffs

Tariffs are government-imposed taxes charged on goods imported into, or exported from, a country. They serve (1) to raise revenues for the country or (2) to protect the country's producers from the competition of imported goods. The tariffs charged on parts are often less than those charged on finished goods. Therefore, foreign assembly operations have become quite popular.

Quotas

A *quota* establishes the maximum quantity of a product that can be imported (or exported) during a given time period. A quota can be set in physical or in value terms. Quotas can be imposed unilaterally, or they can be negotiated on a voluntary basis. Voluntary negotiation generally means that the quotas have been negotiated with threats of even worse restrictions if voluntary cooperation is not forthcoming.

Government Control over Profits

A firm owning facilities in another country naturally expects to receive profits from its operations. The amount of profits the parent company receives is

Figure 9.1 *Effects of Exchange Rates Changes on Importers and Exporters*

Rate Change	Effect When Contract Stated in Importer's Currency		Effect When Contract Stated in Exporter's Currency	
	Importer	Exporter	Importer	Exporter
1. Importer currency strengthens	No effect	Receives more units of domestic currency after conversion	Must pay fewer units of domestic currency	No effect
2. Exporter currency strengthens	No effect	Receives fewer units of domestic currency after conversion	Must pay more units of domestic currency to purchase foreign currency	No effect

Source: Janice James Miller and John A. Kilpatrick, *Issues for Managers: An International Perspective* (Homewood, Ill.: Irwin, 1987), p. 65.

often controlled by the host country's government, which regulates the access foreigners have to its currency.

Taxation

Firms operating in another country are subject to that country's laws and regulations. As taxes are a primary source of government revenue, many countries tax foreign investments located within their boundaries. These taxes may be quite high, since some of these foreign countries have few other businesses to tax.

Coalitions of Cooperating Countries

The basic purpose of coalitions of cooperating countries is to improve the economic conditions of the member countries. Two of the more important of these coalitions are the Organization of Petroleum Exporting Countries (OPEC) and the European Community (EC). The EC, or Common Market, as it is more frequently called, was organized in 1957. Its present membership includes Great Britain, Italy, France, West Germany, Denmark, Ireland, Greece, Belgium, Luxembourg, the Netherlands, Spain, and Portugal. The EC's purpose is to reduce tariffs on goods sold among the member countries. By December 1992, the Common Market nations will eliminate the fiscal, technical, and border barriers between member countries that have, over several decades, increased the costs of goods and services in Europe and reduced the international competitiveness of European companies. Thus, Europe in 1993 should be a single market with exciting potential for multinational corporations.

OPEC is an oil cartel that includes most of the oil-producing countries of the world. Its purpose is to control oil prices and production levels among the member countries. The drastic increases in oil prices in the 1970s that resulted from OPEC pricing decisions significantly influenced the strategic decisions of many American companies. However, today the effectiveness and continued existence of OPEC has come under question since several of OPEC's member countries sell and produce at levels considerably different from official OPEC standards.

Other coalitions of cooperating countries have been formed by lesser developed countries (LDCs). Two of these include the Organization of African Unity and the Latin American Integration Association.

Human Rights

Should international firms close their South African plants as long as apartheid exists in that country? Should Coca-Cola establish minimum labor standards for all of its bottlers around the world to prevent abuses of workers in certain countries? For international firms, such questions present dilemmas that are accompanied by ethical predicaments and hard choices. In each specific situation, the international firm must strike a balance between the interests and ideals of all its various stakeholders. There are no clear and easy choices.

Terrorism

Over the past decade, terrorism has become a critical problem for international firms. Forms of terrorism include but are not limited to kidnapping of executives, bombings, assassinations, and hijackings.

One way international firms defend against terrorism is to increase security. It is now fairly standard practice for executives of MNCs in such high-risk cities as Paris, Rome, New York, and Mexico City to be accompanied by at least one bodyguard. Measures have also been taken to ensure the security of employees and the physical facilities. In addition, all international firms now have substantial insurance coverage to protect themselves against financial losses as a result of terrorism.

GENERIC GLOBAL STRATEGY OPTIONS

Businesses involved in international business operations have many strategic options available to them. Some of the more frequently used strategy options are described in the following sections.

Product Standardization

The basic approach in product standardization lies in developing a standardized product that is to be produced and sold the same way throughout the world.[6] The idea behind this strategy is to take advantage of the economies of scale in producing the product and develop a strong worldwide distribution system to sell to the global market.

Broad-Line Global Strategy

The broad-line global strategy involves competing worldwide in the full product line of the industry.[7] In pursuing this strategy, the firm could attempt to achieve a product differentiation or overall low-cost position in the worldwide market. Obviously, the product standardization strategy could also be employed in pursuing a broad-line global strategy. Furthermore, investments in technology and distribution channels could be shared among products. The development of a strong worldwide distribution system is essential in this strategy.

Global-Focus Strategy

A business using the global-focus strategy selects a particular segment of the industry in which it competes on a worldwide basis. The idea behind this strategy is to select industry segments in which the business can achieve product differentiation or become the overall low-cost producer. Again, product standardization either may or may not be used in the global-focus strategy.

National-Focus Strategy

With the national-focus strategy, a company focuses on particular national markets in order to take advantage of the national market differences. The idea is to achieve product differentiation or become the overall low-cost producer in serving the unique needs of a particular national market.

Protected-Niche Strategy

The protected-niche strategy involves seeking out countries where host government policies exclude many global competitors through high tariffs, quotas, and so on. The business pursuing this strategy operates within the government restrictions and must work closely with the host government.[8]

SELECTING A GLOBAL STRATEGY

Selecting a global strategy from the options available is a complex and difficult choice for any business. Basically, however, the choice is based on the comparative advantages of countries and the competitive advantages of the individual business. A country has a *comparative advantage* when it can produce goods more efficiently or cheaply than other countries. Factors determining a country's comparative advantage include the presence of natural resources, adequate quality and quantity of labor and capital, available technology, and the relative costs of these resources. *Competitive advantage*, sometimes called business-specific advantage, refers to some proprietary characteristic of the business, such as brand name, that cannot be imitated by competitors without substantial cost and risk.[9]

Comparative advantage influences the decision on where to manufacture and market the firm's products. Competitive advantage influences the decision on what activities and technologies along the value-added chain a business should concentrate its resources, relative to its competitors.[10] The *value-added chain* is the process by which a business combines the raw material, labor, and technology into a finished product; markets the product; and distributes the product. A single business may consist of only one link in this process or may be fully vertically integrated.[11] Example 9.3 explains the reasons why Volkswagen of America was established.

ORGANIZING INTERNATIONAL BUSINESS ACTIVITIES

An organization may become involved in international business activities by exporting, importing, licensing, joint ventures, or manufacturing in a foreign country.

Exporting is the selling of an organization's goods in another country; *importing* is the purchasing of goods from a foreign company. Some of the more common reasons for exporting and importing are listed in Figure 9.2.

Organizations that make a commitment to selling their products overseas

Establishment of Volkswagen of America

Volkswagen of America (VWoA) was established more than a quarter of a century ago to import and market the Volkswagen Beetle, the most popular single model in automotive history.

In recent years, the company has established domestic manufacturing plants and activities, first for the Rabbit, and most recently for the new Golf and GTI. This complements its importing of other vehicles by Volkswagen United States and Audi of America.

The United States has traditionally been one of the biggest and most important markets for VW and Audi vehicles outside of Germany. The American market, which represents about 20 percent of VW's worldwide sales, plays an important role in the parent company's prosperity.

Since the first Beetles hit the American shores shortly after World War II, Volkswagens have become firmly established in the American marketplace. The Beetle's quality, dependability and efficiency earned Volkswagen an enviable reputation and a unique niche in the minds of American auto buyers.

Despite its success, Volkswagen knew that even the Beetle would not be able to flourish in the face of changing regulatory and currency activities. Its answer was an all-new successor to the Beetle, the Rabbit.

Born in the early 1970s, the Rabbit represented a complete change in product design compared with the Beetle; from an air-cooled, rear-engined, rear-wheel-drive car to a water-cooled, front-engined, front-wheel-drive car. The only things that were not changed were the quality and product acceptance.

The Rabbit's success in America led to the decision to establish production facilities in the United States. When VW opened its U.S. assembly plant in 1978, it became the first major foreign automotive manufacturer to build cars on American soil. The building of a plant in Westmoreland, Pennsylvania, meant more than steel and concrete—it meant jobs and career opportunities for Americans. The plant presently manufactures the new Golf, Golf Diesel, and GTI, named as 1985 *Motor Trend's* Car of the Year. Volkswagen United States continues to import other Volkswagens, including the all-new Jetta, the Cabriolet, Scirocco, Quantum Sedan and Wagon, and Vanagon and Vanagon Camper.

In the fall of 1970, VWoA established the Audi Division to import and market Audi luxury cars from Audi AG of Ingolstadt, West Germany. Today, Audi of America imports and distributes technically advanced automobiles such as the 5000CS Turbo, the 5000 Sedan and Wagon, the Audi Coupe GT, and the 4000S. Four-wheel-drive vehicles include the 5000CS Turbo Quattro and the 4000CS Quattro. Audi is known for its product innovation, particularly in aerodynamic design.

Even though all Volkswagen and Audi vehicles represent the best in quality and performance in their respective classes, VW employees continue to conduct research and development in Germany and the United States to ensure that VWoA will continue to offer the best in the 1990s and beyond.

Source: Public company documents.

must decide how to organize their exporting/importing activities. The organizational structure that is used depends on how critical these activities are to the overall organization. The organization may establish its own internal structure. This requires special expertise in international accounting, finance, marketing, and law. As a result, many organizations either cannot or do not desire to establish such divisions. Some contract with an outside person who is sometimes called a combination export-import manager. An *export-import manager* serves a group of exporting/importing organizations and handles all activities involved in the exporting/importing of the organization's goods or services.

Over time, many organizations find that it is economically better to expand their production operations overseas than to continue exporting goods to their markets abroad. Furthermore, in recent years, less-developed countries have sought local production of goods. As a result, businesses are finding that they must produce in these countries in order to maintain their overseas markets.

The ways in which international organizations expand their production activities differ in the degree of control retained by the *parent organization* (the

Figure 9.2 *Reasons for Exporting and Importing Goods*

Why Export?

1. If the production process requires high volume to reduce cost per unit, the home market may be too small to absorb the output. Thus, the output may be sold overseas. Stoves, for example, are purchased by households only when needed to replace an old one or when a new home is built. To restrict selling stoves only to the U.S. market could limit the number of stoves demanded below the amount that is cost efficient to produce.
2. The demand for the firm's product may be seasonal and irregular. By expanding the firm's market to other countries, production costs may be lowered by more effective production scheduling.
3. All products undergo what is called the product life cycle: When the product is first introduced, there is usually a big demand and the introducing firm is the only supplier. As the product reaches maturity, this competitive edge is reduced and can be maintained only by creating new markets, where the product reenters the growth stage.
4. In selling goods overseas, the organization may not face competition as stiff as it does in the United States; thus, its marketing costs may be reduced. By selling its established goods in new overseas markets, the organization is also able to increase its profits without risking new product development.

Why Import?

1. The goods may be needed but not available in the importing country (e.g., crude oil).
2. Many foreign-made products have prestige value and are demanded by the home market (e.g., French perfumes, sports cars from Germany).
3. Some foreign goods are less expensive due to lower production costs.

---

organization extending its operations beyond its nation's boundaries). The country it is entering is referred to as the *host country*. The parent company may set up assembly operations in a foreign country: Parts are exported overseas, and the finished product is assembled there. Also, the parent organization may contract with a foreign organization to produce its product, but retain control over the marketing of the product in that country. *Licensing* arrangements are an extension of this latter type of expansion. The parent organization enters into an agreement with a foreign organization, licensing it to produce and market the parent organization's product in return for a set percentage of sales revenues. Often, the parent organization provides technical and/or managerial support to the foreign organization.[12]

Joint ventures can also be used in entering international business activities. Joint ventures, of course, involve a joint ownership arrangement that can vary as to the extent of ownership and involvement of both parties from a 50-50 arrangement to a combination in which one partner is virtually a silent participant. Example 9.4 describes AT&T's joint venture in China.

STRATEGY IN ACTION Example 9.4

AT&T's Joint Venture in China

In June 1989, AT&T agreed to form a joint venture, 50 percent–owned by a unit of the phone giant, to make transmission equipment for China's phone system. That equipment includes fiber optic cable systems, digital multiplexers and channel banks, which convert analog voice signals to digital form for faster, more accurate transmission.

The venture is part of AT&T's efforts to supply equipment for expansion of the Chinese phone system. Several worldwide telecommunications firms are jockeying to sell equipment as China expands its phone system from 7.8 million phones to 33.6 million phones by the year 2000. Now China has only one phone per 133 people, according to AT&T. In the United States, there is about one phone for every two people. Like many countries with underdeveloped phone systems, China is skipping generations of technology to install the latest digital facilities.

AT&T said terms of its venture call for Shanghai Optical Fiber Communications Engineering Corp. to own 28 percent of the venture. Shanghai Optical is owned and managed by the Shanghai municipal government.

Shanghai Telecommunications Equipment Factory, which provides equipment to Chinese telecommunications authorities, will own 22 percent of the venture. Shanghai Telecommunications will provide facilities, most employees, and managers for the venture. Last year, the equipment supplier had sales of $13 million, AT&T said.

AT&T said the chairman of the venture will be a senior executive from China who has not yet been chosen. Two AT&T managers will hold senior positions in the venture, which is named AT&T of Shanghai.

Source: Adapted from Janet Guyon, "AT&T Joint Venture in China to Make Phone System Transmission Equipment," *Wall Street Journal*, June 1, 1989, p. A12.

GUIDELINES FOR SUCCESSFULLY FORMULATING AND IMPLEMENTING GLOBAL STRATEGY

Many factors determine whether a business is successful in its strategic formulation and implementation process in the global arena. The following guidelines are offered to help ensure success:

1. Clarify the international business mission. In addition to the mission statement requirements that were described in Chapter 1, the international business mission should specify the acceptable level of investment, the expected return, and acceptable levels of risk.
2. Develop host country contacts for market assessment.
3. Reach a clear understanding of the partners' objectives. Partners include not only joint venture partners or licensees, but also representatives and distributors.
4. Use local managers to implement the strategy whenever the talent is available.[13]

SUMMARY OF LEARNING OBJECTIVES

1. Outline the basic reasons for international business involvement.
   The four basic reasons for international business involvement are to exploit a technological lead, exploit a strong trade name, exploit advantages of sale, or exploit a low-cost resource.
2. Define global industry and global strategy.
   A global industry is one in which the strategic positions of competitors in major geographic or national markets are fundamentally affected by their overall global positions. Global strategies are the alternatives chosen by a particular organization in order to compete in global industries on a worldwide, coordinated basis.
3. Define multinational corporation (MNC).
   An MNC maintains a production, assembly, sales or service presence in two or more countries; it has a considerable portion of its sales, profits, and assets coming from its international activities; it considers opportunities throughout the world; and it has a worldwide perspective and orientation in managerial decision making.
4. Present the unique environmental forces in global strategy formulation.
   The unique environmental forces are cultural differences, payment for international transactions, tariffs, quotas, government control over profits, taxation, coalitions of cooperating countries, human rights, and terrorism.
5. Outline the generic global strategy options available to a business.
   The strategy options are product standardization, broad-line global strategy, global-focus strategy, national-focus strategy, and protected-niche strategy.
6. Explain comparative advantage.
   Comparative advantage exists when one country can produce goods more efficiently or cheaply than other countries.

7. Discuss competitive advantage in international business.

   Competitive advantage refers to some proprietary characteristic of the business, such as brand name, that cannot be imitated by competitors without substantial cost or risk.

8. Define value-added chain.

   The value-added chain is the process by which a business combines raw material, labor, and technology into a finished product; markets the product; and distributes the product.

9. Define exporting, importing, and licensing.

   Exporting is the selling of an organization's goods in another country. Importing is the purchasing of goods from a foreign company. Licensing is an arrangement in which the parent organization enters into an agreement with a foreign organization permitting the foreign organization to produce and sell the parent organization's product in return for a set percentage of sales revenues.

10. Outline guidelines for successfully formulating and implementing global strategies.

    These guidelines are: clarify the international business mission, develop host country contacts for market assessment, reach a clear understanding of an international business partner's objectives, and use local managers to implement the strategy whenever the talent is available.

REVIEW QUESTIONS

1. What are the four basic reasons for international business involvement?
2. Define the following terms:
   a. Global industry
   b. Global strategy
   c. Multinational corporation (MNC)
3. Define the following terms:
   a. Foreign exchange rates
   b. Tariffs
   c. Quotas
   d. Coalition of cooperating countries
4. Describe the following strategic options:
   a. Product standardization
   b. Broad-line global strategy
   c. Global-focus strategy
   d. National-focus strategy
   e. Protected-niche strategy
5. What is comparative advantage? Competitive advantage?
6. What is the value-added chain?
7. What is exporting? Importing? Licensing?
8. Give some guidelines for successfully formulating and implementing global strategies.

DISCUSSION QUESTIONS

1. What are some of the major risks a business has in going international?
2. Why is it better to use local managers for doing business in a foreign country?
3. Some MNCs seem to be more powerful than their host governments. Do you feel that an MNC could be a potential threat to a host government? Explain your views.

REFERENCES AND ADDITIONAL READING

1. Michael E. Porter, *Competitive Strategy* (New York: Free Press, 1980), p. 275.
2. Ibid., p. 275.
3. William A. Dymsza, *Multinational Business Strategy* (New York: McGraw-Hill, 1972), pp. 5–6.
4. Nancy J. Adler, *International Dimensions of Organizational Behavior* (Boston: Kent, 1986), pp. 8–9.
5. Examples are drawn from Raymond V. Lesikar, *Basic Business Communication*, 4th ed. (Homewood, Ill.: Irwin, 1988), p. 103.
6. See, for instance, Theodore Levitt, "The Globalization of Markets," *Harvard Business Review*, May–June 1983, pp. 92–102.
7. The next four strategies that are described are drawn from Porter, *Competitive Strategy*, p. 294.
8. For additional information on various global strategy options, see Sumantra Ghoshal, "Global Strategy: An Organizing Framework," *Strategic Management Journal*, September–October 1987, pp. 425–440.
9. Bruce Kogut, "Designing Global Strategies: Comparative and Competitive Value-added Chains," *Sloan Management Review*, Summer 1985, p. 15.
10. Ibid.
11. For additional information, see also Bruce Kogut, "Designing Global Strategies: Profiting from Operational Flexibility," *Sloan Management Review*, Fall 1985, pp. 7–38.
12. For additional information on organizing international business activities, see David J. Lemak and Jeffrey S. Bracker, "A Strategic Contingency Model of Corporate Structure," *Strategic Management Journal*, September–October 1988, pp. 521–527.
13. Paul A. Kirkconnell, "Practical Thinking About Going International," *Business Quarterly*, Autumn 1988, pp. 40–44.

Strategy in Action Case Study: Ford Motor Company

Chapter 9: Global Strategies: Formulation and Implementation

Ford entered the international arena early in its career and today is one of the largest multinational corporations.

MAGNITUDE OF INTERNATIONAL OPERATIONS

Ford has undertaken substantial direct foreign investments since it opened its first international units in Canada in 1909 and in the United Kingdom in 1911. Ford's strategy has consisted of looking for internationally competitive countries in which to locate production facilities where international markets could be served. Consequently, Ford Europe was formed in 1967, comprised of manufacturing plants in Spain, the United Kingdom, and Germany. Other plants exist in Australia, Asia, Canada, and Latin America.

Ford's propensity to invest abroad has been based on its technological competitiveness toward rival firms such as GM and European car makers. Today, about 50 percent of Ford's overseas assets produce an estimated 32 percent of its total revenues. In 1988 Ford Motor Company earned an unprecedented $1.6 billion in Western Europe, about three times the total amount of its earnings there in 1986. As can be seen, Ford has been very successful in reaping the benefits of its global strategy (see Exhibit 1).

BARRIERS TO INTERNATIONAL OPERATIONS

Ford's success abroad has not been easy considering the various barriers it has overcome in the course of its globalization process. Constantly, the firm has had to adapt its strategy around the host government. For example, Britain's conservative-oriented government tried to implement an antitakeover barrier in the 1989 Jaguar acquisition, which is described later.

Exhibit 1 *Ford Shares of International Cars and Trucks*

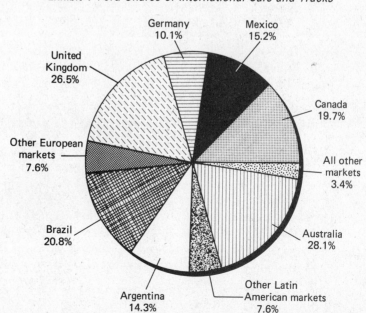

When faced with human rights issues in South Africa, Ford divested its subsidiary, the South African Motor Corporation (Samcor), in the following manner: It used 24 percent of its ownership to set up a trust fund for its 3800-member work force and sold the remaining ownership to Anglo American Corp., South Africa's largest mining and industrial conglomerate. Like every multinational corporation, Ford has also faced such problems as cultural differences reflected in work values.

Despite tariffs and quotas imposed by some foreign governments, Ford has been successful in penetrating markets around the world, thanks to its level of competitiveness. Nevertheless, such issues as interest rates in foreign countries, taxation, and currency exchange rates are still limiting factors for Ford's growth overseas. Foreign operations of U.S. multinationals are subject to tax constraints and are hindered by frequently changing tax systems.

FORD'S "CENTERS OF EXCELLENCE" GLOBAL STRATEGY

In 1987, Ford implemented a new global strategy by unifying all foreign and domestic auto operations. Under the global strategy Ford came up with the program called "Centers of Excellence." The program was initiated to avoid duplication of effort and to capitalize on Ford's engineering centers around the world. The engineers who work in these centers throughout the globe design models in each vehicle series. Ford achieves global integration through its global engineering communication setup, the Worldwide Engineering Release System (WERS). This system allows an engineer in Germany, for example, to be on line with an engineer in Detroit or Britain instantly and have access to computer data on files anywhere in the world.

Ford's objective is to take advantage of the economies of scale and develop a strong worldwide distribution system. The "Centers of Excellence" program identifies with the broad-line global strategy by attempting to achieve an overall low-cost position in the worldwide market.

FORD'S JOINT VENTURES, FOREIGN MANUFACTURING, AND LICENSING

Ford has and still implements other business activities such as joint ventures, manufacturing in foreign countries, and licensing. Like many other global companies, Ford has joined forces with foreign companies to compensate for geographic holes, to fill niches, and to produce mass market cars like the Escort. For instance, Ford owns 25 percent of Mazda and has joint ventures with Nissan Motor Company, Ltd.; Central Glass Co., a leading Japanese glass company; and Kia Motors Corporation in South Korea. Ford also has a joint venture with Volkswagen in South America.

In addition, Ford has opened manufacturing plants in foreign countries such as Spain, the United Kingdom, Taiwan, Brazil, and Mexico. Finally, Ford signed a licensing agreement with Orbital Engine Co. of Australia to power

Exhibit 2 What Will Jaguar Really Cost?

	Millions of Dollars
Purchase price ($14.25 a share)	$2,600
New plant and tooling	650
New model development expense	400
Forgone interest on $2.6 billion cash	1,200
Total cost	$4,850
Less estimated five-year net profit	500
Total five-year cost	$4,350

future small cars with an Australian version of the two-stroke engine made famous in lawn mowers and early Saabs.

FORD'S STRATEGY WITH JAGUAR

Ford Motor Company has been a major player in the European market for quite some time. The company has competed effectively in the low end of the market with some of the European giants like Volkswagen and Fiat. Now, Ford wants to be a contender in the luxury car market. Ford sees a growth in this market from the current 2.3 million units a year to around 3.5 million units by the mid-1990s. This forecast shows that the combined U.S. and European luxury car market has a faster growth rate than the auto market in general.

Ford's objective is to enter the luxury car market. The firm chose to meet this objective by acquiring well-respected and established British makers of luxury cars. In 1987 Ford bought 75 percent of Aston Martin Lagonda, and in 1989 Jaguar PLC was acquired.

Ford's acquisition of Jaguar has raised questions and skepticism around the auto industry. Ford's goal with Jaguar is to expand production and speed up its model development capability. The company wants to compete with rivals such as BMW and Mercedes-Benz. To accomplish this goal Ford needs to invest more than the $2.5 billion it paid for the company, as Jaguar is in need of new auto models and plant investment. Exhibit 2 illustrates an estimate of Jaguar's actual cost.

Three reasons helped make Ford's acquisition of Jaguar strategically viable. First, Jaguar could strengthen Ford's global reach while filling the gap in its premium lines. Second, the lowering of trade barriers in the European Community by 1992 constitutes a nonnegligible growth opportunity for Ford regarding the luxury car market. Finally, the acquisition of Jaguar enables Ford to react against a sudden worldwide threat by new upscale Japanese luxury cars. The primary attractiveness Ford sees in Jaguar, which lags behind West German and Japanese rivals in technology and quality control, is image. Jaguar has developed a brand name that is capable of making buyers spend $60,000 on a car.

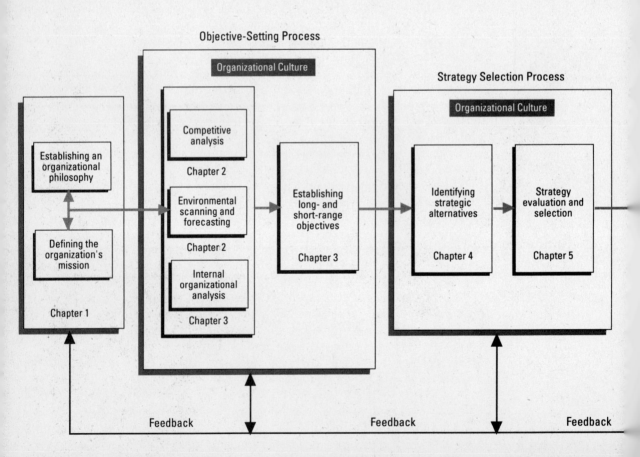

STRATEGIC MANAGEMENT PROCESS

Strategy Formulation

Objective-Setting Process

Organizational Culture

Strategy Selection Process

Organizational Culture

Establishing an organizational philosophy

Defining the organization's mission

Chapter 1

Competitive analysis

Chapter 2

Environmental scanning and forecasting

Chapter 2

Internal organizational analysis

Chapter 3

Establishing long- and short-range objectives

Chapter 3

Identifying strategic alternatives

Chapter 4

Strategy evaluation and selection

Chapter 5

Feedback

Feedback

Feedback

PART SIX

USEFUL INFORMATION FOR ANALYZING STRATEGIC MANAGEMENT CASES

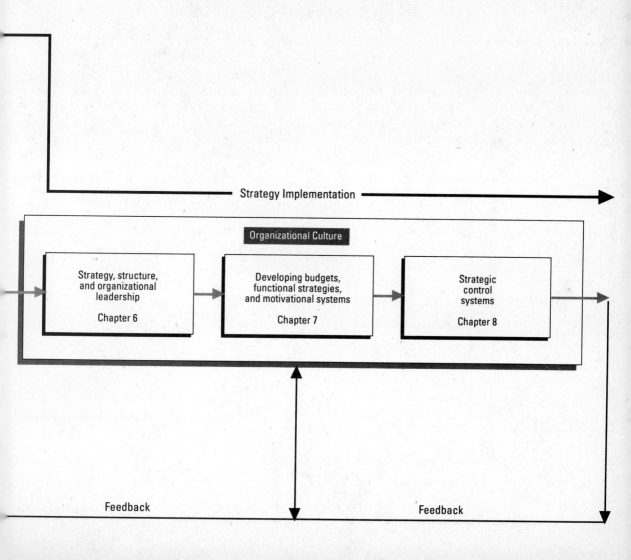

Strategy Implementation

Organizational Culture

Strategy, structure, and organizational leadership

Chapter 6

Developing budgets, functional strategies, and motivational systems

Chapter 7

Strategic control systems

Chapter 8

Feedback

Feedback

APPENDIX A

Preparing a Case Analysis

A *case* is a written description of an organization. A case generally contains a wide variety of information about the organization and may include the history of the organization, environmental forces affecting the organization, current operational data, a description of the management team, the organizational structure, and other general information. The primary reasons for using the case method for instructional purposes are to enable the student to see how actual organizations have performed the strategic management process and to allow students to practice and develop their skills in applying strategic management concepts to actual organizations.

Cases are developed from material taken from actual organizations. The cases in this text are about real organizations. Some cases are disguised in that the real name of the organization is not given. Nevertheless, the problems and challenges faced by the organization are real and should be viewed as such by the student.

OBJECTIVES OF THE CASE METHOD IN STRATEGIC MANAGEMENT

The objectives of a course in strategic management (or business policy) are

1. To develop an appreciation for the interrelationships among the various functional (marketing, finance, production) areas of an organization
2. To understand the importance of timing and sequencing of strategic moves
3. To understand the complexity of the organization as a whole

In the most complete sense, a course in strategic management should cause students to apply the knowledge they have gained in their academic careers or personal experience to an analysis of how organizations develop a strategy for achieving organizational objectives in a changing environment.

The most frequently used vehicle for teaching strategic management is the case method. The following limerick describes what might happen to students without the benefit of cases:

> A student of business with tact
> Absorbed many answers he lacked
> But acquiring a job,
> He said with a sob,
> "How does one fit answer to fact?"[1]

Frequently, much of a student's academic career is devoted to listening to lectures. This, of course, is an essential part of the learning process. Cases, on the other hand, are designed to allow the student to learn by doing. Under the case method, both professors and students read the same basic materials and must determine what analyses are to be made and what decisions are required. Generally, there is no single, right answer to a case.

Under the case method, the professor's role is to assign cases, to participate actively as a member of the class in analyzing the case, to guide the class discussion by raising important questions or critical issues, and (if he or she chooses) to summarize the analysis of the case at the end of the class. The student's role is to analyze the assigned case and to participate actively as a member of the class in discussing the case. The case method of teaching fails totally when either the professor or the student fails to perform his or her role.

When students come to class prepared, several benefits result. First, students learn the value of input from others in making strategic decisions. Students quickly learn that fellow students may have analyzed different issues and may have come to different conclusions. Other opinions must be analyzed and either accepted or rejected. Furthermore, a prepared student quickly learns that the professor does not have all the correct answers. Each student should be free to present and hold his or her point of view. However, students and professors alike should be required to explain the reasoning and basis for their positions.

The case method's primary advantage is that it forces the student to think analytically and constructively. In forcing this type of thinking, the professor may pose such questions as the following:

- Given the available information, what trends do you see developing in the next decade that will affect the organization?
- What are the major opportunities for the organization?
- What are the major risks to which the organization will be exposed through changing social, economic, political, or technological forces?
- What is the current strategy?
- How well does this strategy match current resources?
- What organizational structure is being used?
- Are the control systems adequate?
- What noneconomic purposes are being served or should be served by the organization?
- Is the management team capable of handling the opportunities and risks?[2]

Of course, many other questions can and will be asked. Again, the primary purpose of the question is to cause the student to think creatively.

MISSING OR INCOMPLETE INFORMATION

A frequent criticism of the case method is the absence of or the incomplete nature of data and information contained in the case. Actually, these inadequacies contribute to the reality of the case. Managers who are responsible for making the strategic management decisions for organizations never have all the information needed to make these decisions. And frequently the information available to the manager is contradictory. In these situations, the manager must decide what information is creditable and what information should be ignored.

The necessity to choose the most creditable information should in no way lead the student to feel that he or she might just as well ignore information in making strategy decisions. It is merely meant to emphasize that, even with available data and information, judgments and interpretations must be made.

One challenge in case analysis is for the student to supplement the data and information contained in the case through his or her own research. Throughout the text many sources of data and information are cited.

ANALYSIS OF A CASE

The first step in case analysis is a thorough reading of the case. The student should understand the overall organization and its components as well as all the data and information in the case. After reading the case thoroughly, the student is ready to begin his or her analysis.

One approach to case analysis is composed of five steps:

1. Defining the central issue of the case. Is the main issue strategy implementation or strategic planning? Is the main issue concerned with strategic control? Is the organizational structure the key issue?
2. Determining the pertinent areas of the strategic management process that need to be considered. For example, if an organization's strategy has not been successful, several pertinent areas could be causing this lack of success and would need to be analyzed.
3. Evaluating the available data, gathering and evaluating more data if necessary, drawing conclusions about the central issue, and drawing conclusions about and determining the relative importance of the other pertinent areas.
4. Investigating other, less critical, issues.
5. Drawing a final conclusion or developing an action plan for the organization.

WRITING UP A CASE

Frequently, students are required to prepare a written analysis of a case. Sometimes the professor provides a specific format that is to be followed. On the other hand, quite frequently the student must develop his or her own format. No one format fits all case situations. However, a useful format results when the five steps to case analysis are followed.

Preparation is the key to the growth and development of the student in the use of the case method. Thorough preparation makes the case method one of the best and most enjoyable methods of learning.[3]

REFERENCES AND ADDITIONAL READING

1. Charles I. Gregg, "Because Wisdom Can't Be Told," in Malcolm P. McNair (ed.), *The Case Method at the Harvard Business School* (New York: McGraw-Hill, 1954), p. 11.
2. Some of the questions on this list are adapted from Howard H. Stevenson, "Teaching Business Policy by the Case Method," in Bernard Taylor and Keith MacMillan (eds.), *Business Policy: Teaching and Research* (London: Bradford University Press, 1973), p. 122.
3. For more in-depth discussions of case analysis, see Malcolm P. McNair, *The Case Method at the Harvard University Business School* (New York: McGraw-Hill, 1954); Robert Ronstadt, *The Art of Case Analysis* (Dover, Mass.: Lord Publishing, 1980); and Bernard Taylor and Keith MacMillan (eds.), *Business Policy: Teaching and Research* (London: Bradford University Press, 1973).

How to Conduct Financial Analysis for Business Policy Casework

Manab Thakur, Ph.D.
Professor of Management

Amir Jassim, Ph.D.
Professor of Finance

School of Business & Administrative Sciences
California State University, Fresno

INTRODUCTION

The performance of financial analysis is imperative for the successful dissection of any policy-related case. The analysis provides insights into the past and present, and helps predict the future condition of the organization given a certain set of assumptions. This appendix focuses on five major areas of financial analysis pertinent to analyzing business policy cases:

Area I *Ratio analysis:* A tool used for evaluating a company's performance in relation to itself and its competitors.

Area II *Working-capital analysis:* A type of analysis used for evaluating the company's ability to meet short-term debt obligations and finance current operations.

Area III *Capital budgeting:* A process by which proposals for capital investments are evaluated and selected.

Area IV *Business acquisitions analysis:* A means of determining the value and method of payment.

Area V *Pro forma financial statement analysis:* A comprehensive method of financial forecasting that, in most cases, needs to be made to justify your recommendations.

RATIO ANALYSIS

Who Uses Ratio Analysis?

Users of ratio analysis can be divided into two groups: *outsiders,* such as private investors, corporate investors, bankers, and government agencies, and *insiders,* such as accountants, finance officers, and managers.

How Are Ratios Used in Evaluating Organizational Performance?

Ratios are used to compare an organization's performance with itself and/or with competitors of like size and structure. Primarily, two methods are employed: *cross-sectional analysis,* an analysis of a company's performance with that of similar companies for one given time period, and *time-series analysis,* an analysis of a company's performance with itself and/or with companies of like size and structure covering successive time periods.

What Kinds of Ratios Are Used?

There are five major groups of ratios used for comparative analysis: profitability, liquidity, leverage, activity, and market. The data used in calculating ratios come primarily from the company's financial statements—the income statement (IS) and balance sheet (BS).

How Are These Ratios Calculated?

A. *Profitability ratios* measure the overall effectiveness of management to generate a profit:

1. Gross profit margin $= \dfrac{\text{Gross profit (IS)}}{\text{Total sales (IS)}}$

2. Operating profit margin $= \dfrac{\text{Operating income (IS)}}{\text{Total sales (IS)}}$

3. Net profit margin $= \dfrac{\text{Net income after taxes (IS)}}{\text{Total sales (IS)}}$

4. Return on investment $= \dfrac{\text{Net income after taxes (IS)}}{\text{Total assets (BS)}}$

5. Return on equity $= \dfrac{\text{Net income after taxes (IS)}}{\text{Stockholders' equity (BS)}}$

B. *Liquidity ratios* measure the ability of the company to meet its short-term debts:

1. Current ratio $= \dfrac{\text{Current assets (BS)}}{\text{Current liabilities (BS)}}$

2. Quick ratio $= \dfrac{\text{Current assets (BS)}- \text{ inventories (BS)}}{\text{Current liabilities (BS)}}$

C. *Activity ratios* measure how efficiently the company's resources are being utilized; they focus on the generation of sales with a given asset base:

1. Average collection period (ACP) $= \dfrac{\text{Accounts receivables (BS)}}{\text{Average daily credit sales (IS)}}$

2. Average payment period (APP) $= \dfrac{\text{Accounts payable (BS)}}{\text{Average daily credit purchases (IS)}}$

3. Inventory turnover $= \dfrac{\text{Cost of goods sold (IS)}}{\text{Inventories (BS)}}$

4. Total asset turnover $= \dfrac{\text{Sales (IS)}}{\text{Total assets (BS)}}$

5. Fixed asset turnover $= \dfrac{\text{Sales (IS)}}{\text{Net fixed assets (BS)}}$

D. *Debt (or leverage) ratios* measure the relative amount of long-term debt the company carries and its ability to service it:

1. Debt to assets $= \dfrac{\text{Total liabilities (BS)}}{\text{Total assets (BS)}}$

2. Long-term debt to equity $= \dfrac{\text{Long-term debt (BS)}}{\text{Stockholders' equity (BS)}}$

3. Debt to capital $= \dfrac{\text{Long-term liabilities (BS)}}{\text{Long-term debt (BS)} + \text{stockholders' equity (BS)}}$

4. Short-term liabilities to total debt $= \dfrac{\text{Current liabilities (BS)}}{\text{Total liabilities (BS)}}$

5. Times interest earned (TIE) $= \dfrac{\text{Earnings before interest and taxes (IS)}}{\text{Interest (IS)}}$

E. *Market ratios* measure the performance of the common stock of a firm:

1. Earnings per share (EPS) $= \dfrac{\text{Net income avail. to common stockholders (IS)}}{\text{Number of common stock shares outstanding (BS)}}$

2. Dividend payout $= \dfrac{\text{Dividend per share of common stock (BS)}}{\text{Earnings per share (BS)}}$

3. Dividend yield $= \dfrac{\text{Dividend per share of common stock (IS)}}{\text{Price per share (BS or WSJ)}}$

4. Price/earnings ratio (PE) $= \dfrac{\text{Price per share (BS or WSJ)}}{\text{Earnings per share (BS)}}$

5. Book value per share $= \dfrac{\text{Common stockholders equity (BS)}}{\text{Number of common stock shares outstanding (BS)}}$

6. Price to book value $= \dfrac{\text{Price per share (BS or WSJ)}}{\text{Book value per share (BS)}}$

How Should These Ratios Be Interpreted?

It is important to remember that these ratios do not make much sense unless they are *compared within the industry in which the company conducts its business.* An industry is defined as a group of firms that produce products or services that can be considered close substitutes for one another. For example, an analysis of a case involving 7UP will include a comparison of 7UP's ratios with the averages of the soft drink industry. It is imperative to select the proper industry for making comparisons, or the analysis will be misleading.

It is more difficult to perform a ratio analysis for a conglomerate. In this situation it is necessary to examine the relevant segment(s) of the business being reviewed and then compare the performance of each segment with the appropriate industry average. In other situations, it may be necessary to concentrate on the major product lines of the company to see where most of the revenues are being generated. Relevant industry averages are given by the *Standard Industrial Classification Code (SIC),* a three- or four-digit identification number assigned according to the primary type of business in which a firm engages. Classification descriptions are listed in the *SIC Manual.*

Other references that provide industry data and background information on publicly held corporations are the following:

1. *Moody's.* Data are provided by industry and include consolidated income statements, ratios, capital stock, and long-term debt.
2. *Standard & Poor's Corporation Records.* Same as Moody's, but includes one-page fact sheets on each company.
3. *Value Line Investment Survey.* Includes a wealth of editorial comments on corporations along with pertinent data on each.
4. *Industry Surveys.* Information is arranged by industry and includes comparisons of each company against the industry average.
5. *Annual Statement Studies by Robert Morris.* Prominent industry ratios are provided for comparison.
6. *Dun's Review.* Listings of ratios of *retailers* in the September issue, *wholesalers* in the October issue, and *manufacturers* in the November issue.
7. *5500 Largest U.S. Corporations.* Ratios are provided for publicly held companies that are ranked by sales size within their appropriate industry.
8. *10-K Reports.* Company reports that contain principal products, competitive information, and many other dimensions of various industrial sectors.
9. *Everybody's Business.* Background information on U.S. corporations; an effective tool to obtain an overall feel of the company under study.

In addition, it is important to note the following:

1. Corporations listed in these sources have common stock that is publicly held and traded on the various stock exchanges. No information is given on privately held corporations.
2. Some company cases are "disguised." Naturally, there is no information

available for these organizations because names have been changed to protect the firms' identities. Nonetheless, it should be possible to find the related industry averages for comparative purposes.

3. Data on subsidiaries can be found if the parent company can be located. *Who Owns Whom* (Dun & Bradstreet) provides information.

4. In some cases, it may be difficult to extract ratios from the appropriate industry category because the library may not have the reference you seek. Therefore, it is always useful to consult with the reference librarian and state what specifically is being sought.

5. The method used to compute a given ratio may vary. The formulas used by other sources do not always match up precisely with one's own. To make a proper comparison, the formula employed *must be identical.*

Because of these problems, Exhibit 1 provides rules of thumb for interpreting the ratios. Please note that these rules are for general guidance only.

Now, with an understanding of what some of the key ratios mean, calculate the ratios using Exhibits 2 and 3, and then see if you arrive at the same results as in Exhibit 4.

Exhibit 1 Ratio Interpretation and Its Rule of Thumb

Ratio	Interpretation	Rule of Thumb
A. Profitability Ratios		
1. Gross profit margin	Amount of gross profit generated per dollar of sales.	Industry average, when applicable.
2. Operating profit margin	Amount of profit from operations generated per dollar of sales.	Industry average, when applicable.
3. Net profit margin	Amount of after-tax profits per dollar of sales.	Industry average when applicable.
4. Return on investment (ROI)	Rate of return on total assets employed. This is a measure of management's overall performance in generating a profit.	Should be equal to or higher than market rate of return on Treasury bills during the time period in question.
5. Return on equity (ROE)	Rate of return on stockholders' investment in company. This is a measure of management's performance in generating a profit for the owners of the company.	Should be higher than ROI.

Continued

Exhibit 1 *(Continued)*

Ratio	Interpretation	Rule of Thumb
B. Liquidity Ratios		
1. Current ratio	Ability to cover short-term debt as it comes due.	At least 2 to 1. A ratio above 4 would indicate that the company may not be using its short-term assets effectively.
2. Quick ratio	Expresses degree to which a company's current liabilities are covered by the most liquid current assets.	At least 1 to 1.
C. Activity Ratios		
1. Average collection period	Average collection period for accounts receivable.	Equal to or less than credit period extended to customers by firm.
2. Average payment period	Average payment period for accounts payable.	Equal to credit period extended to the company by its creditors.
3. Inventory turnover	Indicates liquidity or activity of the company's inventory.	Industry average, when applicable.
4. Total asset turnover	Indicates how efficiently company is utilizing its assets to generate sales.	Industry average, when applicable.
5. Fixed asset turnover	Extent to which fixed assets are used in generating sales.	High value indicates productive use of fixed assets.
D. Debt Ratios		
1. Debt to assets	Extent to which funds are provided by creditors.	Industry average, when applicable.
2. Long-term debt to equity	Extent to which funds are provided on a long-term basis by creditors versus owners.	Historical norm tends to be 40:60.
3. Debt to capital	Percentage of a firm's capitalization package that is made up of long-term debt.	Industry average, when applicable.
4. Short-term liabilities to total debt	Percentage of total debt borrowed from short-term creditors.	Industry average, when applicable.
5. Times interest earned	Extent to which earnings can decline without company becoming unable to meet its interest	At least 2 to 1.

Continued

Exhibit 1 (*Continued*)

Ratio	Interpretation	Rule of Thumb
	expense; provides a measure of the degree of security afforded to bondholders.	
E. Market Ratios		
1. Earnings per share	Net income per share available to common stockholders.	Industry average, when applicable.
2. Dividend payout	Percentage of net earnings paid out to common stockholders.	Growth companies generally have low payout ratios because they reinvest most of their earnings.
3. Dividend yield	Shows rate of return stockholders will receive from their investment in the short run.	Industry average, when applicable.
4. Price/earnings ratio	A measure of current price of stock to earnings per share.	High value indicates that company is growing and/or is a stable enterprise.
5. Book value per share	Indicates amount per common share available to stockholders if company's assets are sold at their book value and company's liabilities are paid off.	None exists.
6. Price to book value	Amount stockholders are willing to pay for each dollar of common stock book value.	None exists.

Exhibit 2 Comparative Balance Sheets, 1986–1989 (millions)

	1989	1988	1987	1986
Cash and equivalents	$ 62	$ 41	$ 38	$ 45
Accounts receivable, net	455	410	289	350
Prepaid expenses	35	32	18	21
Total inventories	589	548	608	527
Total current assets	1,141	1,031	953	943
Long-term investments	149	134	121	95
Plant and equipment	3,241	2,915	2,609	2,334
Accumulated depreciation	(1,521)	(1,384)	(1,292)	(1,124)
Net fixed assets	1,720	1,531	1,317	1,210

Continued

Exhibit 2 (Continued)

	1989	1988	1987	1986
Other assets	12	15	14	24
Total noncurrent assets	1,881	1,680	1,470	1,350
Total assets	$ 3,022	$ 2,711	$ 2,405	$ 2,272
Notes payable	61	93	65	52
Accounts payable	106	114	101	96
Income taxes payable	79	71	42	47
Other current liabilities	148	131	126	112
Total current liabilities	394	409	334	307
Long-term debt	622	538	445	492
Other liabilities	127	129	123	114
Total liabilities	1,143	1,076	902	913
Preferred stock	25	25	25	25
Common stock	210	165	165	165
Paid in capital	185	150	150	150
Retained earnings	1,459	1,295	1,163	1,019
Total stockholders' equity	1,879	1,635	1,503	1,359
Total liabilities and stockholders' equity	$ 3,022	$ 2,711	$ 2,405	$ 2,272

Exhibit 3 Comparative Income and Retained Earnings Statements (millions except per share data, 1986–1989)

	1989	1988	1987	1986
Net sales	$3,918	$3,442	$ 3,171	$2,983
Cost of goods sold	3,107	2,737	2,413	2,312
Gross profit	811	705	758	671
Selling, general, and administrative expenses	258	241	232	214
Depreciation and amortization	137	92	168	134
Operating income	416	372	358	323
Other income	12	9	13	11
Earnings before interest and taxes	428	381	371	334
Interest expense	83	76	63	59
Earnings before taxes	345	305	308	275
Income taxes	103	98	92	89
Net income after taxes	$ 242	$ 207	$ 216	$ 186
Retained earnings, January 1	1,295	1,163	1,019	902
Add: net income	242	207	216	186
Deduct: Common dividends	(74)	(71)	(68)	(65)
Preferred dividends	(4)	(4)	(4)	(4)
Retained earnings, December 31	$1,459	$1,295	$ 1,163	$1,019
Closing price on common stock	56.25	52.50	54.625	47.25
Common stock outstanding	49.3	47.1	48.5	46.5
Earnings per share	4.83	4.31	1.46	3.91
Dividends per share	1.50	1.50	1.46	1.40

Exhibit 4 Comparative Financial Ratios, 1986–1989

Ratios	1989	1988	1987	1986
A. Profitability Ratios				
1. Gross profit margin	20.7 %	20.5 %	23.9 %	22.5 %
2. Operating profit margin	10.6 %	10.8 %	11.3 %	10.8 %
3. Net profit margin	6.2 %	6.0 %	6.8 %	6.2 %
4. Return on investment	8 %	7.6 %	9 %	8.2 %
5. Return on equity	12.9 %	12.7 %	14.4 %	13.7 %
B. Liquidity Ratios				
1. Current ratio	2.9	2.5	2.9	3.1
2. Quick ratio	1.4	1.2	1.0	1.4
C. Activity Ratios				
1. Average collection period	42.4	43.5	33.3	42.8
2. Average payment period[a]	17.8	21.7	21.8	21.7
3. Inventory turnover	5.28	4.99	3.97	4.39
4. Total asset turnover	1.30	1.27	1.32	1.31
5. Fixed asset turnover	2.28	2.25	2.41	2.47
D. Debt Ratios				
1. Debt to assets	37.8 %	39.7 %	37.5 %	40.2 %
2. Long-term debt to equity	33.1 %	32.9 %	29.6 %	36.2 %
3. Debt to capital	24.9 %	24.8 %	22.8 %	26.6 %
4. Short-term liabilities to total debt	34.5 %	38 %	37 %	33.6 %
5. Times interest earned	5.16	5.01	5.89	5.66
E. Market Ratios				
1. Earnings per share (EPS)	$ 4.83	$ 4.31	$ 4.56	$ 3.91
2. Dividend payout	31 %	35 %	32 %	36 %
3. Dividend yield	2.5 %	2.9 %	2.7 %	3.0 %
4. Price/earnings (PE) ratio	11.6	12.2	12	12.1
5. Book value per share	$37.61	$34.18	$31.78	$28.69
6. Price to book value	1.50	1.54	1.72	1.65

[a]Assumes that credit purchases equal 70 percent of cost of goods sold.

WORKING-CAPITAL ANALYSIS

By definition, working capital is the excess of current assets over current liabilities, computed by subtracting current liabilities from current assets. It provides an index of financial soundness for current creditors and is one of the primary indicators of short-run solvency for a business. When a financial analysis is performed, a measurement of working capital should be considered in conjunction with the liquidity ratios. The current working-capital amount should be compared with the firm's past figures to determine if it is reasonable. Some caution should be exercised here since the relative size of the firm may be expanding or contracting.

Using the Statement of Changes in Financial Position

Neither the balance sheet nor the income statement tells us anything about the transactions entered into during a given period to finance a firm's operations.

For example, neither would show explicitly the sale of stock, a rollover of debt, or the purchase of land. A statement of changes in financial position focuses one's attention on changes in working capital and can provide information on items such as

- How funds provided by operations were used
- Where the funds used to invest in new plant and equipment came from
- How funds derived from a new bond issue or the sale of common stock were used
- How it was possible to continue payment of a regular dividend in the face of an operating loss
- The method of achieving debt repayment
- What funds were used to redeem the company's preferred stock
- How the increase in working capital was financed
- Why, despite record profits, the working-capital position is lower than last year

The balance sheet shows a variety of assets held by a company at a given time and the manner in which those assets are financed. The income statement gives the results of operations for a specific fiscal period. Since the generation of income will result in an increase in a variety of assets and the incurrence of expense will result in the consumption of assets and/or the creation of liabilities, it should be apparent that net income cannot be equated with an increase in liquidity. It is possible for a firm to be very profitable and still experience difficulty meeting debt obligations or lack funds for future expansion. A business can successfully increase sales and at the same time dry up its liquidity position due to the investment of funds in assets that cannot be converted into cash fast enough to meet maturing obligations.

The statement of changes in financial position (see Exhibits 5A and 5B) discloses the effect of earning activities on liquid resources. It focuses on such matters as what became of net income during the period, as well as what assets were acquired and how they were financed. It highlights clearly the distinction between net income and working capital provided by operations.

The significance of a change in liquidity, whether positive or negative, cannot be determined by the statement of changes in financial position alone. It should be linked to other variables in a firm's financial structure and operating results. For example, an increase in cash may have been gained by selling off assets whose earning power will be missed in the future, or the increase may have been caused by the incurrence of debt that has a high rate of interest expense and/or stringent repayment terms.

The statement of changes in financial position is also of great value to the analyst who wants to project operating results based on present and future productive capacity. In addition, the future potential for expansion and the sources from which this may be met can be forecasted. Using the financial statements as provided earlier, examine carefully how the statements are prepared.

Exhibit 5A *Statement of Changes in Financial Position*

Sources and Uses of Funds

Sources		Uses	
Earnings after taxes	$242	Increase in cash and equivalents	$ 21
Depreciation	137	Increase in accounts receivable, net	45
Decrease in other assets	3	Increase in prepaid expenses	3
Increase in income taxes payable	8	Increase in inventories	41
Increase in other current liabilities	17	Increase in long-term investments	15
Increase in long-term debt	84	Increase in plant and equipment	326
Increase in common stock	45	Decrease in notes payable	32
Increase in paid-in capital	35	Decrease in accounts payable	8
		Decrease in other liabilities	2
		Common stock dividends paid	74
		Preferred stock dividends paid	4
Total sources of funds	$571	Total uses of funds	$571

Exhibit 5B *Statement of Changes in Net Working Capital*

Sources		Uses	
Earnings after taxes	$242	Increase in long-term investments	$ 15
Depreciation	137	Increase in plant and equipment	326
Decrease in other assets	3	Decrease in other liabilities	2
Increase in long-term debt	84	Common stock dividends	74
Increase in common stock	45	Preferred stock dividends	4
Increase in paid-in capital	35	Changes in net working capital	125
Total sources	$546	Total uses	$546

Note: These statements (Exhibits 5A and 5B) are derived from the balance sheet (Exhibit 2) and the income statement (Exhibit 3) for the year 1989.

CAPITAL BUDGETING

A firm's earning power and value often rest on the effective use of its fixed assets (such as its building, plant, and equipment) as well as proper use of its financial sources or funds. Fixed assets become obsolete or abused from time to time and require attention. Since these assets primarily determine the potential of an organization, any decision for overhauling these earning assets has to be made with caution and prudence. Capital budgeting is a process that assists in evaluating the use of assets and funds and helps the firm in selecting the best alternatives with potentials for maximum return.

The capital-budgeting process involves three interrelated steps:

1. *Investment Proposal Generation* Proposals could be generated by anyone in the company. Any proposal put forward must be scrutinized for its value-added contributions. Needless to say, the larger the capital outlays request, the more critical the scrutiny should be.
2. *Estimating Relevant Cash Flows* This is perhaps the most difficult task since the manager is not only examining the numbers but is also judging the feasibility of the project itself in terms of its cash usage. For example, cash outlay associated with the purchase of a new machine would include not only the purchase price but also the following:

   • Machine transportation and installation costs
   • Costs of training employees
   • Costs of changing the administrative procedure (reporting forms may have to be redesigned, for example)

and

   • If the new machine is replacing the existing one, then you should deduct the sales price of the existing machine from the cost of the new one, and consider the tax implications as well. For instance:

$$\text{Old machine's book value} = \$12,000$$
$$\text{Old machine's sale price} = \$15,000$$
$$\text{Tax liability} = \$3,000 \times 0.34 = \$1,020$$

(0.34 is assumed to be the firm's tax bracket and $1,020 should be added to the cost of new machine.)

With the above explanation, consider now the importance of cash outflow and cash inflow with the following illustration.

The Q company is contemplating introduction of a product, and the life cycle of this product is estimated to be five years with a forecast of cash inflows to be:

Year 1	Year 2	Year 3	Year 4	Year 5
$70,000	100,000	150,000	90,000	60,000

Cash outflows (labor, materials, promotion, etc., but excluding the initial investment of $100,000) are:

Year 1	Year 2	Year 3	Year 4	Year 5
$40,000	60,000	90,000	60,000	40,000

The expected net cash flows from the new product are:

	Initial Investment	Year 1	Year 2	Year 3	Year 4	Year 5
Cash in		$70,000	100,000	150,000	90,000	60,000
Cash out	$ 100,000	40,000	60,000	90,000	60,000	40,000
Net C/F	$ − 100,000	30,000	40,000	60,000	30,000	20,000

3. *Project Selection* Given the net cash flow figures as above, management now needs to decide whether to accept or reject the proposal. The following methods are usually used to arrive at a decision:
   a. The *payback period* is the number of years required to recover the initial investment. For the example cited above, $70,000 will be recovered in the first two years, and when the third-year net of $60,000 is added, the payback period becomes 2.5 years. After two years and six months, the project proposal appears to be freestanding (remember, initial investment was $100,000).

   This method, of course, is appealing because of its simplicity and emphasis on the liquidity of the project. However, it presents a problem when management is faced with more than one project with similar payback periods.
   b. The *net present value (NPV)* has to be computed for identical payback periods and, most importantly, for the consideration of time value of money. NPV is calculated by subtracting the initial investment from the present value of the projects' cash inflows. For computation, one first ascertains the firm's cost of capital (i.e., at what rate of interest the company can borrow). Going back to the example in step 2, and assuming 12 percent as the cost of capital, the NPV of the project will be

$$NPV = CF_1(PVIF_{12,1}) + CF_2(PVIF_{12,2}) + CF_3(PVIF_{12,3})$$
$$+ CF_4(PVIF_{12,4}) + CF_5(PVIF_{12,5})$$
$$- \text{ initial investment}$$
$$= 30,000(0.893) + 40,000(0.797) + 60,000(0.712)$$
$$+ 30,000(0.636) + 20,000(0.567) - 100,000$$
$$= 26,790 + 31,880 + 42,720 + 19,080 + 11,340$$
$$- 100,000$$
$$= 31,810$$

The company will add $31,810 to its value by accepting the project. If NPV comes to zero, it will mean that the project will only cover the cost of capital or break even. Alternatively, a negative NPV will denote a loss for the company. Consider another illustration where cash flow projection for ten years is $12,000 per year, the cost of capital is 11 percent, and the initial investment proposed is $80,000:

$$NPV = \text{annual cash flow}(PVIFA_{i,n}) - \text{initial investment}$$
$$= 12,000(PVIFA_{11,10}) - 80,000$$
$$= 12,000(5.889) - 80,000$$
$$= 70,668 - 80,000$$
$$= -9,332$$

The project will result in a net loss of $9,332. The major shortcoming of this method is that it assumes the cost of capital to be fixed for the duration of the project or investment period.

c. The *internal rate of return (IRR)* is the project's annual rate of return. If this rate of return is greater than or at least equal to the firm's cost of capital, the project may be accepted. For example, the project stipulates an initial investment of $40,000 with expected annual cash flow of $7,000 for ten years. To find the IRR:

- Look at an annuity table (given at the back of any finance textbook) for the nearest discount factor of 5.714 which is derived from $40,-000/$7,000.
- The nearest discount (interest) factor is 5.650, which corresponds to a discount rate of 12 percent (actually 5.714 lies between the factor of 5.650 for 12 percent and 5.889 for 11 percent. Through interpolation, one can find that 5.714 corresponds to an IRR of 11.73 percent).

Now, what does it mean? By investing $40,000 now, the company will receive $7,000 per year for ten years. Thus, $40,000, if invested in the proposed project, will earn a rate of return of 11.73 percent. Whether this venture is worthwhile would greatly depend on the firm's employing this capital somewhere else with a higher rate than an 11.73 percent rate of return.

Note that the process of calculating IRR by hand can be difficult when a project's annual cash flows are not equal. Nevertheless, the concept is of critical importance since it takes into account the time value of money and does not assume a fixed cost of capital during the life of investment.

Points to Remember

A. In evaluating investment projects, the company should use a weighted average to compute the cost of capital rather than the cost of a specific source of financing (debt, preferred stock, common stock, and/or retained earnings). The weighted average can be computed by multiplying the specific cost of each source of financing by its weight in the capital structure and adding the weighted values. To illustrate:

Source (1)	Amount (2)	After-Tax Cost (3)		Weight (4)		Weighted Cost (5)
Debt	$6 million	0.08	×	30%	=	0.024
Preferred stocks	$2 million	0.09	×	10%	=	0.009
Common stocks	$2 million	0.12	×	10%	=	0.012
Retained earnings	$10 million	0.11	×	50%	=	0.055
Total	$20 million			100%	=	0.10
						or 10%

$$\text{WACC} = 0.30(0.08) + 0.10(0.09) + 0.10(0.12) + 0.50(0.11) = 0.10$$

Columns 1 and 2 show the sources of capital and their respective amounts. Column 3 tells what the company is paying for these sources of capital. The weight of each source in column 4 is ascertained by the amount in each source divided by the total of column 2 (debt of $6 million/$20 million = 30 percent). The weighted cost is the amount when the weight is multiplied by after-tax cost (30 percent × 0.08 = 0.024). The weighted cost of capital for this company from all sources comes to 10 percent, which means that in order to break even, the company must at least have a rate of return of 10 percent from the projects proposed. Since 10 percent is the minimum return wanted, any proposal for capital investment should be rejected if this rate of return is not achieved.

B. The element of risk can be incorporated into the capital-budgeting process by changing the required rate of return. The higher the project risk, the higher the required rate should be. Risks in capital budgeting result from the uncertainty about the level of future cash inflows. One popular approach to deal with the risk associated with future cash flows is sensitivity or "what if" analysis. Sensitivity analysis uses a number of likely values for a given variable (e.g., sales, cost of materials, cost of labor, tax rates) and assesses the impact on a project's future cash inflow, which could be done easily with Lotus 1-2-3.

C. Capital-budgeting projects can be classified as either independent or mutually exclusive. Independent projects do not compete with each other (e.g., selecting between a computer system and a site for a warehouse) and the organization should accept these projects as long as it has funds to finance them and meet the company's accepted criteria. Mutually exclusive projects, on the other hand, serve the same purpose and thus compete with each other (e.g., selecting between two building sites). As suggested earlier, the organization should select the project that has the higher NPV or IRR.

D. Each firm faces capital rationing since no one has unlimited funds to adopt all possible projects. Hence the company should rank those projects based on their NPVs or IRRs and select the ones that will maximize the value of the company to the stakeholders and that are in line with the corporate strategic direction.

BUSINESS ACQUISITIONS

What Is a Business Combination?

Three types of business combinations can occur in the process of making an acquisition:

1. *Statutory Merger* Company A acquires company B; B goes out of business; A owns 100 percent of B's assets.
2. *Statutory Consolidation* Companies A and B transfer their assets to a newly formed company C; A and B go out of business. C issues its stock to the old stockholders of A and B.
3. *Parent-Subsidiary* Company A acquires a majority (over 50 percent) of company B's outstanding voting stock. The combining companies retain their separate legal identities and separate accounting records even though they have become one economic entity.

Purchase of Assets Versus Pooling of Interests

The terms *purchase of assets* and *pooling of interests* describe accounting methods that deal with statutory mergers and statutory consolidations, and are not concerned with parent-subsidiary relationships. Under the pooling-of-interests method, the ownership interests of the combining companies are united and continue relatively unchanged. Since neither combining company is considered to have acquired the other, there is no purchase, no purchase price, and accordingly, no goodwill is created. The assets, liabilities, and stockholders' equity are carried forward to the combined entity at book values. The Accounting Principles Board has set forth 12 conditions in APB Opinion No. 16 (1970) that must be met before the pooling-of-interests method is employed. The pooling-of-interest method is used if these 12 conditions are met:

1. Each of the combining companies is autonomous and has not been a subsidiary or division of another corporation within two years before the plan of combination is initiated.
2. Each of the combining companies can own no more than 10 percent of the other's voting stock.
3. The combination must be completed in accordance with a specific plan within one year after the plan is initiated.
4. The issuing corporation must offer and issue only common stock in ex-

change for substantially all (90 percent or more) of the outstanding voting stock of a combining company at the date the plan is consummated.

5. If the combining company holds shares in the issuing company, these shares must be converted into an equivalent number of shares of the combining company and also deducted from the outstanding shares to determine the number of shares assumed to be exchanged.

6. None of the combining companies can change the equity interest of the voting common stock in contemplation of effecting the combination within two years before initiation of the plan of combination or between the dates of initiation and consummation.

7. Each of the combining companies reacquires its own shares of voting common stock only for purposes other than the business combination.

8. The proportionate interest of each individual common stockholder in each of the combining companies remains the same as a result of the exchange of stock to effect the combination.

9. The voting rights in the combined corporation are to be immediately exercisable by the stockholders.

10. The combined corporation must not agree to retire or reacquire stock issued to effect the combination.

11. The combined corporation must not enter into financial arrangements for the benefit of the former stockholders of a combining company.

12. The combined corporation must not plan to dispose of a significant part of the assets of the combining companies within two years after the combination.

Under the purchase-of-assets method, the acquiring company receives control of the acquired assets and records them at their fair market value at the time of the business combination. Any excess of purchase price over the fair market value of the assets acquired is allocated to goodwill and is amortized over a maximum period of 40 years. This amortization expense, in turn, will reduce the reported earnings of the firm. One is able to perceive an incentive on the part of management to effectuate a pooling-of-interests transaction rather than a purchase of assets. In spite of this, cash purchases are more common due to the demands of stockholders who increasingly are not interested in just swapping stock.

In determining what price will be paid for a business acquisition, a number of factors should be considered, including earnings, dividends, and growth potential. We will divide our attention between a straight cash purchase and a stock-for-stock exchange, in which the acquiring firm trades its own stock rather than pay cash for the acquired firm.

Cash Purchases

Cash purchases can be viewed as a capital-budgeting decision. Instead of building a new plant or buying additional machinery, the purchaser has opted to acquire a business that has already established itself. For example, Pritchett Industries, Inc., wants to acquire Anderson Amalgamated for $1 million. Anderson has expected after-tax cash flows of $100,000 per year for the next five years and $150,000 per year for years 6 through 20. The synergistic benefits of combined production know-how and management expertise will add $10,000 per year to this after-tax cash flow. If Pritchett Industries has a 10 percent required cost of capital (i.e., its total investment must generate at least a 10 percent return for it to stay in business), calculations show that the proposed purchase would have a positive net present value of $172,690. But how does one figure out how much to pay for Anderson Amalgamated or, for that matter, any firm?

Net Present Value Method   As discussed in the earlier section, the example just given illustrates one of the most widely used tools for determining if an investment will prove viable to a company. As the name suggests, the future earnings that will be generated by the investment in question are "discounted" back to the present via the present value method. Once this is accomplished, the initial investment amount is subtracted from this present value figure to arrive at a net present value, which is positive, zero, or negative. If this value is negative, the investment is viewed as providing a return below the required rate of return of the firm (this rate, occasionally referred to as the internal rate of return, is the rate used to compute the discounted cash flows generated by the investment). If this value is zero, the investment is said to be providing a return that meets the minimum requirement for serious consideration as a possible venture. Similarly, if the net present value is positive, the investment would appear to provide a better than satisfactory return to the firm over its useful life.

Now, let us look at our example again from an analytical standpoint:

1. Pritchett Industries wants to buy Anderson Amalgamated for $1,000,000 cash; the $1,000,000 initial cost is worth exactly $1,000,000 today in present value terms.
2. The investment in Anderson will generate $100,000 per year in *after-tax* earnings for years 1 through 5 and $150,000 per year for years 6 through 20.
3. The combination of the two companies will produce an additional $10,000 per year in *after-tax* earnings for years 1 through 20.
4. Pritchett Industries has a 10 percent required cost of capital.

With this information we can create the following schematic:

	After-Tax Earnings Stream	
Year	1 through 5	6 through 20
Earnings	$100,000	$150,000
	+	+
	$10,000	$10,000

We must discount these figure earnings back to the present using Pritchett's 10 percent required cost of capital figure. We then compare the present value of the earnings stream with the $1,000,000 initial cost to arrive at the net present value.

Present value of earnings for years 1–5	
$110,000 \times PVIFA_{10.5}$	$ 417,010
Present value of earnings for years 6–20	
$160,000(PVIFA_{10.20} - PVIFA_{10.5})$	
$160,000(8.514 - 3.791)$	
$160,000 \times 4.723$	755,680
Present value of earnings stream	$ 1,172,690
Initial cash outlay	(1,000,000)
Net present value	$ 172,690

Our analysis shows that this business acquisition will have a positive net present value of $172,690. Unless Pritchett Industries can come out with a better deal somewhere else, the purchase of Anderson Amalgamated should prove to be a profitable investment.

Determining the Price to Pay for an Acquisition To begin, one may be tempted to look at the book value of the firm under consideration (by definition, book value = assets − liabilities). In reality, book value has become meaningless as a basis of valuation, accept when it is significantly higher than the market value of the firm. In this case, we can compute the ratio of the book values of the two firms and use it as a basis of exchange. Usually this is not done unless the firm is being acquired for its liquidity and asset value rather than for its earning power. By and large, the fair market value of a firm's assets becomes the starting point for negotiations in setting the price for an acquisition. In addition, the firm's future earning potential may play an important part in this process, as was demonstrated by the net present value method.

Stock-for-Stock Exchange

With a stock-for-stock exchange, a slightly different approach is used in determining the value of an acquisition. A ratio of exchange for the common stock of the two entities involved is employed:

$$\text{Price exchange ratio} = \frac{\text{Market price per share for buyer} \times \text{No. shares offered by buyer per share of seller}}{\text{Market price per share for seller}}$$

For example, F&F Enterprises' stock is selling for $60 per share, and it wishes to acquire company B, whose stock is selling for $30 per share. F&F wishes to offer a half share of its stock for each share of B's; therefore, the ratio of exchange would be ($60 × 0.5)/$30 = 1.00. The stock of the two companies would be exchanged evenly; that is, 2 shares of B for each share of F&F. However, there generally is little incentive to swap on an even basis, so the acquiring firm usually must offer a price in excess of the current market price per share of the company it wishes to acquire. Instead of offering 0.5 shares of F&F stock for each share of B, it might offer 0.6 shares at the current market value to persuade B's stockholders to make the swap. Under this arrangement, B's stockholders would receive 6 shares of F&F for every 10 of their own instead of the original 5.

In the case where a business acquires another business whose price-earnings ratio is lower than its own, there will likely be an increase in the acquirer's earnings per share. However, long-term considerations can influence the decision to buy a growth firm with a high price-earnings ratio. The long-term benefits should be evaluated in this instance and found to outweigh any short-term decrease in earnings per share.

In addition to the ideas already offered in establishing a price for an acquisition, there are other sources that may be able to provide some clue as to worth of a firm. Look for a firm of comparable size in the same industry that has been bought recently and see what the purchaser had to pay. If no firm of comparable size can be found in the same industry, then try to locate a firm of comparable size in another industry. Another approach is to find a firm in the same industry regardless of size and compute the ratio of its purchase price to its book value. This ratio is then used to multiply the book value of the firm under consideration. This is similar to the practice used in real estate for determining the value of a house in a given neighborhood. The real estate agent first finds out what other houses in that area have sold for and computes an average price per square foot. This figure is then multiplied by the square footage of the seller's house to arrive at an initial asking price.

EBIT-EPS Analysis   Earnings before interest and taxes (EBIT), also known as operating profit, reveals how efficiently the firm is generating revenues and controlling expenses. When the EBIT is determined, expenses not related to operational matters, such as interest and taxes, are deducted to arrive at net income. Once net income is determined, it is simply divided by the number of common stock shares outstanding to calculate the earnings per share (EPS) of the firm. The relationship between EBIT and the subsequent EPS is affected by the level of EBIT, the size of the firm's interest expense, and the number of shares outstanding. The process of determining what mix of debt and equity to use when a firm is attempting to raise additional funds is known as EBIT-EPS analysis. It is this analysis that reveals the effects of financial leverage on earnings per share.

To illustrate an EBIT-EPS analysis of leverage, suppose that Widget Manufacturing Co. wants to raise an additional $500,000 for expansion through one of three possible financing plans: (1) all debt at 15 percent interest; (2) all common stock at $50 a share; (3) 50 percent debt and 50 percent stock. We will assume that with the expansion, sales will increase by $1,000,000, variable costs by $250,000, and fixed costs by $450,000. We will also assume a 34 percent tax rate and 100,000 shares of common stock initially outstanding. The following table shows the results of the three financing plans on earnings per share:

	Before Expansion	100% Debt	100% Common Stock	50% Debt + 50% Common Stock
Sales	$2,000,000	$3,000,000	$3,000,000	$3,000,000
Variable costs	500,000	750,000	750,000	750,000
Fixed costs	800,000	1,250,000	1,250,000	1,250,000
EBIT	700,000	1,000,000	1,000,000	1,000,000
Interest	100,000	175,000	100,000	137,500
Earnings before taxes	600,000	825,000	900,000	862,500
Income taxes	204,000	280,500	306,000	293,250
Net income	$ 396,000	$ 544,500	$ 594,000	$ 569,250
Number of shares outstanding	100,000	100,000	110,000	105,000
Earnings per share	$ 3.96	$ 5.45	$ 5.40	$ 5.42

The company should favor the combination that yields the highest earnings per share, thereby keeping its stockholders content. Notwithstanding, one must make the decision of financing with debt in light of the availability of credit. If Widget Manufacturing's debt-to-equity ratio is already high (60/40), it would be difficult to finance the expansion through the issuance of bonds. On the other hand, the company must also take into consideration the market demand for its common stock. Will a new issue of stock sell at $50.00 per share? If the market will only pay $45.00 per share, the firm will be forced to sell more stock than it had originally planned to finance the expansion. Consequently, as the number of shares outstanding increases, the corresponding earnings per share will decrease. The trick is, of course, to find the proper mix that everyone can live with.

You will recall here that since the new shareholders will have the right to vote, the current shareholders may not like this "crowding effect" and may prefer the company to issue debt rather than new stocks.

Further, the issuing of bonds has two specific advantages over the issuing of common stocks. First, interest payments on bonds are tax deductible. Second, the bondholders, in general, do not have voting rights and therefore they are not in a position to exercise control over the corporation's affairs.

PRO FORMA FINANCIAL STATEMENTS

Recommendations will carry little weight unless their impact on the financial condition of the firm can be demonstrated. Pro forma financial statements represent the most comprehensive way of forecasting the results of future operations given a specific set of circumstances. Of major importance are the pro forma balance sheet, income statement, and cash budget. The pro forma income statement is a projection of anticipated sales, expenses, and income for given future cash flow requirements given the projected level of operations. The pro forma balance sheet is a projection of future asset, liability, and stockholder equity levels.

The following discussion is a summary illustration of how a forecast income statement, cash budget, and balance sheet are put together.

The Importance of Sales Forecasting

The sales forecast is the most important link in constructing pro forma financial statements. Its accuracy is absolutely crucial for determining production schedules and the subsequent costs to be incurred. When sales forecasting is attempted, the following factors should be considered:

1. Past pattern of sales
2. Estimates and opinions made by the sales force
3. Overall state of the economy
4. Competitors' present activity and possible reaction
5. Effects of target pricing
6. Advertising and sales promotion plans
7. Market research studies

Creating Pro Forma Statements

Once the sales forecast is derived, plans are then formulated to estimate the related costs and cash flow for the specified level of sales. This is usually done through the use of schedules such as cash collections, purchases, and wages and commissions. Exhibit 6 provides an illustration of these schedules.

After these schedules are determined, the next step is to assemble a forecast income statement. Exhibit 7 illustrates this step.

The next step is to produce a forecast cash budget. As Exhibit 8 illustrates, cash receipts and disbursements are predicted on a monthly basis. The ability of the firm's management to foresee accurately what the cash requirements will be is crucial. An accurate forecast will ensure that adequate funds are available to (1) provide for daily operational needs and (2) service all debt obligations as they come due.

The final step is the preparation of the pro forma balance sheet. Each account is projected in harmony with the pro forma income statement, cash budget, and supporting schedules. Exhibit 9 shows the before-and-after results of anticipated operations.

An alternative to going through the process of tracing cash and accounting flows is to assume that the balance sheet accounts will maintain a given percentage of sales. We first estimate the new sales level and then apply the

Exhibit 6 Supporting Sheet for Pro Forma Statements

	Nov. '88	Dec. '88	Jan. '89	Feb. '89	Mar. '89	Total Jan.–Mar. 1989
Forecast sales	$40,000	$36,000	$40,000	$44,000	$50,000	$134,000
Cash sales (0.30)	12,000	10,800	12,000	13,200	15,000	40,200
Collections of A/R						
Lagged 1 mo. (0.50)		20,000	18,000	20,000	22,000	
Lagged 2 mo. (0.20)			8,000	7,200	8,000	
Other cash receipts			1,200	1,200	1,200	
Total cash receipts			$39,200	$41,600	$46,200	$125,800
Purchases (0.6 @ sales)	24,000	21,600	24,000	26,400	30,000	
Cash purch. (0.20)		4,320	4,800	5,280	6,000	
Payment of A/P						
Lagged 1 mo. (0.60)		14,400	12,960	14,400	15,840	
Lagged 2 mo. (0.20)			4,800	4,320	4,800	
Lease expense			1,500	1,500	1,500	
Wages and salaries			4,200	4,350	5,250	
Cash dividends			2,500			
Interest payment					1,800	
Commission (8% of cur. mo. sales)			3,200	3,520	4,000	
Insurance					900	
Misc. expenses (3% of sales)			1,200	1,320	1,500	
Fixed assets purch.				12,500		
Total cash disburs.			$35,160	$47,190	$41,590	$123,940

Exhibit 7 Pro Forma Income Statement (January 1 to March 31, 1989)

Sales		$134,000
Cost of goods sold		80,400
Gross profit		53,600
Operating expenses		
Wages and salaries	$13,800	
Sales commissions	10,720	
Lease expense	4,500	
Depreciation	2,500	
Insurance	900	
Miscellaneous expenses (4% of sales)	5,360	

Continued

Exhibit 7 (*Continued*)

	37,780
Operating profit	15,820
Interest expense	1,800
Profit before taxes	14,020
Tax (0.25 × profit before taxes)	3,505
Net profit after taxes	$ 10,515
Quarterly	
Cash dividends (0.05 per share)	2,500
Increase in retained earnings	8,015

Exhibit 8 Pro Forma Cash Budget (January 1 to March 31, 1989)

	Jan.	Feb.	Mar.
Total cash receipts	$39,200	$41,600	$46,200
Less: total cash disbursement	35,160	47,190	41,590
Net cash flow	4,040	(5,590)	4,610
Add: beginning cash balance	8,500	12,540	6,950
Ending cash balance	12,540	6,950	11,560
Less: minimum cash balance	5,000	5,000	5,000
Required borrowing	—	—	—
Excess cash balance	7,540	1,950	6,560

Exhibit 9A Balance Sheet (December 31, 1989)

Assets			Liabilities	
Cash		$ 8,500	Accounts payable	$ 17,760
Accounts receivable		33,200	Taxes payable	3,100
Inventories		12,000	Notes payable	4,500
Other current assets		5,000	Other current liabilities	9,700
Total current assets		$ 58,700	Total current liabilities	$ 35,060
Fixed assets	$130,000		Long-term debt	40,000
Acc. depreciation	36,200			
Net fixed assets		93,800	Stockholders' equity	
			Common stock (50,000,	
			par $1)	50,000
			Retained earnings	27,440
Total assets		$152,500	Total liabilities and	
			stockholders' equity	$152,500

percentage relationships to arrive at the projected figures on our balance sheet. This is known as the percentage-of-sales method. It is a broad-brush approach that is not as meaningful as the pro forma approach described earlier.

Cost-Volume-Profit Analysis

In addition to presenting pro forma financial statements to back up recommendations, it may be helpful to employ cost-volume-profit, or break-even, analysis, to lend more clarity to the argument. Using this technique, one is able to

Exhibit 9B *Pro Forma Balance Sheet (Mar. 31, 1989)*

Assets			Liabilities		
Cash[a]		$ 6,560	Accounts payable[f]		$ 29,280
Accounts receivable[b]		43,800	Taxes payable[g]		3,390
Inventories[c]		20,000	Notes payable		4,500
Other current assets		6,400	Other current liabilities		9,700
Total current assets		$ 81,410	Total current liabilities		$ 46,870
Fixed assets[d]	$142,500		Long-term debt		40,000
Accumulated depreciation[e]	38,700		Total liabilities		$ 86,870
Net fixed assets		103,800	Stockholders' equity		
			Common stock	$ 50,000	
			Retained earn.[h]	35,455	
					85,455
		————	Required new funds[i]		12,885
Total assets		$185,210	Total liabilities and stockholders' equity		$185,210

[a]Cash: $9,910 from pro forma cash budget.
[b]Accounts receivable:
  Feb. sales 44,000 × 0.20 = 8,800
  Mar. sales 50,000 × 0.70 = 35,000
                              43,800 supporting sheet

[c]Inventories represent about 40% of sales. Inventories consist of $4,000 or 20% in raw material and goods in process and $16,000 in finished goods.
[d]Fixed assets consist of $130,000 balance on December 31 and $12,500 bought on February of next year.
[e]Accumulated depreciation is $36,200 at December 31, 1989, and $2,500 depreciation for the next three months from the pro forma income statement.
[f]Accounts payable ($5,280 from February purchases, 26,400 × 0.20, and $24,000 from March purchases, 30,000 × 0.80).
[g]Taxes payable assumed to equal next quarter taxes of $3,390 from the pro forma income statement.
[h]Retained earnings increased by $8,015 from the pro forma income statement.
[i]This is the required new funds necessary to balance the company's balance sheet. The company has to plan to raise these funds by borrowing or issuing new common stocks to support the forecast sales of $134,000 for the next quarter.

demonstrate the relationship of revenue, expenses, and net income as well as what happens to overall profit if a specific level of sales is achieved.

With the following information, we can derive the break-even point:

Selling price per unit	$ .50
Variable cost per unit	(.40)
Contribution margin per unit	$ .10
Monthly fixed expenses	$1,000.00
Rent	4,000.00
Wages and salaries	500.00
Other fixed expenses	500.00
Total fixed expenses per month	$6,000.00

Using the equation

$$\text{Net income} = \text{sales} - \text{variable expenses} - \text{fixed expenses}$$

We get

$$\text{Sales} = \text{net income} + \text{variable expenses} + \text{fixed expenses}$$

Letting X = the number of units to sell to break even, we get

$$\$.50X = 0 + \$.40X + \$6,000.00$$

(*Note:* To break even, our revenue should be exactly equal to our expenses, thereby yielding *zero net income.*) Solving for X, we get

$$\$.50 - \$.40X = 0 + \$6,000.00$$

$$\$.10X = \$6,000.00$$

$$X = \frac{\$6,000}{\$.10}$$

$$= 60,000 \text{ units}$$

We must sell 60,000 units to break even. Our break-even dollar sales is simply 60,000 units $\times$ $.50 sales price per unit = $30,000. Using this equation, we can determine how many units need to be sold to obtain a given net income; conversely, we can also determine what our net income will be given the number of units sold.

For example, if we want to know how many units must be sold to generate $75,000 in net income, we simply plug that figure into the equation:

$$X = \frac{\$6,000 + \$75,000}{\$.10} = \frac{\$81,000}{\$.10} = 810,000 \text{ units}$$

If, on the other hand, we sold 500,000 units, what would our net income be? Letting I = net income, we substitute into the same equation and solve for I:

$$500,000 = \frac{\$6,000 + I}{\$.10}$$

$$\$.10 \times 500,000 = \$6,000 + I$$

$$\$50,000 = \$6,000 + I$$

$$\$50,000 - \$6,000 = I$$

$$I = \$44,000$$

By now it should be apparent that the form of the equation used in both cases is

$$\text{Units sold} = \frac{\text{fixed expenses} + \text{net income}}{\text{contribution margin per unit}}$$

Exhibit 10 illustrates the graphical application of the cost-volume-profit analysis.

In summary, you should attempt to present pro forma financial statements following your recommendations. In some instances, however, you may not be able to provide them due to lack of financial information contained in the case. Should this occur, it is suggested that you seriously consider presenting a financial impact statement. The impact statement in this instance would be a brief summary of the company's projected financial affairs given the student's set of recommendations.

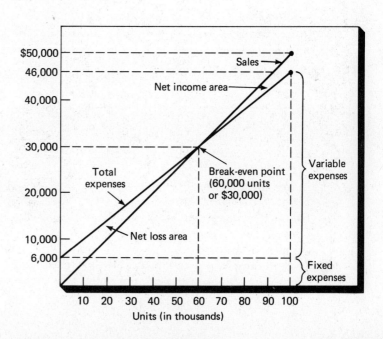

INDEX

Acquisition, 108–112
Activity ratios, 263
Adler, Nancy J., 250
American Express Company, 70, 100, 236
American Telephone & Telegraph (AT&T), 11, 247
Ansoff, H. Igor, 193
Apple Computer, 224–227
Applied research, 200
Aquilano, Nicholas J., 199
Arbitrageur (arb), 111
Audit committee, 169
Auditing, 220–221
Auld, Deborah, 79
Avon, 106

Backward integration, 98
Bacon, Jeremy, 174
Baird, Lloyd, 200, 206
BankAmerica Corporation, 236
Baptist church, 5
Basic research, 200
Bear hug, 111
Bemelmans, T., 203
Bettis, Richard A., 144
Betts, Michael A., 79
Blaine, Charley, 112
Blau, Peter M., 174
Board of directors, 167
Boston Consulting Group (BCG), 124
Boy Scouts of America, 70
Bracker, Jeffrey S., 250
Brano, Albert V., 144

British Petroleum, 236
Broad-line global strategy, 243
Brown, James K., 174
Buchele, Robert B., 78
Budgeting, 188–190
Budgets, 220
Burns, Tom, 173
Business acquisitions analysis, 261
Business judgment rule, 170
Business policy, 5
Business portfolio analysis, 124
Business unit stategies, 13, 18, 92–94, 114, 130
Business Week, 45
Byars, Lloyd L., 51

Caldwell, Philip, 177
Campbell Soup Company, 237
Cannon, J. Thomas, 173
Capital assets, 195
Capital budgeting, 195–196, 261, 271–276
Cary, Frank T., 6, 22
Case analysis, 257–258
Cash cows, 125
Cash flow analysis, 196–197
Catch-up R&D strategy, 201
Celler-Kefauver amendment, 99
Chandler, Alfred D., Jr., 154, 158, 173
Channel strategy, 194
Chapter 11 (federal bankruptcy laws), 104
Chase, Richard B., 199

Child, J., 173
Christensen, H. Kurt, 144
Chrysler, 44, 52
Clemons, Eric K., 223
Coca-Cola Company, 5, 139, 140
Code of ethics, 19
Combination strategies, 105
Common Market, 242
Comparative advantage, 244
Compensation committee, 169
Competitive advantage, 244
Competitive analysis, 36–37
Competitive gap, 95
Competitive response profile, 54
Competitive strategy analysis, 135
Competitor response profile, 40–41
Compustat, 217
Concentric diversification, 97–98
Concentric mergers, 108
Concentric strategy, 115
Condition of facilities and equipment, 67
Conglomerate diversification, 100–101, 115
Conglomerate mergers, 108
Conn, Carolyn, 206
Contingency approach to organizing, 157–158
Control process, 214
Cooke, Robert A., 174
Cooper, Arnold C., 144
Cooper, Thomas A., 12
Corporate strategies, 13, 18, 92, 114
Cost leadership strategy, 106

Cost-volume-profit analysis, 285–287
Creeping tender offer, 111
Critical external factors, 128–129
Critical success factors, 128–129
Crozier, Michael, 173
Culture, 8–9, 18, 240
Customer departmentation, 157

Daft, Richard L., 51
Dalton, D. R., 22
Data Research, Inc., 45
David, Fred R., 23
Davids, Meryl, 51
Davis, Peter S., 117
Debt (or leverage) ratios, 263
Decentralization stage, 158
DeGive, Ghislaine, 200, 206
DeKluyver, Cornelis, 144
Delphi technique, 47–48
Delta Air Lines, 10
Departmentation, 155–157
Department of Defense, 5
Department of Justice, 99
DePorras, Richard A., 79
Dess, Gregory G., 117
Development research, 200
Differentiation strategy, 106–107,
     115
Digital Equipment Corporation
     (DEC), 167
Disney, Walt, 9
Disney, Walt, Productions, 9
Distribution gap, 95
Diversification marketing strategy,
     193–194
Divestment strategy, 104
Dogs, 125
Drucker, Peter F., 11, 22, 95, 116,
     161, 174, 204, 206
Due care, 170
Dun and Bradstreet, 217
Dun's Review, 217
DuPont, 154, 216
Dyer, Lee, 206
Dymsza, William A., 250

Eastman Kodak, 236
EBIT-EPS analysis, 281–282
EC. See European Community
Econometric modeling, 48–49
Endgame strategies, 101, 115
Entrepreneurial stage, 158
Environmental scanning, 41, 45–46,
     49–50
Ethics, 19–20
European Community (EC), 242
Executive committee, 169
Export-Import Bank, 44
Export-import manager, 246
Exporting, 244
Exxon, 236

Falbe, Cecilia, 174
Federal Communications
     Commission (FCC), 44
Federal Trade Commission (FTC),
     43–44
Fiedler, Edgar R., 51
Filley, Alan, 173
Finance committee, 169
Financial position, 64–65
Financial strategies, 195
First Nationwide Financial
     Corporation, 29
Flexible budgets, 189
Focus strategy, 107, 115
Food and Drug Administration
     (FDA), 44
Forbes, 45, 218
Ford, Henry, 24, 177
Ford, Henry, Jr., 141, 177
Ford Aerospace Corporation, 29
Ford Foundation, 5
Ford Microelectronics, Inc., 29
Ford Motor Company, 23, 52, 79,
     117, 141, 145, 175, 207, 228, 250
Ford Motor Credit Company, 29
Ford Motor Land Development
     Corporation, 29
Ford New Holland, Inc., 29
Forecasting techniques, 47–49
Foreign exchange rates, 240
Fortune, 4, 45, 218
Forward integration, 98
Freeman, E. A., 22
Freund, York P., 145
Friendly mergers, 109
Friendly takeover, 111
Functional departmentation,
     155–156
Functional development stage,
     158
Functional strategies, 13, 18, 92,
     114, 130, 190

GAAP. See Generally accepted
     accounting practices
Geneen, Harold, 141
General Accounting Office (GAO),
     221
General Electric (GE), 9, 16, 17,
     128, 135
Generally accepted accounting
     practices (GAAP), 221
General Motors (GM), 5, 52, 142,
     154
Geographic departmentation, 156
Georgia Tech, 5
Giallourakis, Mike, 23
Gitman, Lawrence J., 216
Global industry, 236–238
Global strategies, 238
Global-focus strategy, 243

Golden parachute, 111
Gonzales, Monica, 51
Government auditors, 221
Greenley, G. E., 22
Greenmail, 111
Gregg, Charles I., 260
Growth-share matrix, 124, 145
Growth strategy, 94–95, 114
Guth, William D., 206
Guyon, Janet, 247

Hall, William K., 144
Hambrick, Donald C., 117, 145
Harrigan, Kathryn Rudie, 103, 116,
     117
Hartman, Curtis, 42
Harvest strategy, 101
Harvey, Edward, 174
Hax, Arnoldo C., 127, 144, 174
Henderson, Bruce D., 144
Herold, David, 22
Hertz Corporation, 29
Hofer, Charles W., 134, 144, 145
Honda, 52
Horizontal diversification, 99–100,
     115
Horizontal mergers, 108
Hosmer, LaRue Tone, 166, 174
Host country, 247
Hostile mergers, 109
House, Robert, 22, 173
Hudson Institute, 45
Human resource/personnel
     strategies, 197
Human resources, 66
Human rights, 242
Hurwich, Mark R., 206
Huss, W. R., 51
Hussey, David E., 79

IBM, 4, 5, 9, 141, 142, 158, 236,
     238
Importing, 244–245
Incentive pay plans, 202–203
Independent auditors, 221
Individual competitor analysis,
     37–41
Industry attractiveness-business
     strength matrix, 128, 147
Industry structure analysis, 37
Innovative R&D strategy, 201
In play, 111
Internal auditors, 221
Internal organizational analysis, 64
Internal Revenue Service (IRS), 44,
     221
International Harvester, 4
Interstate Commerce Commission
     (ICC), 44
Ireland, R. Duane, 79
ITT, 100, 141

Jaguar, 253
Jain, Sabhash C., 51
Jassim, Amir, 261
Johnson, F. Ross, 168
Johnson, Robert Wood, 9
Johnson & Johnson, 7, 9
Joint venture, 112–114, 247
Junk bond, 111

Kaplan, Eileen E., 174
Kaplan, Jack M., 174
Kerin, Roger A., 194
Khandwalla, Pradip N., 174
Kilpatrick, John A., 241
Kimberly, John R., 174
King, William R., 79
Kirkconnell, Paul A., 250
Kiwanis International, 5
Kogut, Bruce, 250

LaForge, R. Lawrence, 22
Lawrence, Paul, 173
Leadership, 164–165
Leadership strategy, 101
Leidecker, Joel K., 144
Leisner, Richard M., 174
Lemak, David J., 250
Leontiades, Milton, 174, 206
Lesikar, Raymond V., 250
Leveraged buy-out, 111
Levitt, Theodore, 250
Licensing, 247
Life-cycle approach, 131–132
Liquidation strategy, 105
Liquidity ratios, 262
Little, Arthur D., Inc., 131
Lockheed, 44
Lockup, 111
Long-range objectives, 12, 18, 69
Long-range planning, 5
Lorsch, Jay, 173

McDonald's, 9, 96
McGinnis, Michael A., 145
McIlhenny Company, 94
McKesson Drug Company, 223
McKinley, William, 174
McKinsey and Company, 128
MacMillan, Ian C., 206
MacMillan, Keith, 260
McNair, Malcolm P., 260
Maidique, Modesto A., 206
Majiluk, Nicholas S., 127, 144, 174
Management audits, 221
Management information system
    (MIS), 223–224
Market development strategy, 193
Marketing, 191–192
Marketing capability, 65–66
Marketing mix, 194
Marketing penetration strategy, 193

Marketing strategies, 191–192
Market ratios, 263
Mary Kay Cosmetics, 199, 201
Mayo Clinic, 5
Mechanistic systems, 159
Merger, 108–110, 111
Meshoulam, Ilan, 200, 206
Meyers, C., 206
Migliore, R. Henry, 68
Miller, Janice James, 241
MIS. See Management information
    system
Mission, 11–12, 17
Monsanto, 46
Multinational Corporation (MNC),
    238
Murphy, Patrick E., 7

NAACP (National Association for
    the Advancement of Colored
    People), 5
National-focus strategy, 244
Nestlé, 236
Net present value method, 278
Niche strategy, 101
Nissan, 52
Nominating committee, 169
Nonparticipative budgets, 189

Olivetti, 236
Olsen, Ken, 164, 167
Olson, James E., 12
OPEC. See Organization of
    Petroleum Exporting Countries
Operations planning and control,
    197
Optimum strategy report, 136
Organic systems, 159
Organization, 154
Organizational culture, 9, 18, 21,
    141
Organizational mission, 11, 18, 21
Organizational philosophy, 5, 18,
    21
Organizational policies, 8
Organizational purpose, 11
Organizational structure, 66
Organization of Petroleum
    Exporting Countries (OPEC),
    242
Overall cost leadership, 115

Pac-man defense, 111
Paine, Frank T., 145
Parent organization, 246
Parks, Don, 51
Par ROI report, 136, 138
Participative budgets, 189
Past objectives and strategies, 67
Pearce, J. A., 22
Penney, J. C., 6

Peters, Thomas J., 6, 22, 98, 116,
    162, 174
Petersen, Donald E., 178, 229
Peterson, Robert A., 194
Pfeffer, Jeffrey, 173
Philip Morris Companies, Inc., 101,
    102
Phillips, 236
PIMS analysis, 135–137
Planning committee, 170
Poison pill, 111
Polaroid, 198
Policies, 8
Poling, Harold A., 178, 229
Pooling of interests, 276
Porter, Michael E., 37, 38, 39, 51,
    103, 135, 136, 137, 145, 250
Powell, William J., Jr., 117
Power, 141
Price strategy, 194
Principle
    of individual rights, 19
    of justice, 19
    of utilitarianism, 20
Problem children, 125
Procter, Harley, 9
Procter & Gamble, 9, 221
Product development strategy, 193
Production/operations strategies,
    197
Product line gap, 95
Product-market evolution matrix,
    133–135
Product or service
    departmentation, 156
Product positioning, 65, 194–195
Product standardization, 243
Product strategy, 194
Profitability ratios, 262
Pro forma financial statement
    analysis, 261, 281
Prokesch, Steven E., 117
Promotion strategy, 194
Protected-niche strategy, 244
Protective R&D strategy, 201
Purchase of assets, 276
Purpose, 11

Quaker Oats Company, 131, 132
Quick divestment, 101
Quota, 241

Raider, 112
Ralston Purina, 165
Ratio analysis, 261
Recentralization stage, 159
Regression modeling, 48
Reimann, Bernard C., 138, 140, 145
Reorganizing, 162–163
Research and development
    capability, 66

Research and development strategies, 199–202
Restructuring, 162–164
Retrenchment strategies, 102, 115
Rewards, organizational, 202
Rhyne, L. C., 22
Ringness, Ronald C., 68
Rizzi, Joseph V., 206
RJR Nabisco, 167, 168
Robin, Don, 23
Robinson, R. B., Jr., 22
Roman Catholic church, 161, 221
Ronstadt, Robert, 260
Rothschild, William E., 23
Rousseau, Denise M., 174
Row, Michael, 223
Rue, Leslie W., 51
Rumelt, Richard, 144, 173

Salancik, Gerald, 173
Salter, Malcolm S., 173
Schecter, Steven M., 117
Schendel, Dan E., 134, 144, 145
Schmidt, Jeffrey A., 225, 228
Sears, Roebuck & Co., 154
Section 7, Clayton Act, 99
Securities and Exchange Commission (SEC), 44
Self-tender offer, 112
Sen, Shruba, 228
Shanks, David C., 174
Shared experience, 127
Shark repellent, 112
Sheth, Jagdish N., 51
Short-range objectives, 12, 18, 21, 69
Shoshal, Sumantra, 250
Shrader, C. B., 22
Sieban's River North Brewery, Inc., 42
Sigma Mu Fraternity, 5
Singhvi, Surendra S., 117
Skinner, Wickham, 206
Smith v. Van Gorkom, 170

Social responsibility committee, 170
Sormanen, Juhani, 51
South, Stephen C., 79
SRI International, 45
Stable growth strategy, 92–94
Staff proliferation stage, 158
Stakeholders, 5
Stalker, G. M., 173
Standard and Poor's (S&P) Corporation, 217
Standard Industrial Classification Code (SIC), 264
Standard Oil Company, 154
Standstill agreement, 112
Stars, 125
Stata, Ray, 206
Steiner, George A., 23
Steiner, John F., 23
Stevenson, Howard H., 79, 260
Stock buyback, 112
Strategic Planning Institute (SPI), 135
Strategic business units (SBUs), 16–17, 74, 126
Strategic management, 4, 18, 20
Strategy, 5, 13, 18, 21
    formulation, 5, 18, 20
    implementation, 5, 18, 20
    report, 136
    review, 224
Stroup, Margaret A., 46
SWOT analysis, 36
Synergy, 100
System design, 197

Tandy Corporation, 72
Target company, 109–112
Target marketing, 195
Tariffs, 241
Taylor, Bernard, 260
Taylor, L., 22
Technology, 43
Ten-day window, 112

Tender offer, 109, 112
Tennican, Michael L., 174
Terrorism, 243
Thain, Donald H., 173
Thakur, Manab, 261
Thoenig, Jean-Claude, 173
Thornhill, William T., 228
Thune, Stanley, 22
Time-series analysis, 48
Toyota, 52, 236
Tracy, Phelps K., 174
Trans Union Corporation, 170
Trapani, Cosmo S., 206
Turnaround strategy, 103–104
Two-tiered tender offer, 112

Umapatny, Srinivasan, 206
United States Leasing International, Inc., 30
Usage gap, 95

Value-added chain, 244
Value-based planning, 137, 139
Value Line, 217
Vertical integration, 98–99, 115
Vertical mergers, 108
Vesey, Joseph, 117
Volkswagen of America, 236, 245

Wal-Mart, 192
Waterman, Robert H., Jr., 6, 22, 98, 116, 162, 174
Watson, Thomas J., Jr., 6, 8, 22
Watson, Thomas J., Sr, 6, 9, 141
White knight, 112
Woo, Carolyn Y. Y., 144
Wood, Robley D., Jr., 22
Woodward, Joan, 173
Working-capital analysis, 261, 269–271

Zakon, Alan J., 144
Zero-based budgeting, 189